Making
Democracy

Making Democracy

Leadership, Class, Gender, and
Political Participation in Thailand

■ ■ ■ ■ ■ ■ ■ ■ ■

James Ockey

University of Hawai'i Press
Honolulu

Library of Congress Cataloging-in-Publication Data

Ockey, James.
Making democracy : leadership, class, gender, and
political participation in Thailand / James Ockey.
p. cm.
Includes bibliographical references and index.
ISBN 0-8248-2781-3 (hardcover : alk. paper)
1. Democracy—Thailand. 2. Political participation—
Thailand. 3. Politics and culture—Thailand.
4. Thailand—Politics and government. I. Title.
JQ1749.A15O25 2004
320.9593—dc22
2004003471

University of Hawai'i Press books are printed on acid-free
paper and meet the guidelines for permanence and durability
of the Council on Library Resources.

Designed by University of Hawai'i Press Production Staff
Printed by The Maple-Vail Book Manufacturing Group

CONTENTS

PREFACE

I have been working on this manuscript for nearly a decade now. At first I did not even realize that this book would be the eventual result. Indeed, I thought I was working on three different projects: one on political parties, one on the middle classes, one on poor people. However, each project led me to some of the same conclusions regarding the nature of Thai democracy. At that point I realized that the seemingly discrete projects were really one, that they were the foundations of this manuscript. Since that time, I have been struggling to fit the pieces together—an interesting challenge.

At about the same time I realized that these projects were all one, I was interviewing community leaders in a Bangkok congested community, or to use the common term, slum community. The community leader I was interviewing was a *hua khanaen,* a vote canvasser for a popular Bangkok politician, and very much aware of the flaws of the Thai democratic system due to his involvement in the election process. Yet he proudly informed me that he had been present at the 1973, 1976, and 1992 democratic uprisings. I found this rather jarring, since popular opinion held that these were middle-class uprisings, and that the lower classes were not interested in democracy. By no stretch of the imagination could this community leader be described as middle-class. Indeed, he was so ashamed of his home that he always met me in the community center. This contradiction lies at the heart of this book. Are the lower classes really apathetic? Why does popular opinion maintain that the uprisings were middle-class? Are democratic attitudes the province of the middle classes? And how can those involved in the notoriously corrupt *hua khanaen* system be so proud of Thai democracy? I already had some tentative answers to these questions, as they were the common elements in the projects I had undertaken. And so the seeds of this manuscript were planted.

One cannot hope to repay ten years of intellectual debts in a preface. In my own case, the debt seems unusually high. I would like to thank, first and foremost, all those people in Thailand who gave of their time for interviews, who were unfailingly polite, who struggled to understand just what I was trying to say, and who tried to answer both thoughtfully and completely. I found that, in Thailand, the vast majority of people I met, with social statuses ranging from cabinet minister to slum dweller, from journalist to godmother, were generous, kind, and helpful. I must admit that I was more surprised to find such characteristics in the cabinet ministers than in the slum dwellers.

I would also like to thank all the support staff who have provided assistance along the way. That includes, among others, the staffs at the Government Department, the Southeast Asia Program, and the library at Cornell University; the Political Science Department and the library at Canterbury University; the Law School, the Office of International Programs, and the library at Kwansei Gakuin University; and the parliament, the National Library, the Ministry of the Interior, and the Thammasat, Chulalongkorn, and NIDA libraries in Bangkok. Thanks also to Dean Toshimasa Moriwaki and Professor Ikuzo Maeno of Kwansei Gakuin University for arranging such a hospitable environment for me while I was struggling to write this book, and to Mark Francis and John Henderson, the heads of department at Canterbury during this time, who assisted me in so many ways. Sunh Arunrugstichai and Paul Bellamy have been highly capable research assistants. Jill Dolby of the Canterbury University Political Science Department deserves special thanks.

I have had much advice on and assistance with various chapters. Those who have read and helped to shape one or more of the drafts include Ben Anderson, Thak Chaloemthiarana, Thamora Fishel, Tami Loos, Ruth McVey, Gary Ockey, Michael Pinches, Craig Reynolds, Jim Scott, John Sidel, Yao Souchou, Naimah Talib, Curtis Thomson, Carl Trocki, Erick White, David Wyatt, and a number of unknown reviewers. In addition, Mike Montesano has often discussed and helped shape my ideas over the years; and Douglas Kammen endured many hours of obsessive complaints and still made many helpful suggestions during the process. The anonymous reviewers of the University of Hawai'i Press were also very helpful. None of them have read all the drafts, nor have I always had the ability to fully incorporate their advice; I alone remain responsible for the many flaws that remain.

Along the way I have enjoyed the support of many friends in Ithaca, in Christchurch, and in Thailand. It would be impossible to name them all. I have had the encouragement of two families: my own, and that of my wife, best friend, and favorite scholar, Naimah Talib. I also wish to thank my daughter, Aminah Anne, who more than made up for the brief delay in publication that her arrival occasioned by the joy she has brought into my life.

Finally, I wish to thank the "Gentle Reader" so aptly described by Nathaniel Hawthorne in his preface to *The Marble Faun:* "I never personally encountered, nor corresponded through the Post, with this Representative Essence of all delightful and desirable qualities that a reader can possess. But, fortunately for myself, I never therefore concluded him [*sic*] to be merely a mythic character. I had always a sturdy faith in his actual existence, and wrote for him, year after year. . . ."

Portions of this book have previously appeared elsewhere in different forms. Some parts of Chapter 2 appeared in "Political Parties, Factions, and Civilian Rule in Thailand," *Modern Asian Studies* 28, no. 2 (1994): 251–277, and "Change and Continuity in the Thai Political Party System," *Asian Survey* (forthcoming). Another version of Chapter 4 appeared in "Chaopho, Capital Accumulation, and Social Welfare in Thailand," *Crossroads* 8, no. 1 (1993): 48–77. Chapter 5 is an edited version of "God Mothers, Good Mothers, Good Lovers, Godmothers: Gender Images in Thailand," *Journal of Asian Studies* 58 (Nov. 1999): 1033–1058. Chapter 6 is based on two earlier articles, "Weapons of the Urban Weak: Democracy and Resistance to Eviction in Bangkok Slum Communities," *Sojourn* 12 (April 1997): 1–25, and "Eviction and Changing Patterns of Political Leadership in Slum Communities," *Bulletin of Concerned Asian Scholars* 28 (April–June 1996): 46–59. Much of Chapter 7 appeared in an earlier version as "Constructing the Thai Middle Class," in Michael Pinches, ed., *Culture and Privilege in Capitalist Asia* (London: Routledge, 1999), 230–250.

CHAPTER 1

Changing Patterns of Leadership, Culture, Power, and Democracy

The ruler [of Siam] was a reincarnated deity. . . . The king's person was unapproachably sacred and his authority absolute. He was owner of all the land and also of the bodies of his subjects, who were legally his chattels. . . . The ruler's autocratic control was unqualified.
— (Cady 1964:326).

In theory, Thai monarchs were absolute. The king was not only *phrachao phaendin* (lord of the land), he was also *chao chiwit* (lord of life). He was both the physical receptacle of morality for the kingdom and the embodiment of the state. His word was law, state revenue his private purse. The king stood at the apex of a vast pyramid of status relations, the *sakdina* system, where all had their place in relation to the king and, by extension, to each other. Each individual was given a certain number of *sakdina* points by the king, which determined position in the pyramidal structure. Thus, leadership in Thailand, in theory, was authoritarian and absolute.

As is well known, in practice leadership in Thailand was quite different, both in Bangkok and in the provinces. And yet much of the literature on Asian democracy, and on democratization in Thailand in particular, is predicated on the notion of traditional authoritarian rule. Scholars such as Pye (1985) and Huntington (1991: 300–307), and political leaders such as Sarit Thannarat, Lee Kuan Yew, and Mahathir Mohammad have argued that democracy in Asian cultures is at best problematic, if not entirely inappropriate. Pye (1985) has perhaps stated this argument most clearly and powerfully. "Asian cultures . . . share . . . the common denominator of idealizing benevolent, paternalistic leadership and of legitimizing dependency" (1985:vii). "For most Asians the acceptance of authority is not inherently bad but rather is an acceptable key to finding personal security. . . . For Asians the search for identity means finding a group to belong to—that is, locating an appropriate paternalistic form of authority" (1985:x). While Pye did allow for some degree of cultural change, he argued that continuity is by far the more important aspect. Therefore, since democracy is not part of the enduring Asian culture, he argued, it is not likely to develop there. "Any thrust for democracy that exists tends to result from the desire to appear respectable in Western eyes" (1985:340). Thus, the argument goes, democratization is both unlikely and inappropriate, since it is not culturally relevant.[1] However, this conceptualization is based on court culture, and an idealized model of court culture at that.

Most scholars of Thai politics have avoided this claim that democracy is inappropriate to Asian cultures. Yet many scholars and politicians who believe in the possibility and desirability of democracy in Asia have nevertheless implicitly accepted this underlying notion of traditional authoritarian culture. Consequently, rather than seeking for indigenous roots of participation and democracy, they turn to foreign influence, arguing that democratization has only come to Asia in general and to Thailand in particular through the middle classes. In this most common explanation for democratization in the literature, it is the middle classes who are exposed to Western lifestyles and to Western ideas of political participation and democracy, and it is the middle classes and Western ideas that bring about democracy.[2] For example, in one of the most influential analyses of Thai politics, Wilson (1962:274–275) argued that the Thai political system was remarkably stable and nondemocratic *because* it had no middle class. Thai society had "a simple structure, consisting of an extremely large agrarian segment and a small ruling segment . . . in which the classes are physically as well as economically separated, and differential status is satisfactorily justified" (ibid.). As for the future, he thought that change could possibly occur, based on the role of some incipient middle-class elements and the spread of Western ideas:

> The generation of constitutional government since 1932 has created within
> the groups of parliamentary politicians, journalists, and intelligentsia a cadre
> of potential leadership which, under sufficient inducement, perhaps could and
> would disrupt the consensus which sustains the ruling class . . . there are signs
> of incipient demands among the rural population; and increasing penetration
> of education into the lives of these people . . . may, indeed, be weakening the
> hold of tradition. (Wilson 1962:282)

It is quite striking that Wilson clearly identified deep divisions between agrarian and ruling segments yet assumed they shared a common culture. It is this flawed assumption that has focused attention in the democratization debate on the influence of Western ideas, and on the role of the middle classes in perpetuating those Western ideas, obscuring the role of indigenous culture and the lower classes.

Given that leadership and participation in practice varied considerably from the model that forms the basis of these contentions, reconsideration is in order. While I do not wish to overlook the contribution to democratization of Western ideas, I will argue that support for democracy also has indigenous roots in Thai vil-lage culture. Because political participation is a part of traditional village culture, as we shall see, support for democracy has gone well beyond the middle-class ele-ments. This has important implications for democratization. For if democratiza-tion comes entirely from foreign ideas assimilated by the educated middle classes, then the lower classes, especially in rural areas, may be an obstruction to democ-ratization: only when they are educated can they effectively participate. When democratization is understood in this way, rather than encouraging rural and lower-class participation, building on indigenous participatory patterns, such broad-based participation is subverted. Then, middle-class Western-influenced democratic ideals are (unsuccessfully) imposed from above. This has long been the case for Thai democracy, from the time of the first constitution in 1932, which allowed appointed M.P.s until educational standards could be improved, through to the 1997 constitution, which required a university education for all M.P.s. How-ever, if participation and elements of democracy are part of Thai village culture, as I contend, then participation should be encouraged, and the problems and solu-tions may lie elsewhere. Of course there are also nondemocratic elements present in both village culture and middle-class culture. It is therefore important to exam-ine how differences between village culture, court culture, and Western ideas of political participation have shaped not only the emergence but also the nature of democracy in Thailand.

The focus on the middle class and the foreign origins of democracy is often intensified by a tendency to concentrate on the development of democratic insti-tutions rather than democratic attitudes and political participation. This contrib-utes to the tendency to overlook indigenous traditions of participation, as there were no parliaments or political parties in Thailand prior to the arrival of the West. To see the democratic elements in Thai political culture, we must look instead to participation in decision-making and to patterns of leadership.

Traditional Patterns of Leadership and Participation in Thailand

In traditional Thai society, the pattern of leadership in any community, and the pattern relevant for any given individual, varied considerably.[3] At the top of the societal pyramid, in the capital, we find that, in practice, the king often had his power constrained by the *sangha*, by princes, and even by high-ranking nobility. In extreme cases, kings were killed and replaced by other members of the royal family in early Thailand (Wood 1982:74–75, 108–112, 174–175, 189–190). Akin (1996:70) pointed out that the early Chakri kings believed the fall of Ayutthaya was due to the excessive power of the princes and sought to circumscribe their power. King Taksin, who restored Thai rule after Ayutthaya was sacked and burned by the Burmese, was deposed after a conflict with the *sangha* (Wyatt 1984:143–144; Tambiah 1976:183). Throughout most of the nineteenth century, the Bunnag family controlled the most powerful ministries and much of the revenue of the kingdom, placing significant constraints on the power of the king (Wyatt 1979).

For other residents of the capital, the presence of the royal family and much of the nobility meant that the *sakdina* system held considerable sway. Nevertheless, there were ways to avoid it. According to Akin, during the early Bangkok period there was an increase in informal patron–client relationships, particularly between *nai* (nobility) and *phrai* (commoners), which existed outside of the *sakdina* structure. These informal relationships were dependent on mutual support and obligations, not on status bestowed by the king. While such patron–client ties were paternalistic and exploitative, nevertheless, because they involved mutual support and obligations, they did allow clients some input into decision making. These informal relationships indicate the complex nature of leadership at all levels of society in the capital city.

Outside the capital the patterns were even more complex and less like the formal *sakdina* system. Perhaps the most important distinction was geographical.[4] The capital ruled directly in only a few nearby areas. Beyond those easily accessible areas were a number of provinces where local nobility, ostensibly appointed by the king, but in practice generally hereditary, had control (Pasuk and Baker 1995: 212–214). In most cases, the king did not (could not) select rulers in these provinces, but recognized and sanctioned existing leaders. Generally speaking, the more remote the province the greater the independence of local leaders.[5] In many places, the power of the absolute monarch meant little compared to the power of the local leader. In the tributary states, the king could only demand tribute, which was paid only intermittently, on threat of war.

Below the provincial level, generally the local nobility appointed their own leaders within their own areas, although a few important officials may have had the king's writ to recognize their authority. At the top levels of the provincial hierarchy, local nobility often appointed their own relatives to positions (Bunnag 1977:21). Outside the provincial capital, local nobility often had to accept existing leadership arrangements in their areas, just as the king had to accept the local nobility. In some cases, even "bandit leaders" had to be accepted (Bunnag 1977: 23). Again, the more remote the town or village, the less control exercised by the local nobility.

It was in the villages, where the majority of the population dwelt, that patterns differed most from the theoretical absolutism of the king. Particularly with the expansion of settled agriculture in the 19th century, peasants had a great deal of independence (Pasuk and Baker 1995:396ff.). The king could not even provide security in villages; he left it to village leaders. Although patterns varied from village to village, generally there were two types of leaders in village communities.

First, there was the *phuyaiban*, or village headman.[6] According to Steinberg et al. (1987:28):

> Headmen generally were informally elected from among the elder men in the village. Their age gave them an automatic high status and their experience gave their judgments weight. Being the wise old men they were, however, they employed consultation and persuasion to perform the acts required of them by central authority [mainly labor conscription and taxation] and to settle disputes by conciliation and compromise. These were part of a style of leadership inculcated by folk tradition and encouraged by the values of village society.[7]

Second, there were the *nakleng* or "bandit leaders" mentioned by Bunnag, who were responsible for the protection of the village. In some cases, the *nakleng* and the headman were the same person, though generally the headman was an elder, the *nakleng* a young tough. Such leaders are discussed in more detail in subsequent chapters. The point to be made here is that the experience of villagers was entirely different from the absolutism that the king, theoretically, exerted over their lives. The lived experience of the villager within the village was generally participatory, and even somewhat "democratic," though leadership was narrowly restricted by age, gender, and wealth.

Another crucial difference between the court and village cultures can be discerned in the pattern of gender relations. In the palace, polygyny, seclusion, virtue, passivity, and subordinate status were the rule.[8] The nobility and the wealthy sought to emulate this court culture. In village culture, though women were not equal, they "had freedom and authority, for example, to control the family purse strings and share in decision making in the household" (Darunee and Pandey 1991:16; see also Bencha 1992:17). Juree (1993:179–180) argued that, "as the social and political elite strengthened its hold on society, the values and norms that elite society saw as appropriate for itself were disseminated to the rest of society." Darunee and Pandey (1991:17–18), on the other hand, have argued that recently evolution toward greater equality has taken place, due to education and Western influence among middle-class professionals. It is striking that here we see the same assumption of the dominance of court culture over village culture, and the need for foreign influence to break it down. In the chapters that follow, I will argue that the reverse also took place: that as villagers were increasingly brought into contact with government, women accustomed to the patterns of gender relations in village culture, including participation in decision making, contributed to the demands for democratization.

In addition to providing useful background information, this glance at the past suggests the need to look beyond central governmental institutions and their formal power and to examine carefully the patterns of leadership at various levels of society if we are to understand the nature of political participation and democratization. In the pages that follow, I shall examine patterns of leadership, political participation, and democracy in modern Thailand. Particular attention will be paid to the differences between village and urban culture, which have been especially stark, and to the related influence of Western ideas on the (primarily urban-based) middle-class elements.

Leadership and Participation

Although much has been written of democratization in Thailand, relatively little literature exists concerning the relationship between leadership, participation, and democracy. The only book-length analysis is that of Yot Santasombat (1986; 1990).[9] Yot interviewed some twenty Thai political leaders and presented results of interviews with four of those leaders. In the earlier version, his dissertation, Yot's theme had been the necessity of studying personality in order to understand leadership. He wrote that Thai leaders tended to have certain personality traits, including strong achievement motivation, a well-developed self-identity and sense of competence, a willingness to accept responsibility, and the ability to manage patron–client ties successfully. These traits, he argued, were the result of the psychological development of a leader, particularly in the formative years.[10] In the revised version published in Thai, Yot shifted his focus slightly to emphasize the importance of patron–client ties. He argued that Thai leadership is based on "uncertain" patron–client ties. Leaders who successfully manipulate those ties, both as clients and later as patrons, will rise to the top. This shift in focus allowed Yot to pay more attention to the relationship between leader and followers, and is the key to the political participation that interests us here. Nevertheless, Yot's primary focus remained on the importance of personality in understanding leadership in Thailand.

Yot later returned to this theme in a volume on leadership and national security (1989). Here he made two additional important points relevant to this study of leadership. First, he pointed to the "damage" done to legitimacy by the 1932 coup. According to him, this sudden dramatic break with the past left the nature of the legitimacy of the new government suspect (Yot 1989:84–85). Second, he pointed to the erosion of patron–client ties, arguing that such ties have "become more instrumental, less expressive, and hence less resilient," as well as "of less intensity" (Yot 1989:89). These two changes opened the way for transitions to new forms of participation—including, eventually, democracy.

Another article by Sombat Chantornvong and Montri Chenvidyakarn (1991) is part of the same series. It emphasized the close relationship between institutions and styles of leadership, and the impact of that relationship on legitimacy. As we shall see, one key aspect of democratization has been exactly this struggle to legitimize democratic institutions with democratic styles of leadership. Sombat and Montri also provide some very useful analysis of the personalities of former prime ministers Prem and Chatchai; however, the comparison is not done in a systematic way but as part of the more general theme of institutionalization of leadership.[11]

Another approach, taken by Montri (1984), has been to examine the characteristics of Thai prime ministers to determine what factors have made political leaders successful over the years. Montri examined the socioeconomic backgrounds and career paths of these leaders. He categorized prime ministers as military or civilian and organized his material into two periods, 1932–1957, when all prime ministers came from the group that overthrew the absolute monarchy, and 1957–1983, when they did not. He then examined their performance. He concluded that military leaders entered politics when civilian politicians failed to perform well, and that civilian prime ministers needed strong personalities to survive. His primary focus was on the influence of occupational background and strength of personality on performance.

Surin Maisrikrod (1993) also examined differences in styles of political leaders. The main theme of his analysis seems to be that Thai society is becoming "polarized" between two groups characterized variously as "conservatives" and "reformists," "pro-military" and "pro-democracy," and "traditional military/ bureaucratic power holders and the new business-based power-seekers" (Surin 1993:85, passim). In contrast to Yot, who had argued that personality shapes leadership, Surin held that "pro-democracy" leaders "emerge[d] largely because of changes in the different 'environments,' specifically in education, the media, the corporate world, the bureaucracy and the international security and economic arena" (Surin 1993:92). In other words, the political culture shaped the nature of the leader.[12] Like Yot's attention to patron–client ties, this focus on political culture allowed a careful consideration of the relationship between leader and follower, here combined with an analysis of the institutions that shape such relationships. This concentration on the role of institutions is reminiscent of Sombat and Montri; however, Surin considered political culture more generally rather than legitimacy specifically. In the analysis that follows, both are considered.

My own earlier work (Ockey 1996), which I draw on here, attempted to combine elements of these approaches. Since Yot and Montri had found personality of the leader to be the most important factor, at the risk of oversimplification I attempted to provide a culturally relevant typology for the personalities of leaders, dividing past prime ministers into those who exhibited *nakleng*-style characteristics and those who exhibited *phudi*-style characteristics. The *nakleng* as described by Thak (1979:338–340), is a type of traditional Thai leader who is tough, charismatic, and above all loyal to friends. The *nakleng* is often on the wrong side of the law, or perhaps above the law, at least in his own mind. He is also closely associated with manliness and *decha*, or power. The *phudi* (literally "good person") style of leadership is associated with *khunna,* or moral goodness. Originally this term was used primarily to describe members of the aristocracy, and it retains those connotations; but it also refers to the "well-mannered" and to "good" people in general, and is not linked to gender. *Phudi* prime ministers have been consummate compromisers or mediators. This, I argued, made them more suitable to democratic styles of government. Historically, *nakleng* were most successful prior to the 1970s, while *phudi* have been more successful since that time. This, I believed, indicated that a change in the nature of legitimacy had taken place, a change to styles of legitimate leadership conducive to democracy. More recently, *nakleng* have also had to adapt to changes in the nature of legitimacy.

While this argument highlighted the importance of changes in political culture and the nature of legitimate leadership, it did so by drastically oversimplifying. As I pointed out at the time, leaders are complex, and their personalities cannot be easily characterized by a simple typology. I should also have pointed out that both the *nakleng* and the *phudi* styles of leadership have elements of paternalism and of participation. In its aristocratic version, the *phudi* was the wise leader who knew best what to do for social inferiors. Popular participation in politics was not necessary, nor did *phudi* think it necessary to listen to the opinions of social inferiors; acting wisely was enough. This legacy remains for the *phudi* of today, who conceive of democracy in terms of representation rather than participation (Ockey 1999). At the same time, while *nakleng* are decisive, they also depend on reciprocal relationships with their followers that require them to understand and look out for the needs of their followers. This is particularly true of the new-style *nakleng,* who has to shore up weak patron–client ties with loyalty and generosity. Thus the *nakleng* and *phudi* traditions are both paternalistic and participatory, in different ways.

As for patron–client ties, I argued that, while they were eroding everywhere, they remained stronger in rural than in urban areas. Weakened patron–client ties were being shored up by institutional structures, particularly in the military and the bureaucracy, and, especially in rural areas, by generosity, often in the form of cash payments for participation in demonstrations or elections.

While all these themes are important to understanding Thai leadership, it remains to draw them together and to relate them to participation and democratization. Although we shall explore the relationships among culture, leadership, participation, and democracy from a broad-based perspective, there will be six main tasks for this examination. First, we shall consider how political culture—particularly the differences in urban, rural, and Western cultures—shapes leadership, participation, and democracy in contemporary Thailand. Second, evolution over time has been a consistent theme in the discussion of leadership, participation, and democracy. We begin with a brief examination of periods of change in Thai history and continue to focus on change in our analysis of the contemporary era. Third, in terms of leadership and participation, we shall examine the nature of leadership by loosely dividing leaders into our categories of *nakleng* and *phudi* styles, keeping firmly in mind that we can only identify broad patterns using this typology; where necessary, individual leaders will be assessed in more detailed and nuanced terms. Fourth, we shall look at the effects of the erosion of uncertain patron–client ties and its impact on participation and democracy in Thailand. Fifth, we shall investigate the nature of political institutions, and how they relate to political culture, leadership, and participation. Finally, we will consider the role of gender, class, and, given the focus of previous work on the middle classes and on Western culture in the democratization process, of Thai village culture and its impact. I shall begin by briefly sketching the historical development of leadership, participation, and democratization in Thailand prior to the period under study here.

The Historical Evolution of Leadership, Participation, and Democratization

Changes in attitudes toward leadership and participation tend to be incremental; however, as Yot pointed out, there can also be some periods of accelerated shifts. We can identify at least four of those since the late nineteenth century. First, the efforts of King Chulalongkorn to strengthen the power of the central government, combined with the endeavors of his son Vajiravudh to strengthen the visibility and power of the monarchy through nationalism amounted to an attempt to expand the leadership tradition of the court to a wider segment of society. Second, as Yot pointed out, in 1932 there was a collapse of traditional monarchical leadership. The collapse was not complete, however, because the monarch remained as a figurehead for the new regime. Furthermore, the state was strengthened while, at the same time, the new parliament was weakened, as political parties were banned and half the members of the legislature were appointed. The third accelerated shift took place in 1957, when Sarit overthrew the Phibun government. Sarit briefly allowed elections and a parliament but then turned to centralized authoritarian rule, all but abandoning even the rhetoric of democracy and participation. Finally, in the 1970s, parliamentary rule returned, and with it new ideas of leadership and participation.

Increased contact with the West after the Bowring Treaty of 1855 established the preconditions for the attempts of King Chulalongkorn and King Vajiravudh to shift patterns of leadership and participation in Thailand. The Bowring Treaty opened the economy to foreign trade, and increasingly to foreign ideas. In reshaping the economy, it began to bring villages into closer contact with the market and the state. As colonialism continued to spread through Southeast Asia, King Chulalongkorn reacted by seeking to centralize power in the kingdom by rationalizing and centralizing the bureaucracy, and attempting to extend court views of leadership and participation to the regions and the villages. The bureaucracy was divided into functional ministries (rather than a mix of functional and regional ministries). Civil servants were made subject to the ministry rather than to the locality. From that time, civil servants were placed on salary paid by the ministry and were subject to transfer, making it difficult for them to build up a local power base. The bureaucracy also expanded dramatically. The models for this reformation were the colonial administrations in neighboring countries during the same period.[13]

Villages could not escape either the political or the economic impact of these changes, most notably the beginnings of the erosion of patron–client ties Yot (1989) discussed.[14] Structures of leadership and participation in the villages underwent two important changes. First, the Ministry of the Interior began to organize formal elections. Second, as part of the attempt at centralization, these newly elected headmen became increasingly responsible to the state, but without becoming civil servants or receiving any salary. As the task became increasingly onerous, and as it came to depend increasingly on interaction with the state rather than with other villagers, many were reluctant to stand for elections. Those elected were often civil servants accustomed to dealing with the state, whereas villagers continued to rely on the same *nakleng* and village elders for leadership in the village.[15] Thus a gap began to open up between the ostensibly democratic institutions initiated by the state, which were concerned with the interests of the center, and informal (participatory) leadership, which continued to deal with the everyday concerns of villagers (Bunnag 1977:188ff.).[16]

King Chulalongkorn also began a process of making the monarchy more accessible; his son, King Vajiravudh, took up this task in earnest. Vajiravudh sought to popularize the monarchy through developing a conservative pro-royalist nationalism (Vella 1978). This early attempt at nationalism was confined largely to urban areas, and to the educated. While generally considered to have been successful, it was aimed at preserving the status quo rather than implementing change. It did little to enhance the ability of the monarchy to impose its version of leadership and participation on either the villages or the elite. Rather, it was so ineffective at popularizing the monarchy that, not many years later, the absolute monarchy was toppled.

In 1932, another accelerated shift in attitudes toward leadership, participation, and democracy was initiated. In the midst of the depression, the absolute monarchy was overthrown by a group of mostly young, mostly Western-educated nationalists led by Pridi Phanomyong on the civilian side and Phibun Songkhram from the military. It was this group which had been most affected by Westernization and the rapid changes taking place in Southeast Asia. As Yot pointed out, the 1932 overthrow of the absolute monarchy marked the collapse of the traditional monarchical form of leadership at the top. New attitudes led to the development of new Western-style institutions and new types of leaders. A parliament was instituted, with half of its membership appointed, half elected. This composition reflected the ambivalence of the new Western-educated leaders. While they were open to somewhat greater participation, they were not convinced that the people of Thailand were educated enough to participate effectively. Furthermore, shortly after the new system was established, political parties were banned. Thus there was no democratic or participatory structure to mediate between the people and the new institutions. Instead, political leaders turned to the state itself, which was decidedly nonparticipatory (Riggs 1966), so the gap between the demands of the state and the culture of participation we noted in the election of village leaders also emerged between parliament and people. As an institution ostensibly based on participation but with little basis in indigenous forms of participation, the new parliament struggled to develop any semblance of legitimacy, especially outside urban areas. The result was that, in this initial period following the overthrow of the absolute monarchy, the state was strengthened even as it was taken away from the royalists, and consequently participation was weakened even as Thailand became, formally, a "democracy."

In the late 1930s, Prime Minister Phibun, like Vajiravudh before him, turned to nationalism to shore up support for his leadership, but this time the effort was aimed at the masses. Phibun was a leader in the *nakleng* style. He also sought to appropriate the monarchical tradition of leadership, designating himself *phunam* (leader) and focusing much of the nationalism on himself. This mass-oriented nationalism did organize and mobilize people throughout much of Thailand. Of particular importance were the organizations designed to mobilize women. But again, this was mobilization for the purposes of the state, not for political participation. As with Vajiravudh, the nationalism that developed did little to preserve Phibun's personal authority.

While Yot argued that the 1932 overthrow of the absolute monarchy led to a sharp break in the nature of legitimacy, in fact the shift was not so sudden. King Prachathipok continued as a figurehead for several years, and then was replaced by King Ananda. Patron–client ties also continued to erode, but again, without a sharp break. Instead it was the disruptions associated with World War II that accelerated the breakdown of patron–client ties and the process of bringing middle-class elements, villagers, and Western ideas together in support of greater participation and democracy. The most important aspect of this was mobility: villagers moving to the cities, middle-class elements temporarily fleeing Bangkok, and, at the end of the war, Westerners arriving in larger numbers. After the war, economic disruptions led increasing numbers of people to leave the countryside for cities, especially Bangkok, many temporarily, some permanently. During this period, Bangkok grew by an estimated 7.1 percent annually (Siffin 1962:135).[17] All this movement broke up patron–client ties and brought different attitudes toward leadership and participation into closer contact.

In the aftermath of the war, politics in Thailand became more participatory than at any point in the past. Political parties were allowed, and campaigning was quite vigorous. A range of political parties and newspapers representing all parts of the political spectrum developed. Labor unions were organized. Even the Communist party was legalized. Parties supporting Pridi Phanomyong, who was on the political left and a strong opponent of colonialism, easily won the election. This political participation was soon interrupted, however, when a military coup returned Phibun to power.

The reinstatement of Phibun meant that unions and parties were banned and the press faced censorship. Nationalism was again promoted, and the military was expanded to fight the Cold War. During his second stint as prime minister, Phibun depended on the support of others who directly controlled the armed forces and the police. Within a few years, two men, General Sarit Thanarat, army commander, and General Phao Siyanon, police chief, had built up large and powerful bureaucratic institutions. Phibun was left looking for a way to find support of his own, and he looked to the people. That meant actively encouraging participation in politics. Relying on his experience in mobilizing the people during the war through the use of nationalism, this time Phibun attempted "democracy." He revived elections, instituted press conferences, and opened Hyde Park–style "speakers' corners" (where free speech and political debate were allowed) throughout Thailand. As in the period immediately after the war, participation was widespread and enthusiastic. Unions and political parties formed, and tens of thousands of people turned up at political rallies in Bangkok and in the provinces. Students became politicized. During this period came the election of the first women M.P.s and the nationwide organization of women's cultural associations as women grew politically active. Furthermore, public prominence was accorded to La-iad Phibunsongkhram, wife of the prime minister and leader of the cultural associations, to the Queen Mother, and to the young queen, especially at the time of the royal wedding. Participation among various social groups—lower classes and professionals, migrants and residents—in Bangkok and other urban centers reached a new high (Kasian 2001; Ockey 2002). Unfortunately for Phibun, little of this support was for him. Instead, most of the support went to the opposition Democrat Party, to a host of smaller leftist parties, and to his rival, General Sarit.

This period between the end of the war and the Sarit coup of 1957 demonstrates the various traditions of participation coming together in complex ways. In the institutional structures of the parties, the parliaments, and the labor unions, for example, we see the influence of Western ideas. Many of the politicians who participated in the political institutions were from middle-class backgrounds, while those in labor unions were from the lower classes, and in many cases either recent migrants or temporary migrants.[18] Election rallies and the Hyde Park–style speakers' corner attracted tens of thousands of people, including students, workers, bureaucrats, hawkers, and *samlo* drivers. Speakers appealed primarily to the tastes of lower classes (Ockey 2002). Furthermore, election rallies and speakers' corners were also held in the provinces, as participation spread in new ways to rural areas.

In 1957, army commander General Sarit, with the support of students, Hyde Park demonstrators, the monarchy, and the Democrat Party, carried out a coup and removed Phibun from power. Sarit made a brief, halfhearted attempt of his own at democracy; then, in 1958, he instituted the most repressive regime, led by the military and supported by the bureaucracy, and initiated the most sudden and drastic shift in patterns of participation in modern Thai history. Development replaced democracy as the stated priority of politics. The bureaucracy and the military expanded further. Local and parliamentary elections were eliminated, and authoritarian leadership, appointed from the top, was instituted at all levels of society. Participation was forcibly suppressed, or channeled into development activities directed by the state.

Sarit put into place a regime that established its legitimacy by appealing to the most authoritarian tendencies in Thai political culture in a number of closely intertwined ways. First, he eliminated Western-style democratic institutions, including parliament and the political parties, as well as other organizations such as labor unions and the free press. Second, Sarit reestablished the prominence of the monarchy as a symbol. By doing so, he ensured that there was a symbolic absolutist leader to legitimize his own authoritarian regime. That the monarchy had no formal power, and could not therefore be blamed for any of the problems of society, removed it from any criticism regarding the lack of opportunities for participation and helped to ensure its popularity (Anderson 1978). Indeed, later, when demands for participation emerged, appeals for support were made to the monarch. Third, Sarit appealed to the least participatory elements of the *nakleng* tradition to further legitimize his rule. He exemplified decisiveness, risk taking, loyalty to friends and ruthlessness to enemies, and debauchery (Thak 1974:432). Furthermore, Thak (1974) pointed out, Sarit sought to portray himself as a benevolent father figure, "to make decisions independent of the wishes and desires of the public. . . . Development in the political sense of expanding political participation, political mobilization, and the building of new political institutions was no part of the Sarit regime's goals" (Thak 1974:280). This style of rule Thak designated "despotic paternalism." Sarit's regime was therefore symbolically masculine, and with the military and the top levels of the bureaucracy being entirely male-dominated, women were marginalized from national-level politics. Fourth, Sarit relied on the institutional structures of the military and the bureaucracy to strengthen patron–client ties. The system of ranks and the obedience to authority provided concrete structure to these ties, and a sense of camaraderie that solidified what Yot called the "uncertain" patron–client ties of Thai society. (Of course, a narrowing of participation also helped to make the remaining patron–client ties more effective.)

Finally, Sarit's *nakleng* style was particularly effectual during wartime, and Thailand was increasingly drawn into Cold War rhetoric and the war against communism in Indochina. With the country in a state of war, a soldier and *nakleng* style-protector made an attractive leader for many people.

Under Sarit, the authority of the village headman—once based on popular support and elections—derived from appointment by the national government. At the same time, to counter insurgency, Sarit made rural development a priority of the national government. This changed the nature of the gap between local concerns and national politics. Sarit was interested in rural development and did initiate some policies that benefited villages, so national politics and local concerns did coincide on development. However, these development concerns were separated from the tradition of participation and leadership, as local leaders were all appointed by the state. Furthermore, the rural economic growth initiated by Sarit's policies opened the way for the development of a new style of *nakleng*. The ability of new *nakleng* to span the gap between national politics and local concerns and to bring resources and development to their villages ensured their position in village society. With headmen appointed, and development initiated by the state, participation was eroded—except through these new *nakleng*. In these ways, Sarit subtly shifted the balance between participation and authoritarianism in village society.

While Sarit's use of the monarchical tradition and the most authoritarian and paternalistic aspects of the *nakleng* tradition provided some legitimacy in the short term, it did not last. Sarit died in 1963. His successor, General Thanom Kittikachon, carried on for another ten years, though he lacked Sarit's personal charisma. However, beneath the economic success, and in part because of the economic success, the culture was slowly changing in ways that made the legitimacy of authoritarian leadership increasingly problematic. First, economic development meant large-scale migration to the cities, especially Bangkok. People from the countryside with different attitudes toward participation and politics were more easily mobilized than in the past. Furthermore, having uprooted themselves from their villages, and their past, and having been forced to learn many new things in order to survive, the migrants were in a malleable state. Second, economic development and the Vietnam War brought many foreigners with new ideas and attitudes into the country. Third, and closely related, the developing economy required a more educated workforce. There was a tremendous expansion in higher education in the 1960s and early 1970s. Some of these students went abroad, were exposed to other cultures and ways of thinking, and returned to teach in Thai universities. Such young university lecturers were an important component of the 1973 uprising. Others learned of other cultures and ways of thinking through books and newspapers. So Western ideas became an important force for change. Fourth, economic growth led to changes in the social structure. The most often noted has been the expansion of middle-class elements. A large number of newly rich emerged who wanted greater participation in politics. However, the working class also expanded rapidly during this period, as did the urban poor. While the successors of Sarit worked to preserve their legitimacy and power, these new groups began to challenge the regime.

These underlying changes were accompanied by an opening up of opportunities in the late 1960s. In 1968, political parties were allowed to operate, and elections in Bangkok were followed by national elections in 1969. Again, campaigning was vigorous, and people were widely exposed to participation and to democratic styles of leadership. Other groups that sought to strengthen participation also formed, most significantly the National Student Center of Thailand, which organized students. For most Thais, this was not new, but a return of elections after ten years without them. Authoritarian leadership styles again had competition. Electoral arrangements were rigged so that Thanom was returned to power, but with a parliament and an opposition. Although just two years later Thanom eliminated the parliament and the opposition, this brief two-year period went far toward reviving the desire for participation. It set the stage for the democratic uprising of 1973, led by students and joined by women and men of all classes.

Since that time, Thailand has been governed by an elected parliament for all but five years, including the year or so it took to write a constitution and elect a parliament after the 1973 uprising. Twice more during that time, Thais risked their lives to defend their right to participate in elected government. It is my contention that this shift to participation and parliaments, and the willingness of Thais from all classes and both genders to risk their lives to secure it, is best understood when taken in the context of long-standing traditions of participation, rather than considered simply the result of short-term growth of middle-class elements and the arrival of Western ideals. Furthermore, I contend, while all classes and both genders have such traditions of participation, those traditions vary, and those variations continue to shape the democracy that has developed. It is this period since the shift to parliamentary rule in the 1970s that I shall discuss in detail in the chapters that follow.[19]

Participation, Parliament, and Types of Leadership

The development of parliamentary institutions and political parties meant that traditional forms of leadership and participation had to be adapted. How that was done and how it has shaped Thai democracy is a major theme of this book. In an earlier work (Ockey 1996) I identified two broad styles of traditional leadership: the *phudi*, based on *khunna*, or virtue, and the *nakleng*, based on *decha*, or power. Both types have elements of participation and paternalism, and both have been employed over the years by political leaders and adapted to fit existing political and bureaucratic institutions. During the 1980s and 1990s middle-class elements, which had been most affected by Western ideas, tended to support *phudi*-style politicians. In the countryside and among some of the urban poor, a new style of *nakleng* politician developed to take advantage of the new parliamentary and party structures. Before turning to a more detailed examination of democratization, participation, and leadership, it is worthwhile briefly to outline the nature of these types of leadership styles since the shift to parliamentary rule in the 1970s.

As we have observed, the rise of the *phudi* type of leadership style correlates well with parliamentary rule (see also Ockey 1996). The two longest-serving prime ministers since the 1970s, Prem Tinsulanon and Chuan Leekphai, can both be characterized in this way. The parliamentary politician has to deal with many groups that provide support only conditionally. Here any patron–client ties are indeed "uncertain," and the deliberative style of leadership of the *phudi* reflects the difficulties in balancing the needs of various loosely tied clients and their factions. Prem and Chuan excelled at this. By nature, a *phudi* must seem to be incorruptible, a reputation both leaders enjoyed. However, this calm, deliberative style also opens up politicians to charges of being aloof, indecisive, and, in Chuan's case at least, unable to control the corruption of subordinates. Furthermore, both Prem and Chuan exhibited distaste for populist politics. This combination of perceived indecisiveness, distaste for populism, and the need to win the support of other politicians also made it virtually impossible for Prem or Chuan to gain credit for policies designed to help people in rural areas. That went to the local M.P.s, many of them *nakleng*, who claimed personal credit for the bridges, roads, and other benefits their constituents received. It was this weakness which Thaksin would later exploit.

The new *nakleng* style is deeply rooted in the changes of the Sarit era. By appointing headmen to represent the national government, Sarit further eroded the ethic of participation in village politics. At the same time, he made resources available for rural development, and villagers found that certain individuals with good connections to bureaucrats could procure those development funds for the village. Those same individuals, due to their relations with the bureaucracy, were able to develop economic enterprises, often based on government concessions. Naturally, the people with good connections to bureaucrats were often those engaged in illegal enterprises who needed protection. These individuals became the new *nakleng*.

In national politics, the *nakleng* style, in the version promoted by Sarit at least, worked well with a more rigid structure of loyalties where patron–client ties were reinforced by bureaucratic and military institutional structures. This style was most effective when the number of actors in the political arena was relatively limited. The arrival of parliamentary rule expanded the numbers of actors and made it impossible to rely on bureaucratic and military structures alone. Thus, after the development of parliamentary rule, the *nakleng* style had to be adapted somewhat from the style that had developed under Sarit.

The new *nakleng* is generally a provincial politician, whose (disintegrating) patron–client ties are unreinforced by institutional structures. Furthermore, he cannot possibly have face-to-face patron–client ties to all his constituents. Consequently, he is expected to exhibit, not just manliness or power, but, above all, generosity, whether in the form of vote buying, charitable contributions, or privileged access to government resources, as a means of extending those ties. In this sense, the new *nakleng* can be seen to embody both the traits of the old *nakleng* loyal to his own—now generalized to an entire constituency—and the benevolence of the *phudi*. Former prime minister Banhan Silapa-acha, for example, had the nickname of "the mobile ATM" because of his generosity to colleagues and constituents. He has established a charitable foundation in his home province, has been accused by political rivals of vote buying on several occasions, and has consistently succeeded in obtaining a disproportionate share of government development budgets for his province (*Bangkok Post*, 3 November 1995, 5). Key to the generosity of the *nakleng* is giving constituents what they want—whether it be a bridge, a road, or cash—so that, at some level, consultation and participation exists. For the rural voter, both the *nakleng* style and especially practical (economic) reasons make the new *nakleng* an attractive candidate. The power of the new *nakleng* depends in large part on convincing voters that he can deliver benefits that alternative forms of democratic participation, such as a public hearing or support for a political party, could not. The new *nakleng* has found that perpetuating the gap between local concerns and national politics is in their interest, as it allows them to take the powerful position of mediator between the two. Thus, for villagers, the gap between central government policy and local needs has been reinforced under this style of leadership.

In addition to the increased emphasis on generosity, the new *nakleng*, like the *phudi*, must be willing to listen and to compromise at the parliamentary level in order to aspire to national leadership. These talents are necessary skills for maintaining some degree of unity within political parties, which are based on factions, and for supporting often-fragile governing coalitions. Here again, generosity comes into play, as it can help to ease conflicts. Yet this generosity is often sustained through corruption. For example, the Banhan government was plagued with allegations of corruption. While this may not have mattered in Banhan's home province of Suphanburi, it did matter in Bangkok, where people were increasingly frustrated with the new *nakleng* style of politics.

Prime Minister Thaksin Shinawatra, on the other hand, at least in the initial period of his term, has succeeded where Banhan could not: as a new *nakleng*-style politician acceptable to Bangkok.[20] Thaksin's ancestors, like Banhan's, migrated to Thailand, eventually settling in Chiang Mai in the north in 1908. Thaksin's ancestor Ku Sun Saeng was a tax farmer and silk trader, and the family business gradually expanded to include banking, real estate, bus routes, schools, a cinema, and a department store (Plai-Oh 1987:53–54, 104–105; Ukrist 1998:67). By the time Thaksin was born in 1949, the family was already wealthy and prominent in the north.

Thaksin began his career at the police academy. He graduated at the top of his class (1973) and was given a scholarship for graduate study in the United States, where he earned first an M.A. and later a Ph.D. in criminal justice. On his return to Thailand after earning his M.A., Thaksin married the daughter of a top police general, and his bureaucratic career was off to a strong start. His career with the police department lasted until 1987, when he resigned to devote full time to his business activities. It included a stint attached to the Prime Minister's Office, giving him connections with some top politicians to complement his friendships in the police department.

Although Thaksin had limited experience with computer technology—he had taken some classes during his Ph.D. study—with the alleged support of his father-in-law, he won the contract to supply computers to the police department in the early 1980s (Ukrist 1998:67–68). On this foundation, Thaksin built a business empire through concessions won from the government. Like Banhan, he had extensive connections he could call upon in his applications for those concessions. His uncle, Suraphan Shinawatra, was for a time deputy minister of communications. Subsequently, Thaksin was able to win several monopoly concessions from that ministry. For instance, he obtained a concession for a cable television channel—perhaps, one report alleged, with the help of a fellow former police officer who then chaired the Mass Communications Organization of Thailand (see *Khao phiset,* 3 May 1989, 12). Thaksin parlayed these government contracts and concessions into billions of dollars when he listed his companies on the stock exchange in the early 1990s.[21] By the mid-1990s, he had become one of the richest people in Thailand.

Also like Banhan, Thaksin began his career in politics partly to protect his business interests from competitors, who were actively supporting political parties (Ukrist 1998:69). His first political party was Chamlong Simuang's Phalang Tham party, which was then quite popular with Bangkok middle-class elements. Thaksin became foreign minister under the Phalang Tham quota in 1994. However, he was forced to resign just a hundred days later when it was discovered that he still held shares in companies that had contracts with the government. When parliament was dissolved in May of 1995, Thaksin became the new leader of the party. Although he served again briefly as a cabinet minister, he was unsuccessful in his attempts to enlarge the party. In 1998, Thaksin formed a new party of his own, the Thai Rak Thai party, and began once again to prepare to contest an election. Like Banhan, he was the major source of financial support for his party.[22] And like Banhan, he was under suspicion: the National Counter Corruption Commission (NCCC) had found, in an 8 to 1 decision, that he had concealed some of his assets in a declaration made in relation to his position of minister in a previous government.

In terms of leadership style, Prime Minister Thaksin has described himself as a "Genghis Khan"–style manager, one capable of setting out a "vision and forc[ing] everyone to work like barbarians" (*Nation*, 8 January 2001, A1, quoting from *Asian Business* 1995). According to the *Bangkok Post* (7 February 1995, 3), he has "no fear" and demonstrates "toughness and reliance." "He is never afraid of making decisions, although caution is not one of his strong points" (*Nation*, 8 January 2001, A1–2). He is also said to delegate well, but "has a tendency to think that money will solve problems" (ibid.). While described primarily in business terms acceptable to the middle-class elements, this is not significantly different from the *nakleng* style of leadership, except in that, perhaps appropriately to a new *nakleng*, money is discussed while loyalty is not.

Although, like Banhan, Thaksin originally accrued his vast wealth in large part through government connections and concessions,[23] the overwhelming victory of his Thai Rak Thai party in the January 2001 election both in Bangkok and in the provinces indicated that he is perceived quite differently. In part, this is probably because Thaksin only entered politics directly after he became wealthy. However other factors are also important. Banhan began by selling chlorine and sewer pipes; Thaksin sold computers. Banhan got his degree through a correspondence course, and his M.A. came with accusations of plagiarism; Thaksin obtained his M.A. and Ph.D. in the United States. As prime minister, Banhan still betrayed his lower-class provincial origins in his mode of speech and mannerisms; Thaksin was never lower-class, and spoke and acted like the Bangkok elite. In short, Thaksin won his overwhelming victory because he was able to portray himself not only as decisive in the manner of a *nakleng*, but as the model "middle-class" success story and as an effective CEO. Banhan can be seen as someone who attempted to reach that same level of legitimacy following a similar path but without similar success, as he never left his provincial lower-class origins behind.

This new style of leadership tells us much about changes in Thai political culture. It reflects the decline in the strength and rigidity of patron–client ties. Whereas in the past, these ties were strengthened by bureaucratic or military structures, current leaders must deal with a wide variety of groups, and no overarching structure exists to confirm patron–client ties. Money has emerged, particularly in the provinces, to help support patron–client ties. However, while structures provided long-term reinforcement of the ties, money provides only short-term reinforcement and must be renewed periodically within a competitive environment.

As Mulder (1992b:chap. 2) pointed out, the *khunna*-based legitimacy of the *phudi* tends to be associated with femaleness and the *decha*-based legitimacy of the *nakleng* with maleness.[24] If *khunna*-based *phudi* styles of leadership are increasingly seen as more legitimate than *nakleng* styles, then we might expect to see more women attaining leadership positions. In fact, in the parliament, there is a trend of slowly rising numbers of women M.P.s. But thus far the change has been very slow. The number of women in parliament increased in the 2001 election, quite substantially in absolute terms (to forty-four), but only slightly in percentage terms (to 8.8 percent), as the parliament increased in size. Interestingly, the increase was mainly in the provinces, and not in Bangkok nor on the party lists. The associations of *khunna* with femaleness, then, have only slowly begun to benefit women in elections.[25] Nevertheless, although women have only slowly begun to enter the parliament, they have played an important role in the evolution of male politicians from *decha*-based legitimacy to *khunna*-based legitimacy. *Decha*-based prime ministers relied on the male-dominated military and bureaucracy as the primary source of their legitimacy. *Khunna*-based prime ministers have largely relied on the election and the public opinion poll, where women make up half of their constituency.

Much has been made of the differences between urban and rural voters, or alternatively, middle-class and poor voters, and their attitudes toward democracy and participation.[26] Often it is argued that urban voters are democratic, basing their votes on parties and policies, while rural voters are apathetic and willing to sell their votes to the highest bidder (Suchit 1996; Anuson 1998). Anek (1996: 220–223) takes a more charitable view of rural voters, arguing that they expect different results from their M.P.s. Vote buying, he holds, is not as important as the underlying patron–client ties. Rural voters expect their M.P. patrons to address their "parochial" issues, leading to direct benefits such as roads or bridges, rather than "abstract" interests like policies or the public good. "For the educated middle class, influenced by Western thought" (1996:221), the "national" interest takes precedence; and yet, as Anek pointed out, the middle class does not have a privileged position in determining the "national" interest. Indeed, as we shall see in the next chapter, parties have rarely designed policies to appeal to rural voters, leaving the way clear for rural M.P.s to seek votes as individual patrons. As in earlier periods, there is a gap between local interests and national politics, so rural voters have little choice but to choose according to their local interests. Thus, new *nakleng* quite frequently win election to the parliament in the provinces by bridging the gap and bringing benefits to their constituents. This has led to a great deal of frustration for the urban middle-class elements who see parliamentary rule being undermined by the election of new *nakleng* in rural areas.[27]

This combination of village-level support for democracy and middle-class frustration is clear in the survey research of Albritton and Thawilwadee (2002). They report that support for democracy is stronger in rural areas than in urban ones, and weakest in Bangkok, where the middle classes are concentrated. Furthermore, they found that, while more educated people were less likely to participate (a trend they attributed to cynicism about democracy), this relationship was much less important than the difference between Bangkok and rural areas. Taken together with the evidence indicating that both middle and lower classes have participated in democratic uprisings, this phenomenon may indicate that both groups support democracy in principle, but have some difficulties with the way it is practiced. Finally, the survey research of Albritton and Thawilwadee (2002) indicates that, relative to other Thai political institutions, trust in political parties is low. Again, this supports the contention that parties have not successfully appealed to the interests of either urban or rural voters, of any class.

In Chapter 2, I turn to the parliament, to the electoral system, and to political parties and their relationship to voters, particularly in rural areas. It is in the parliament and the political parties that leadership and democracy are most visibly linked. Parties have struggled to develop organizations compatible with both parliamentary institutions and local patterns of leadership.

In Chapter 3, I examine the nature of female leadership, the difficulties faced by women leaders, and the factors that seem to allow some women to become leaders in Thailand. I observe in Chapter 3, and argue more fully in Chapters 5 and 6, that space is opening up for a greater leadership role for women as culture, stereotypes, and socialization change. However, progress has been slow.

In Chapters 4 and 5, I discuss a traditional style of local leadership, the *nakleng,* and examine how it is changing under the aegis of political, economic, and social change. I examine the rise of the *jaopho* (godfather) and *jaomae* (godmother), their relationship to the traditional *nakleng,* and their roles in politics.

In Chapter 6, I analyze changing patterns of leadership in urban poor communities. In some communities, traditional *nakleng* are still the leaders and patrons of the community. In others, new forms of leadership have emerged to take advantage of democratic institutions. I find that when poor communities have a clear stake in the democratic process, when they stand to benefit or to lose, they quickly learn democratic methods of participation.

In Chapter 7, I turn to the middle-class elements. It has often been argued that middle-class elements are the strongest supporters of democracy. But it is less often recognized that their economic interests can come into conflict with their desire for democracy. I conclude that while the middle-class elements do play an important role in initiating democracy, they also seek to place limits upon it.

After examining leadership and democracy in these contexts—Thai political institutions, cities and countryside, and their relationship to different genders and classes—I return in the Conclusion to the broader issues confronting Thailand and to the lessons that can be learned for expanding our understanding of the democratization process.

CHAPTER 2

■ ■ ■ ■ ■ ■ ■ ■ ■ ■

Leadership, Political Parties, Factions, and Patronage

Political parties form a key link between the institutions of democracy borrowed from the West, such as parliaments and cabinets, and the voters, by providing leadership at the top, in the cabinet and the parliament. They do so by appealing to voters within the framework of the prevailing culture, norms of participation, and styles of leadership. The political parties and their workings are thus the most appropriate place to begin a study of leadership, participation, and democracy.

A considerable number of articles, dissertations, and books have been written in attempts to explain the Thai political party system. Duncan McCargo (1997b) has usefully summarized this literature by dividing it into two categories: works that focus on parties and those that focus on factions.[1] In the first category he placed scholars who have assessed Thai political parties by examining their formal structures, comparing them to idealized Western models, and sometimes to specific Western political parties. This approach has led to cataloging the areas where Thai political parties fail to measure up to those ideal models, and has contributed to attempts to force political parties to change through political party laws, electoral laws, and even constitutional provisions.[2] In the second category, scholars have focused on the internal dynamics of political parties, and particularly on their factions. Rather than comparing Thai parties to Western parties or models, these scholars have focused on the way Thai political parties actually function. They "seek to explain parties in terms of resource allocation: parties exist to marshal funds and appropriate power. Their studies emphasize the role of factions, the importance of regional groupings *(sai)* and the close links between politicians and the business sector" (McCargo 1997b:118). These scholars see vote buying and corruption as the methods of resource allocation that are central to the functioning of parties. However, McCargo maintained that studies that focus on factions and resource allocation within parties cannot explain some of the conflicts that have occurred both within and between political parties. Drawing on Panebianco, he argued that the ideology of the party, however vaguely expressed, has some relevance to how parties and politicians act. Studies that focus on resource allocation and factional alignments ignore the roles played by ideology and organization.

As useful as this categorization of the literature is, it suffers from two flaws. First, somehow McCargo lost track of his own accurate representation of the work on the formal structures of political parties. Scholars in this category do not posit idealized parties; rather, they assess Thai parties against idealized standards. Similarly, scholars who focus on factions do not admire the workings of Thai parties and often conclude their analyses with suggestions for improving them. Indeed, scholars in both McCargo's categories conceive of Thai parties in similar ways and suggest similar remedies. The effect of McCargo's categories, then, is to downplay the overwhelming consensus in the literature: that Thai parties have been deficient, and that they can and should be improved. There is widespread agreement that parties have been too weak while their factions have been too strong. Weak party organization has led to vote buying; vague policy platforms; unstable, ideologically incoherent coalition governments; and patronage politics.[3] The importance of this consensus in the literature cannot be overstated, as it underlies the attempts at the reform of the party system and the recent rhetoric regarding the need for fewer parties and greater stability. Second, while McCargo is certainly right in encouraging the study of both the parties and their factions, he gives little concrete guidance as to how we might go about it, aside from what we can interpret from his case studies.[4] Criteria for assessing the relative importance of parties and factions have not been provided.

Despite these weaknesses, McCargo rightly highlighted the importance of paying attention to the ways in which party policies and structures relate to factional structures and the allocation of resources. This second challenge was almost simultaneously taken up in the work of Dan King (1996: esp.191–200). In a comparative case study of the Phalang Tham (Palang Dharma, or PDP) and New Aspiration (NAP) parties, King characterized the NAP as a party based on factions, and the PDP as innovative, seeking to strengthen party structure. He concluded that the NAP, despite pretensions to a national network of branches and members, was organized around the individual M.P.s and factions. Nevertheless, he found that while NAP decision making was made by an oligarchy of faction leaders, national-level policy positions did affect decision making. The innovative PDP, he concluded, had a more developed branch network, but that network did not participate in the decision-making process, which was dominated by the party leader (see also McCargo 1997a). Other parties, he believed, were not following the innovations of the PDP in regard to party structure, so that the change had not affected the party system more generally.

To understand the nature of participation and democracy in Thailand, then, we begin with the political parties and their factions. Since the parties play a crucial role in the selection of national leadership, it is certainly worthwhile to examine carefully the ways in which they function, how they are organized, how they are funded, how they select their leaders, and how they change. Many of the faction leaders in the parties are the provincial politicians who appeal directly to voters. The ways they interact with village leaders and voters will reveal much about the nature of participation. In this chapter we will undertake a detailed study of Thai political parties.

Legacies of the Past

During the sixty-year period since the toppling of the absolute monarchy, parties have emerged six times to participate in elections and parliamentary government; however, before the latest parliamentary experiment, these parties had never governed for more than three years.[5] In each case—except the most recent—following a coup, parties were ultimately dissolved, their assets confiscated, and their organizations dismantled. Up until the 1975 parliament, each election was won by a government party, which, by using the bureaucracy, had a ready-made organization and adequate financial support.

Some of the most important legacies inherited by political parties stem from the early years of democracy, before and after World War II. After 1932, one piece of the pattern was set in place when political parties were banned in Thailand. Originally the Promoters, the group who overthrew the absolute monarchy, called themselves the People's party and began to organize. However, shortly thereafter an opposition party came together and sought to register. At that point, rather than accept competition, the People's party turned itself into an association and outlawed political parties. This ban on political parties prevented the formation of centralized electoral organizations and entailed two related effects. First, it led to the use of government ministries and bureaucrats in support of candidates, which reached a peak in the form of government parties, most prominent in the 1950s and 1960s. At the same time, each candidate was left to create an ad hoc organization at the local level, consisting of clients, friends, and anyone else whose support could be assured in seeking votes. The candidate then became dependent on these supporters. This second effect became increasingly important after the disappearance of government parties in the 1970s.

After World War II, parties appeared in Thailand for the first time. For the most part, they organized within the parliament in support of particular leaders, with the prominent exception of the Communist party. For example, two parties organized to support Pridi Phanomyong, then the most influential politician. The new political parties had only a brief time to organize before elections were held, and of necessity fell back on the same two types of organization mentioned above: the bureaucracy, and the networks of local candidates and notables. During the period between the end of the war and 1958, parties were sometimes allowed, sometimes banned. While it may well be that parties would have been underdeveloped anyway,[6] this historical pattern precluded any possibility of developing strong central party organizations or party-based electoral organizations, had any party wished to do so. After he abolished parliament in 1958, Sarit banned all political parties and confiscated their assets as he turned to strongly authoritarian patterns of leadership.[7] Parties disappeared from the political scene for nearly a decade.

The elections of 1969 and 1975 saw two related changes that together altered both future parliaments and political parties of Thailand. The first of these changes was the increased competition for seats in parliament, as more individuals and groups sought to play a role in politics. The 1969 election differed from past elections, as the high level of competition for parliamentary seats by factions within the governing coalition ensured the importance of those able to deliver votes in return for money. As candidates scrambled to form electoral organizations, election methods based on *hua khanaen* (voting chiefs) and vote buying increased. Where in the past patrons might have been able to deliver their clients' votes through mere persuasion, with the weakening of traditional patron–client ties and greater competition, vote buying became increasingly necessary to ensure support. In some cases, vote buying reinforced patron–client ties; in other cases, it was used to overcome the stronger patron–client ties of a rival. These *hua khanaen* were generally patrons, *nakleng*, local leaders, or respected individuals, and served as intermediaries between voters and candidates by encouraging voters to elect particular candidates. The importance of these *hua khanaen* expanded further with the disappearance of government parties after the 1973 uprising: ultimately, no candidate could hope to win without an effective *hua khanaen* structure.

The second change, after 1973, came about as a direct result of the demise of government parties. The dramatic uprising of 1973 discredited the old military regime, and the caretaker government, led by Sanya Thammasak, chose not to contest the ensuing election. Consequently, there was no party able to monopolize the resources of the government in the election. Instead, individual bureaucrats could be recruited into the *hua khanaen* structures of the various candidates. Concurrently, economic development increased the quantity of potential *hua khanaen* as the number of the village-level notables expanded and as more cooperatives and factories (whose owners became potential *hua khanaen*) began to appear in some provinces. New types of *hua khanaen* developed, leading to the creation of complex electoral networks made up of various types of *hua khanaen* formed by the candidates of leading political parties. This enhanced the importance of the campaign methods that had arisen in 1969 and increased the number of parties competing for power. As a result, more parties won seats than ever before, and no party was able to win a majority. Coalition governments became the norm for Thai politics.

Some forty-two parties contested the 1975 election and twenty-two won seats in the new parliament. After an unsuccessful attempt by Seni Pramot and the

Democrat party (Prachathipat) to form a minority government, Khukrit Pramot of the Social Action party (Kitsangkhom) organized a coalition government that included sixteen parties, twelve with fewer than ten seats each. Khukrit's own party held just eighteen seats in the 269-seat parliament. Khukrit was able to put together a cabinet through astute maneuvering and through distribution of cabinet seats to the parties in the coalition by means of a quota system. He left several cabinet positions open, and was able to maintain a precarious grip on power by dangling the empty portfolios as rewards to cooperative members of the government and the opposition and by granting key faction leaders control over their own ministries. Patronage flowed from cabinet positions to the factions and then to the members of the parliament. Khukrit's sixteen-party coalition lasted just one year. It collapsed when some members of factions within the coalition parties, disgruntled at not being awarded cabinet positions, destabilized the government—demonstrating the influence of the faction over the party and the weakness of party discipline.

With the emergence of a quota system, cabinet positions became based on the number of M.P.s a minister could control and not on experience or seniority, and factions grew in power: by building a faction of seven members, an M.P. could hope to gain a cabinet seat. Any individual able to control enough seats to meet the quota might successfully join the cabinet, regardless of background or ideology. This further strengthened the factions and hindered the development of strong party organizations. Finances and electoral organization were coordinated by the party but remained in the hands of faction leaders. The leader of the party was generally the most powerful faction leader. In the event of a coup, this limited the assets that could be seized; it also allowed the party to organize rapidly, though haphazardly. However, the parties had come to depend on the faction leaders for electoral organization and finance. The faction had become the building block for the party, as each party put together a group of factions in order to expand rapidly and thus join the cabinet.

So, at least since the 1970s, parties have been built from factions, based on personalities rather than ideologies, without effective central electoral organizations, mass bases, or assets. A substantial decentralization of power has occurred as the government has become dependent not on parties but on powerful factions. The quota system made the necessary constituency for a cabinet seat dependent on controlling a specific number of seats in the parliament within a party that is a part of the governing coalition. The power of the cabinet was then used to enhance the position of the faction and the minister or his patron. Consequently, the cabinet—consisting of faction leaders or their nominees—was subject to frequent turnover as a result of conflict within and among factions and sought to limit the role of parliament as much as possible to minimize conflict.[8] Faction leaders who succeeded in gaining a position in the cabinet attempted to employ the resources and patronage of the office as rapidly and effectively as possible in order to strengthen the faction before the next cabinet reshuffle. The weakness of coalition government and the frequent changes led to considerable corruption and a focus on short-term goals.

Although power resided largely in the cabinet and the factions, the party did play some important roles. Even when the election laws were not in place to force factions to bond together to form large parties, the need to form a coalition government often accomplished the purpose. The leader of the largest party was the most likely to become prime minister. And the largest parties were most likely to be invited to join a coalition government, since the smaller the number of parties in the coalition, the easier it was for the government to control the coalition. The difficult task of controlling the factions was left to the parties. There was, then, a tension between the desire to build a small, cohesive faction large enough to win a cabinet seat and the need to join with other factions and individuals to form a larger party—at the risk of weakening both the faction and the party. The result was fluidity both among factions and among parties, as individuals and groups maneuvered to improve their positions and chances of gaining a cabinet seat.

Thai political parties, then, have been made up of powerful factions. The factions, and their individual M.P.s, depend on *hua khanaen* to connect them to the voters. Given the importance of these intermediary levels between voters and parties, it is worth examing them, and the way they function, in a bit more detail, beginning with the *hua khanaen* system.

The *Hua Khanaen* System

The *rabop hua khanaen* (literally "vote-chief system") has been a result of several societal factors; these factors, and the *rabop hua khanaen,* are strongest in rural Thailand. First, due to the gap between local concerns and national politics, there has been considerable apathy regarding political parties and national politics in Thailand. With a few rare exceptions, many voters have been unaware of any differences between competing candidates or parties that actually matter in their daily lives. As we shall see, this may be changing under the Thai Rak Thai government. Second, there is a respect for authority figures, particularly those involved in issues of local interest, including teachers, monks, *phuyaiban,* and other influential persons in the community. Given the lack of differences between candidates or parties, the recommendations of these authority figures translate into a large number of votes from villagers, who may see no concrete benefit in participation in national politics or may simply trust or fear the voices of these figures.[9] Third, the patron–client ties, which have become increasingly uncertain, still exist, and when effectively reinforced, can sway voters. Finally, the lack of effective local-level political party branches[10] means there is no continuing organization to support a particular party or platform at the local level. Thus each candidate puts together a network of *hua khanaen,* relying on respect, apathy, and patron–client ties, reinforced by gifts where necessary. Nelson (2002) argued that these networks, or major segments of them, have become so powerful that they, rather than the candidates, the factions, or the parties, are the key link. By switching their support from one candidate to another, these *phuak* (groups), to use his term, can control election outcomes in an election district. Of course this system discourages participation and benefits *hua khanaen,* as it enables them to maintain their influence in elections and beyond.

Hua khanaen vary by type and by level, ranging from a village teacher with limited influence to a wealthy tycoon with business interests and employees spread throughout an entire region.

Types of *Hua khanaen*[11]

GOVERNMENT OFFICIALS

Retired government officials have often won the respect of many of the people formerly under their jurisdiction. Furthermore, they may also have supporters among active government officials who are in a position to benefit candidates. Even more important than the retired government official is the working government official, who may be able to influence many of his subordinates to support a candidate. In addition to campaigning among subordinates, government officials can often use their positions to the advantage of the candidate. A new independent agency, the Election Commission, has been established to supervise elections in the hope of controlling such abuses, but it has limited resources both in terms of finance and personnel, and is still quite dependent on the Ministry of the Interior. Over time, however, this change may decrease the effectiveness of government officials as *hua khanaen.* The Ministry of the Interior, and in particular the District Officer (Nai Amphoe) has the responsibility for keeping all the records, including household registration, which is used to generate the list of registered voters. Though the 1997 constitution and the election laws that stem from its provisions have made it more difficult, manipulation of the records in favor of a candidate has often contributed greatly to that candidate's success in the past.[12] A police chief may send officers to protect and aid favored candidates, threaten rival candidates, or even have a candidate arrested (Sombat 1987b:64–65; *Bangkok Post,* 13 December 2000, 2). In the run-up to the 2001 election, fourteen high-ranking police officers were transferred after their neutrality was questioned, and several more were transferred as the election approached (*Bangkok Post,* 31 December 2000, 3; 4 January 2001, 3). Government resources, such as medicines from the Department of Public Health, may also be distributed in such a way as to benefit a particular candidate.

ELECTED OFFICIALS

Elected officials, like government officials, are not allowed to campaign for candidates. However, this restriction has been widely ignored. Elected officials have proven their ability to win votes and have become increasingly important as *hua khanaen* over the last decade. They range from those whose influence is fairly widespread, such as members of the provincial council, to those with a narrower base of support, such as members of the village administrative committee.[13]

Provincial councilors. The provincial councilor, and particularly the president of the provincial council, who has won the support of a majority of the council, has the widest base of support of the elected provincial officials. Provincial councilors may be seeking to expand ties to their constituencies by campaigning for a candidate and may also benefit financially from the transaction. Many provincial councilors, however, donate their own time and money to the campaign in order to develop a close relationship with a winning candidate. The ties formed during the campaign may progress into a symbiotic relationship as the candidate seeks to ensure electoral victory for his *hua khanaen* in later elections. The provincial council has also become an important route to running for parliament as the provincial councilor builds an election network in his own campaign and acquires broader connections by helping with the election campaigns of parliamentary candidates.

Mayors and *thesaban* councilors. *Thesaban* councilors are elected in a single citywide district and can gain election with a relatively small number of votes. Consequently, their constituency, in many cases, is small and not as well developed as the constituencies of the provincial councilors. A *thesaban* council position is, therefore, not a common political pathway to a position as a member of parliament. The most influential *thesaban* councilor is chosen by the council as mayor. A mayor can be a powerful *hua khanaen*. The mayor has the support of most of the *thesaban* councilors and as their patron can often arrange for other councilors to assist in the election effort. More important, the mayor can employ many of the city government resources in the campaign in the same way as government officials can employ government resources. The mayor is leader of a large number of city employees and has control over a wide array of equipment and services that can be quietly used in support of a candidate.

Kamnan. The *kamnan* (head of the *tambon*, which consists of about five to ten villages), along with the *phuyaiban*, or village head, is generally the most important link in the chain of *hua khanaen*. The *kamnan* has a relatively large constituency, though smaller than that of the provincial councilor. Unlike the provincial councilor, the *kamnan* serves as a direct link between the villager and the district office—the level of government most directly concerned with the villager. Consequently, villagers are accustomed to respecting or even fearing the *kamnan* and the *phuyaiban* for their knowledge of the government and their influence in the village, and their opinions carry weight. Furthermore, the smaller constituency of a *kamnan* (who is elected from among the *phuyaiban*) allows a *kamnan* to develop stronger ties to his constituents than a provincial councilor. The role he or she plays in maintaining law and order in the *tambon* also allows the *kamnan* to use intimidation if he or she chooses. Recognizing the importance of their position in the *hua khanaen* system, *kamnan* and *phuyaiban* in many areas have formed associations to attempt to exploit that influence (Ockey 2000; Phichai, Somchaet, and Worawit n.d.:59; Suchit 1985:57). Finally, most *kamnan* and *phuyaiban* are influential in the community for other reasons: financial resources, ties with powerful figures, or control over violence. Also, like the members of the provincial council, *kamnan* often develop close relationships with members of parliament in economic activities (Ockey 1992:chap. 4). A *kamnan* may also have higher political ambitions.

Phuyaiban. The *phuyaiban*, like the *kamnan*, is in close contact with a constituency. However, the constituency is much smaller than that of the *kamnan*, covering a single village. The importance of the *phuyaiban* in the *hua khanaen* system is clear: associations always include both *kamnan* and *phuyaiban*. *Kamnan* and *phuyaiban* often work together politically and economically. At other times they may compete for the loyalty of villagers, allowing candidates from more than one party to secure support at these two different levels.

Village council members. Members of the village council also serve as *hua khanaen*, although they are less influential than *kamnan* and *phuyaiban*. Members of the village council have little influence with the government, making them less effective than *phuyaiban*. However, when working together with other more powerful *hua khanaen*, they can be valuable because of the respect they command within the village, and because they can directly supervise the voting of small groups of voters.

Defeated candidates for elected office. In cases where a candidate cannot win the support of a *kamnan* or *phuyaiban*, he may enlist the support of a losing candidate for the office, hoping to win the votes of those who dislike the *kamnan* or *phuyaiban*.

LOCAL GANGSTERS AND CRIMINAL GROUPS

As campaign methods have changed over the last thirty years, the importance of this type of *hua khanaen* has grown markedly. The frequent use of vote buying and the privatization of intimidation led to the use of criminal groups in the election process, as they have broad political and economic ties that can be useful in an election. These ties reach both upward to government officials and downward to the people. The operator of the underground lottery is particularly important due to the continuing organization of ticket sellers that extends into nearly every village (Phoemphong and Sisomphop 1988:30–31). Criminal elements may be able to cooperate with or coerce election officials, policemen, and opposing candidates, and even voters come under the threat of violence to property or person if the wrong candidate is victorious. Despite the new constitution designed to eliminate corruption and vote buying, violence may have increased during the 2001 election, although naturally the evidence is sketchy. Police sources claimed that, with still two weeks to go before the election, more than thirty people had been killed for political reasons (*Bangkok Post* (Perspective), 24 December 2000, 3; see also *Nation,* 11 January 2001, A2; *Bangkok Post,* 29 December 2000, 2).

BUSINESS LEADERS

Local business leaders are in a position to supply both financial resources and equipment, such as printing equipment, sound equipment, vehicles for transportation, and goods for distribution, to potential voters. Business leaders who are involved in the distribution or marketing of goods are able to draw on a network of paid employees to advance the campaign of a candidate, and factory owners are in a position to urge the support of their workers for a particular candidate[14]— perhaps even with the promise of a bonus if the candidate is victorious. Liquor distribution, construction, and banking entrepreneurs have been particularly important in elections because of the nature of their networks and the goods they control (Ockey, 1992:chap. 5). Business leaders often have the respect of customers, and may also wield influence over debtors and those dependent on them for the distribution of goods or the marketing of crops. The importance of business leaders with these resources can be seen in the large numbers of candidates who are business leaders themselves (Anek 1988; Ockey 1992:chap. 6).

RELIGIOUS LEADERS

Prominent local monks, Islamic religious leaders, and in a similar fashion, leaders of Chinese lineage associations, command a great deal of esteem among their followers and can provide an aura of respect to a candidate. The support of Islamic leaders is particularly important in the south, where the leadership may be organized at the provincial level.[15] A religious leader may support a candidate of the same religion, out of kinship ties, or, in some cases, in return for a donation, either in cash or in the form of construction work. Although in some cases a religious leader will actively support a candidate,[16] more frequently support will be more subtle: the candidate and the religious leader will be seen together; the candidate will make a public donation to the temple; or the candidate may visibly support improvements to the temple. Religious symbols may be used in campaigning or rallies held at temples, where the candidate may be able to associate himself or herself with the temple. Muslim candidates often speak at the mosque after evening prayers. And in some cases, villagers who sell their votes are required to swear before a revered religious icon that they will vote for the candidate who has provided the money.[17]

TEACHERS

Teachers are respected for their knowledge and for their efforts in educating the youth. A teacher who recommends a candidate to students, who in turn tell their parents, can command votes (Kramon, Sombun, and Pricha 1988:59). An administrator may also be able to make buildings and equipment available.

HUA KHANAEN RAP JANG

One final type of *hua khanaen* should be mentioned, the *hua khanaen* for hire. Such *hua khanaen* are experienced campaigners with no particular ties in a community. Instead they rely on money to create loyalties, generally by trying to buy *hua khanaen* who do have influence rather than by trying to buy voters directly. Such *hua khanaen* are not tied to a territory and can be used in areas where the candidate has no personal influence.

Levels of *Hua Khanaen*

I have outlined the types of *hua khanaen* in rough order of importance, beginning with government officials who may have influence throughout a province or entire region, down to village councilors and teachers, who may only be able to influence a few people. It is necessary to develop a campaign organization with *hua khanaen* at all levels in order to succeed. The hierarchical structure reflects both the needs of an electoral campaign and the nature of patron–client ties. Before turning to the nature of the factions that make up the political parties, it is necessary to show how the *hua khanaen* structure and the factions are linked through the top level of *hua khanaen*.

Regional-level *hua khanaen*, and in some areas provincial-level *hua khanaen*, are at the peak of the *hua khanaen* hierarchy. This type of *hua khanaen* is often influential in the selection of candidates in his own area and may finance the campaigns of many of those candidates. Many of the regional-level *hua khanaen* are themselves members of parliament and thus work through their own political parties. By supporting other candidates, they develop a faction of M.P.s within the party. In return, the *hua khanaen* gains influence in the party through the support of his candidates and often obtains a cabinet position. Other regional-level *hua khanaen*, though not M.P.s, may support sons, daughters, or loyal subordinates in the party and develop a faction through them. Still other regional *hua khanaen* may support candidates from a number of parties in areas under their control.

Typically, this last type of *hua khanaen* is not interested in political opportunities or prestige but is seeking protection for illegal activities and privileged access to government resources. By supporting candidates in several parties, the *hua khanaen* maximizes the chances of getting some allies into a coalition government. There is heavy competition from parties to enlist the support of these *hua khanaen*. Regional- and provincial-level *hua khanaen* are the most coveted because of their financial resources, their existing networks of important connections, and their ability to recruit other *hua khanaen* at lower levels of the election network. These types of *hua khanaen*, as faction leaders, may have more control over the selection and election of candidates than the parties or the candidates themselves.

Factions and Political Parties

As we have mentioned, one source of the contemporary powerful factions is the quota system established for gaining cabinet positions. Nevertheless, factionalism is not new to Thai politics. The Democrat party, the only one to survive the periodic bans on party activity between 1945 and 1978, has split some ten times because it could not control internal factionalism. Since 1978, constitutions have sought to limit the number of political parties in the parliament in order to ensure stability. As a result of these provisions, it is difficult for a single faction to become large enough to contest an election as an independent party, and the number of parties contesting elections has fallen from thirty-eight in 1976 to about fifteen in the 1990s. The 2001 election saw the rise of many small parties, but the party list system put in place has limited the number of successful ones. As of 2003, there were forty registered political parties, but only eight held seats in parliament, and only four held more than two seats. Rifts continue to occur in Thai political parties and factions to split off from parties; however, one important result of the constitutional provisions favoring large parties has been an increase in mergers of small parties with larger ones, in particular with the powerful Thai Rak Thai party.

If constitutional provisions managed to decrease the number of successful political parties, they failed to eliminate the problem of factions. The smaller factions were forced to bond together to form larger parties or to merge with larger parties in order to survive; however, within these expanded parties the factional bonds remained. By rebelling, or threatening to rebel, the faction presents a problem out of proportion to its numbers and enlarges its power as a faction. In a recent case, the Democrat Party managed to form a coalition by giving cabinet seats to a faction from an opposition party, in return for its support. The party, Thai Citizen party (Prachakon Thai), then attempted to expel this renegade "Cobra" faction for violating a party resolution to support another candidate for prime minister, only to face delay after delay. Eventually, the Constitutional Court ruled that the faction could be expelled, but that members would retain their seats in parliament if they joined another party. Most Cobra faction members joined the Rassadon party, the coalition government survived, and the faction retained its ministerial positions. The Chuan coalition government was able to retain power for four years, initially due to the support of this ostensibly opposition party faction.

TYPES OF FACTIONAL LOYALTIES

Factions within Thai political parties vary in both type and degree of loyalty among members. A single member of parliament may owe loyalty to several factions, with different degrees of loyalty owed to each, or may owe loyalty to none. In general, factional ties can be divided into several types, and are here described in order of increasing cohesiveness or shared loyalty.

Ideological ties. Among the weakest types of factional ties are factions based on ideology. For brief periods during the fifties and the seventies, left-oriented political parties flourished. However, in both cases these parties were destroyed after coups. The coup of 1976 in particular was bloody by recent Thai standards, and was caused by ideological conflict. Reluctance to reopen this violent conflict and laws that have made it difficult to form small parties have largely prevented ideologically based parties from reemerging. However, ideology has not disappeared from the Thai parliament. Many of the individuals involved in the ideological conflict of the 1970s have returned to politics, although they have been dispersed over a number of parties. Factions based on ideology tend to be situational, may cross party lines—limiting their ability to gain a cabinet position by meeting the necessary quota—and have rather tenuous ties. Activities seem to consist largely of discussing ideas and working behind the scenes to influence policies.[18] Ideology-based factions are stronger when limited to a single party. Since the economic crisis, ideology, or at least policy, has become more important for political parties, with the Thai Rak Thai party promoting populist policies, and the Democrat party promoting neoliberal policies. Such differences seem to have had little effect on struggles among factions, however.

Regional ties. Regional ties, which may also cross party lines, have a long history in Thailand, especially in the northeast (Keyes 1967:chap. 5). However, the large number of M.P.s in each region has made strong cohesive regional factions impossible. Although some regions appear to be dominated by particular parties, in most cases, the domination is the result of shared *hua khanaen* structures rather than regional ties. Factions based purely on regionalism are no more cohesive than those based on ideology. Like ideological factions, regional ones are concerned with specific policies. Also like ideological factions, regional factions are stronger when they exist within a single party where they can meet the quota for a cabinet position, or are strengthened by other ties. Finally, it is worth noting that regional ties can be exploited in electoral campaigns. Party leaders often appeal to voters in their region by claiming that having a prime minister from their region will benefit them. Sometimes party leaders even appeal to more than one region on this basis. In the 2001 election, for example, Thaksin Shinawatra made such regional appeals both to voters in the north, where he was born, and to voters in Thonburi, where he resided.

Personal ties. More focused than the regional ties are personal ones. Since Thai political parties originated as organizations established to promote certain leaders, it is not surprising that the personality-based faction is still important in Thai politics. Some respected senior politicians are able to retain factions through their influence within the political system, through the respect of other politicians, and through their broad-based popularity. Members of the faction may remain loyal out of respect, ideological affinity, or as a means of gaining influence and support for themselves through the prestige of the faction leader, either locally or nationally. True personality-based factions—those that do not also involve financial support by the leader for members of the faction—have become less common as competition for election increases and elections become more expensive. The departure from the political scene of longtime politicians and founders of political parties such as Khukrit and Seni Pramot, Praman Adireksan, and Chatchai Chunhawan has also undermined the significance of such ties.

Kinship ties. In many cases, personal ties are strengthened by kinship. An examination of parliamentary records shows that 21.6 percent of all the members of parliament since 1932 have shared a surname with at least one other member. While some of those relationships may be distant, counting shared surnames actually underestimates the number of relationships, as it does not account for name changes, in-laws, or married daughters. To take a few examples, Niphon Promphan, a timber magnate in Nakhon Ratchasima, his wife, Sisakun Thechaphaibun, and her brother, Phonthep Thechaphaibun, from a family known for its role in developing Bangkok's World Trade Center, its control of the now defunct Bangkok Metropolitan Bank, and once prominent in the liquor industry, among other business activities, have all entered the parliament in northeastern constituencies. In at least one case, that of the Saphawasu family, father Pramuan (Chat Thai) and son Kumphon (Ruam Thai) ran for different parties. In the 1988 election, "between 150 and 160 candidates [were] on record who have some sort of blood or legal link with other candidates." "The [Chat Thai] party [had] about 13 families with at least two members running" (*Nation*, 20 July 1988, 31; *Khao phiset*, 13 July 1988, 53–54). This tendency may have increased with the new constitution, as senior party members moved to the party list and sponsored relatives in their former constituencies. These included close relatives of prominent politicians such as Sanoh Thienthong, Surin Phitsuwan, Pongphon Adireksan, Banhan Silapa-acha, Suphatra Masadit, and the northeastern *hua khanaen* and *jaopho* Sia Leng, among others.[19]

Financial ties. With the burgeoning costs of elections, money has become increasingly important as a basis for factionalism. While the less affluent M.P.s find themselves unable to finance a campaign, the more affluent see an opportunity to enhance their own power by financing the campaigns of others. In this way, a rich member of parliament becomes powerful by gaining the support of a number of less affluent M.P.s who could not win without financial support. Others who choose not to run for parliament themselves also finance the campaigns of a number of M.P.s—at least until 2001, often in several parties to ensure that at least one of their M.P.s join the government—in order to gain protection, access to information, and influence within the parliament and, if their power extends that far, the cabinet. Although these types of factions, based as they are on a concrete exchange of benefits, are much more cohesive than those based on ideology, regionalism, or personal loyalty, they have still been subject to betrayal. When a number of potential sources of campaign finances are available, an M.P. may be willing to leave his current financier for another if the reward outweighs the risk. Furthermore, in many cases, the M.P. will obtain financial support from several sources and the tie to any particular patron is thus weakened. In the wake of the 1997 financial crisis, the importance of financial support increased dramatically, as both provincial notables and many Bangkok tycoons felt the effects of the crisis. As one analyst put it, "Most backers now have to think very seriously about which party to get behind since they no longer can afford to hedge their bets by giving to all . . ." ("Inside Politics," *Bangkok Post,* 28 December 2000, 15). With fewer alternative sources of support available, the importance of monetary ties has increased, at least temporarily. However, as money is not directly tied to the election district, it is not as strong a tie as a network of local *hua khanaen.*

Business ties. In some cases business ties will link members of a faction. The Social Action party, for example, originally included a faction led by Bunchu Rochanasathien, many of whose members were associated with the Bangkok Bank. The Soi Ratchakhru clique that established the Chat Thai party is another frequently cited example. In the 1990s, some telecommunications conglomerates became closely associated with political parties (Ukrist 1998:69). Since the business ties exist independently of the political ties, betrayal in this type of relationship also risks a rift within the business.

Electoral ties. Some of the strongest factions are based on the *hua khanaen* system. As already noted, local election networks are not controlled by the parties but by individual *hua khanaen* at various levels. While the number of possible sources of financing may be relatively high, the number of individuals able to control the *hua khanaen* in each election district is much more limited. An individual who can control enough *hua khanaen* to determine the outcome in an election district, or in several election districts, can choose the future members of parliament in those districts. This type of faction is quite strong and betrayal is unusual; effective alternative *hua khanaen* are often difficult to find and moving to a new district also involves building a new network of *hua khanaen*. Up until 2000, election districts elected as many as three M.P.s, and small tightly knit district-level factions, usually connected through financial support to a larger faction, were quite common. The 1997 constitution changed this system to single-member election districts. Over time, this may undermine the tightly knit district-level factions. However, *hua khanaen* structures often fall within a specific area larger than a district, such as a province. In addition, the senate is elected on a province-wide basis. So such tightly knit local factions will likely remain in some form. The importance of this type of faction also helps to explain the strong territorial basis both of factions and of political parties, as individuals able to dominate a large number of *hua khanaen* usually do so in adjacent provinces within a single region.

The strongest factions are those which combine more than one of the elements of factionalism listed above. In many cases, the faction leader who is able to control *hua khanaen* is also the financier for the candidates in his safe districts. In order to insure against betrayal, the faction leader chooses candidates who feel ideological or personal loyalty to the faction leader—often supporting a wife, son, daughter, or other relative. The members of any faction may be loyal to the leader for different reasons: for one member it may be because of personal loyalty; for another, it may be because of finances or shared *hua khanaen*. All of these factions, as well as individuals loyal to no faction, and the linkages among them must be considered in forming a cabinet and in taking important votes in the parliament.

THE FLUID NATURE OF FACTIONS

While factions tend to cluster around individual leaders, the relationship between each individual member of the faction and the leader may have different bases. For core members of the faction, there may be a close personal tie, shared *hua khanaen,* and financial support. For peripheral members or smaller allied factions, there may be only personal loyalty, financial support, or promises of mutual support for cabinet positions when the party joins the government. Some individuals may owe personal loyalty to one faction leader and receive financial support from another, as long as the two factions are not at odds. Relationships between factions, like relationships between individuals, vary in strength and type. A small faction may be entirely or partly subsumed within a larger one, with members of the smaller faction supporting not only the leader of their own faction but also the leader of the larger one. Two factions may have overlapping memberships. Members of a faction may even have loose ties to a faction leader in another party, facilitating the formation of coalitions. It is only at times of conflict and struggle for leadership that factional lines and loyalties are clearly drawn. After the crisis passes, the fluidity is restored, though new allies and enemies have emerged, some may have departed, and new factions may have formed.[20] This fluidity is the basis of chances to rise in the party, to realize aspirations for a cabinet position, and to pursue opportunities for financial gain.[21]

FACTIONS AND THE CABINET

Although the basis for factionalism varies from individual to individual and from faction to faction, the goal of each faction is the same: to attain a lucrative position in the cabinet. Many M.P.s are willing to change factions and even split parties for the sake of cabinet positions. The cabinet quota system instituted by Khukrit Pramot and the resulting dispersal of power and concentration of patronage within the factions enhanced the importance of gaining a cabinet position for one's faction. While the largely arithmetically determined cabinet quota for parties focuses debate among party leaders on the awarding of important (and lucrative) ministries in the formation of a governing coalition, the fluidity of the factions within each party creates conflict and debate over the distribution of each seat within the party quota, with the winners able to use their new access to resources to build their factions, and the disgruntled losers often seeking to topple ministers within their own parties. For example, when deputy New Aspiration party leader Chalerm Yubamrung was denied a cabinet seat after the January 2001 election, he went on the offensive, criticizing the policies of the government, even though his party was part of the coalition (*Bangkok Post,* 26 February 2001; *Nation,* 7 February 2001).

Once in the cabinet, ministers can seek to build their factions in order to gain even more power within the party and more lucrative cabinet positions.[22] One means of building influence is through the appointment of potential allies and *hua khanaen* to advisory positions and to positions of political importance. A large number of paid advisory positions are divided up among the coalition parties for distribution, mainly to those M.P.s who fail to secure cabinet seats.[23] In addition, each minister is allowed to appoint an unlimited number of unpaid advisers, who are then able to print up official name cards specifying their advisory position and assuring others that they have the ear of the minister. Perhaps the most extreme example occurred after the 1988 election, when Minister of the Interior Praman Adireksan appointed some 149 of these advisers.[24] During the 1980s and 1990s, the most prestigious position offered to key party supporters was membership in the senate. Since 2000, the senate is elected; however, many other types of patronage-oriented appointments remain. Less prestigious but more lucrative appointments are made to the boards of state enterprises and governmental promotional and regulatory agencies. Under the catch phrase of "political suitability," boards are reorganized generally either at the beginning or at the end of a minister's term in office. Accusations of nepotism, patronage, and corruption in the appointments of these boards have been frequent (see, for example, *Bangkok Post,* 22 December 2000, 3;

23 December 2000, 3; *Matichon,* 26 December 2000:1ff.). For government departments, civil servants amenable to the minister may be transferred to important and lucrative positions (Bidhya 2001).

A second means a minister can employ in expanding a faction is the use of political favors to build relationships with important *hua khanaen* and entrepreneurs. Favors to *hua khanaen* may include assistance in gaining government concessions or contracts, or cooperation in getting a government official transferred to another province.[25] Favors done for businessmen may be similar, though often with higher stakes—for example, implementing regulations that result in a virtual monopoly for one business or exempting a certain business from obligations to the government.

A third means of constructing a larger faction through a cabinet position is to use the office to develop the financial means to lure cash-strapped M.P.s to the minister's faction, to support more candidates in later elections, and to build prestige within the party by donating to party expenses—often at the request of the party. The importance of money in building a faction and the resultant activities of ministers in seeking funds have led to almost continuous allegations of corruption by members of the cabinet and their appointees. The number of projects rushed through by lame-duck administrations just prior to elections remains suspiciously high. Prior to the dissolution of parliament in 2000, the government pushed through projects related to a new airport, telecommunications, paddy silos, and irrigation. Key personnel were transferred in the police, military, and Ministry of Education (*Bangkok Post,* 17 September 2000).

The crucial role of factions can be illustrated by a brief examination of the faction of Sanoh Thienthong. Sanoh, dubbed the *Jaopho Wang Nam Yen* (Godfather of Wang Nam Yen), first won election to parliament in 1976 as a Chat Thai party member from Prachinburi. In 1976, Sanoh was the only Chat Thai party member among Prachinburi's four M.P.s. He gradually expanded his faction in Prachinburi and other provinces, until by 1988 all six Prachinburi seats belonged to Chat Thai, and Sanoh had become deputy party leader. In 1986, Sanoh was rewarded with the position of deputy minister of agriculture, and in 1988 was given a post as deputy minister of interior.

Sanoh's business activities are strikingly similar to those of the *jaopho* described in the next chapter. Initially, his entrepreneurial activities included agriculture, timber concessions, and the franchise for the distribution of whisky in his province. Later, he also became involved in construction, receiving most of the contracts for the highway department in his region, real estate, transport, and service industries in the region, and secured highly sought after and difficult to obtain permission necessary for two quarries (*Matichon sutsapda,* 30 June 1991, 14–15; Pasuk and Baker 1995:333–334). It is also worth noting that Sanoh's home region is strategically located along the Cambodian border, although he has denied involvement in the border trade (*Matichon sutsapda*, 30 June 1991, 14). After the coup of 1991, Sanoh was investigated for being "unusually wealthy" along with other politicians accused of corruption by the coup government.

By 1995, Sanoh had built up one of the largest factions in the Chat Thai party, some thirty members, using his wealth and his influence in his home region. With his help, Chat Thai won the most seats in parliament, and party leader Banhan Silapa-acha became prime minister. As a reward for his efforts, Sanoh sought the highly prized minister of interior post, which then controlled the police, the land department, and local government, among other things. However, Sanoh had two rivals for the office, Watthana Asawahaem, the leader of the Cobra faction, and northern tobacco tycoon and powerful faction leader Narong Wongwan. Banhan sought to prevent conflict by retaining the position himself, a solution unsatisfactory to all three contenders. The Sanoh faction would later bring down the government in its efforts to gain the post.

In September 1996, just over a year into Banhan's administration, he faced a no-confidence vote in parliament. At that time, two coalition partners, New Aspiration and Nam Thai, together with Sanoh's faction, agreed to support Banhan only if he would resign, allowing the New Aspiration party leader to become prime minister. Sanoh would then become minister of the interior (Ockey 1997). Ultimately Banhan chose to dissolve parliament and call new elections rather than resign.

Sanoh again demonstrated his power in the ensuing elections. Angry with Banhan, he and his faction switched to the New Aspiration party (NAP) of General Chawalit Yongchaiyut. With Sanoh's help, the NAP won the most seats in the election; General Chawalit became prime minister; and Sanoh was rewarded for his crucial support with the interior ministry. Again, however, the governing coalition lasted just a year, falling victim to the Asian economic crisis in 1997. When Watthana Asawahaem's Cobra faction of the Thai Citizen party defied a party resolution to support a Democrat-led coalition government, the NAP found itself in the opposition.

For the 2001 election, Sanoh and his faction again switched parties; and again his support proved important. This time Sanoh joined the Thai Rak Thai party of billionaire Thaksin Shinawatra. Thai Rak Thai won in a landslide, as Sanoh's faction increased in size to about seventy members (*Nation*, 18 January 2001, 1). This most recent election and its implications for leadership and democracy are discussed more fully below. The important point here is that Sanoh and his faction played a crucial role in bringing three different governments to power between 1995 and 2001, and the Cobra faction was the determining factor in the formation of the only other government of the period. Thus one can see that the factions retain considerable influence in Thai political parties.

OPPOSITION POLITICS

With cabinet offices contributing so heavily to the success or failure of each faction, and by extension to each party, no party can afford to remain long in the opposition. Faction leaders need to be in the cabinet; the future of the faction and the politician is at stake. Factions in power grow and factions out of power shrink. During the 1980s and 1990s, this need to join the ruling coalition led to a further decline in the importance of ideology: parties that wished to be in a coalition could not be choosy about the ideology of a potential partner, and opposition politics became skewed. While some opposition parties, and some factions in government parties, sought to attack the government at every opportunity to bring it down and necessitate a new coalition, most parties and factions acted not as watchdogs but as partners-to-be, balancing the criticism necessary to overthrow the government with the tolerance necessary to avoid making enemies in coalition parties that might preclude entrance into a future government. Powerful faction leaders frequently cultivated members of other parties to open channels for negotiations on joining the government. Consequently, there has been a constant jockeying for position by factions within the parties and by parties within the parliament, all seeking cabinet posts in order to survive and grow. Indeed, it is exactly this need that Thaksin exploited in building up his grand coalition government.

Although factions in power grow while factions out of power shrink, there is a further paradox involved. As factions grow, faction members often expect a greater share of the resources available or see the opportunity to form a faction of their own. So, by being in power a faction grows, but increasing conflict caused by that growth can lead to a split. This has created further instability in the political party system and has contributed to the frequent changes in cabinet ministers, which have increased under the Thai Rak Thai coalition.

I have gone into considerable detail regarding the *hua khanaen* system and the factions to underline just how important they have been to the political party system in Thailand. Since the economic crisis and the new constitution seemingly changed the party system so dramatically, it is worthwhile to reemphasize the strength of the factions and the *hua khanaen* system as we examine change, so that we do not overlook the equally important continuities. Both factions, and especially the *hua khanaen* system, remain important elements despite the changes.

THE 2001 ELECTION: CHANGES AND CONTINUITIES

The new constitution promulgated in 1997 aimed to reform the electoral system by eliminating corruption and vote buying through a number of reforms that sought to strengthen monitoring institutions and political parties. (The provisions of the new constitution and their implications are discussed in Chapter 7.) The first election of a House of Representatives under the new constitution took place on 6 January 2001. Of course, it is impossible to extrapolate a trend from a single data point, so that no firm conclusions can yet be drawn regarding the long-term impact. Nevertheless, it is worth examining some of the changes and continuities apparent in this first election under the new constitution.

In the wake of the January 2001 election, much attention was paid to the number of new politicians who had succeeded in gaining seats. These new faces were optimistically seen as the harbingers of a new style of politician who would eventually push aside the "corrupt" politicians of the past. This view was given added impetus by the losses of prominent provincial notables, including candidates from the Asawahaem, Prachuapmoh, Tangthong, and Hansawat families who had long dominated politics in their provinces. While many first-time M.P.s were elected, it should be recognized that the new parliament, with 500 seats, is more than 25 percent larger than the old one. This expansion of the size of the parliament, combined with the usual number of incumbents who lose their seats, guaranteed a large number of new M.P.s. Between the elected M.P.s and the replacements for those who resigned to join the cabinet, some 534 were chosen. Since the previous parliament comprised only 393 seats, 141 of those chosen had to be new M.P.s. If we exclude those 141 newly created seats from consideration, just over three-fourths of the remaining elected MPs were former M.P.s.[26] This rate of turnover is similar to the turnover rate in other elections.[27] Moreover, many of the new M.P.s were relatives or close aides of former M.P.s who had moved to the party list, to the senate, or had chosen this opportunity to retire.[28] Thus, while nearly half of the M.P.s were new faces, there was also a surprisingly high degree of continuity in the parliament, obscured by the large number of new seats. To put it differently, the new commissions and election rules did little to limit the ability of former M.P.s to retain their seats, and in some cases benefited them as they moved to the party list and also retained their constituency through a relative or an aide. Either the changes had little impact on successful campaign methods, or most politicians successfully adapted.

Perhaps the most remarkable change is the tremendous success of the fledgling Thai Rak Thai party, which won 248 seats in the initial election, just three fewer than an absolute majority.[29] No party has won such a large share of the seats in parliament since the days of government-sponsored political parties. This gave the Thai Rak Thai party unprecedented bargaining power in forming a coalition, choosing a cabinet, and pushing its policies through parliament. It is worth examining some trends in party size and numbers of parties.

The new constitution seems to have had little effect on the number of parties with more than twenty seats, other than to reward them with party list seats.[30] Indeed, the number of parties with more than twenty seats has varied from four to six, which is remarkably consistent over the years, particularly when we take into account the number of different parties that have had at least twenty seats in any one election (thirteen parties since 1979). Of course the number did shrink *after* the election, but the first election provided little evidence that the new constitution by itself could reduce the number of parties in parliament.

As for party size, the second largest, the Democrat party, is virtually the same size as in the last election, and the same size as the second largest party in the last election (see Table 2.1). Of course, that represents a smaller proportion of the expanded parliament. So the dramatic growth in party size is limited to a single party in the 2001 election and has not benefited other large parties. After a decade with the two largest parties nearly equal in size, the Thai Rak Thai party doubled the size of the second largest party. Also interesting is the general trend we see in the gradual growth of the largest parties since 1988. Part of the reason for this growth is the departure of the military from the cabinet in that year. This meant more rewards for civilian politicians and made it possible to support larger factions and larger parties. Another factor driving the growth in size of parties and factions through the 1990s was control over the Ministry of the Interior. With the ministry then responsible for the land department, the public works department, the department of town and country planning, the prisons department, provincial and metropolitan waterworks and electricity, the National Housing Authority, the Expressway and Rapid Transit Authority, and most important, local government administration and (until very recently) the national police force, minister of the interior became by far the most valuable cabinet position other than prime minister. Heavy competition for the post led to larger and larger factions, and naturally political parties grew as well.

We may question whether the sudden dramatic growth of Thai Rak Thai represents a new trend, or whether the trend lies in the gradual growth in previous

Table 2.1. Size of Largest Political Parties

Parliament (Year)	Largest Party	Seats	Second Largest Party	Seats	Combined Seats	Total Seats
1979	Social Action	83	Chat Thai	38	121	301
1983	Social Action	92	Chat Thai	73	165	324
1986	Democrat	100	Chat Thai	63	163	374
1988	Chat Thai	87	Social Action	54	141	357
1992a	Samakkhitham	79	Chat Thai	74	153	360
1992b	Democrat	79	Chat Thai	77	156	360
1995	Chat Thai	92	Democrat	86	178	373
1996	New Aspiration	125	Democrat	123	248	393
2001	Thai Rak Thai	248	Democrat	128	376	500

elections of other large parties. We must also ask how much the growth in the size of political parties matters. Increase in the size of parties does not necessarily undermine the importance of factions.

PARTIES AND THEIR FACTIONS

As we have seen, and as the concensus in the literature indicates, there are four key areas of contention between parties and their factions. First, parties have always had to rely on factions, and individual M.P.s, to establish their own electoral networks. When competition for *hua khanaen* and votes increased, even as patron–client ties further weakened, vote buying expanded. Second, parties have failed to develop clear and convincing policies designed to benefit rural voters, allowing factions and individual M.P.s to seize the initiative in promising benefits to rural voters and claim personal credit for improvements delivered. (While policies designed to benefit business are equally important, these have generally been better articulated.) Third, coalition building in Thailand has been based on a quota system dependent on the size of individual factions. While the quota has varied, generally it has been about five to seven seats for a cabinet position. In order to satisfy all factions, the goal of coalition building has been to create a minimum winning coalition, so that cabinet positions are shared among the smallest group possible. Fourth, patronage that flows from cabinet seats has been left under the control of the factions for distribution. Thus the factions have had the upper hand in all of these areas. In assessing how the party system has changed, these are the relationships that must be examined.

Electoral Networks and Vote Buying

Despite the establishment of new laws and institutions designed to eliminate vote buying and corruption, and to strengthen parties, many of the same patterns continued. Preparations began earlier than usual, partly because the new Thai Rak Thai party could focus its attention entirely on campaigning rather than on the parliament. More important, the Election Commission, which seeks to prevent vote buying, was largely inactive until the parliament was dissolved; goods distributed before that time were gifts rather than vote buying. Vote buying was widespread, despite the efforts of the Election Commission and other monitoring groups, with the price of votes ranging from 50 to 1,000 baht,[31] 500 baht being perhaps the most common amount. On the whole, vote buying was done much more carefully than in the past, often through gifts rather than in cash.[32] One community-level informant claimed that in his Bangkok community the cash was going only to *hua khanaen* (vote canvassers) rather than to voters, in order to limit the risk of being caught.[33] Other reports have this money eventually making its way to voters, but not until election day.[34] It is difficult to estimate the total amount of vote buying as much of it was done before the campaign officially started. Thai Farmers Bank Research Center estimated that about 25 billion baht was put into circulation during the election campaign itself, up 25 percent from the 1996 election. Of course, only a part of that money went to vote buying, but it is worth noting that if the total were divided equally among all the candidates, each would be spending about nine times the limit set by the Election Commission.[35] False accusations of vote buying, complete with manufactured evidence to present to the Election Commission, were the most widely employed new tactic.

Electoral networks remained under the control of individual M.P.s and factions, rather than the parties. Thai Rak Thai engaged heavily in the recruitment of M.P.s and *hua khanaen*, convincing about a hundred M.P.s and former M.P.s to join and bring their personal election networks with them. Thai Rak Thai also recruited local politicians, such as provincial councilors, who had their own electoral networks in place. So effective was Thai Rak Thai in this recruiting that it had more former M.P.s contesting the election than any other party. As in the past, candidates switched parties in large numbers, apparently basing their decisions on the willingness of parties to contribute to their election campaigns and on the likelihood of the party doing well. Thus, the key role of *hua khanaen* in linking individuals and voters did not change significantly, although with vote buyers risking disqualification, trust between the candidate and the *hua khanaen* was at a premium. Party organizations remained secondary to such personal networks in the campaign process.

Party Policies

While electoral networks remained in the hands of the factions, for the first time since the 1970s, party policies played a major role in the election. In particular, Thai Rak Thai developed populist policies that were clear and concise and aimed at the lower classes, particularly in rural Thailand. These included a debt moratorium for farmers, a revolving fund of 1 million baht for every village, and subsidized medical care. These policies were popular and easily understood. They would make a clear difference in the lives of the poor, particularly the rural poor. Furthermore, as a new party, Thai Rak Thai did not face as much skepticism as the existing parties in regard to its policies. The Democrat party countered with a campaign based on the continuation of its economic policies. Those policies had become closely associated in the public mind with the unpopular IMF structural reforms and were neoliberal in character, so that the Democrat party was pursuing a clearly losing strategy. Nor were there any clear concrete benefits for rural voters such as those Thai Rak Thai offered. Aware that its economic policies were unpopular, the Democrat party downplayed the role of the finance minister, Tarrin Nimmanahaeminda, but refused to abandon him entirely. Thus policy platforms—and even ideological differences—clearly divided the two leading parties to a degree unseen for two decades.

In all regions but the south, the stronghold of the Democrat party, Thai Rak Thai did well. These policies certainly played an important part. Of course the new constitution did not enter into the decision by Thai Rak Thai to develop such populist policies. The more relevant factor was the economic crisis, which forced rural poverty onto the political agenda. If poverty could no longer be easily ignored, it certainly could be used to win votes. The economic crisis may have been important in another way as well: provincial notables, and indeed many wealthy Bangkok entrepreneurs, suffered heavily from the crisis. This eroded the power of the provincial notables in the election process, as they became increasingly dependent on external financing, and from a more limited set of patrons. Thai Rak Thai was best positioned financially to take advantage of the weakness of the provincial notables and took them on board in large numbers. This greater dependency of the local notables on the party for financing may have been crucial in allowing the party to take credit for assisting the poor with its policies rather than, as in the past, leaving it to the provincial notables to take personal credit for rural development projects.

Although the most striking aspect of the Thai Rak Thai party policy platform was the scope and clarity of its policies aimed at the rural poor, it also targeted the support of the wealthy. Two aspects of that policy, both responses to the financial crisis, are noteworthy. First, the party proposed to set up a Thai Asset Management Corporation to assume bad debts. Since many leading entrepreneurs were deeply in debt, this policy had widespread appeal. While the policies to assist the rural poor received more publicity, the establishment of the Thai Asset Management Corporation to assist the rich was more costly. Second, the Thai Rak Thai party promised preferential treatment for domestic entrepreneurs. This second promise allowed the party to seek support from entrepreneurs who would otherwise have been in competition with each other and therefore might have chosen to support competing parties. Thus Thai Rak Thai was able to consolidate the support of many financiers who had previously supported other parties. This second policy also provided the cement that held the entire policy platform together: nationalism. The IMF and its policies became the enemy, and promotion of Thai interests in business and in the countryside became the rallying cry.

Coalition Building

Past democratic parliaments in Thailand have been characterized by numerous small and medium-size parties, organized internally around powerful factions. In the past, the maximum size of parties, and of factions, has been constrained by the preference for a minimum winning coalition in the parliament, since the smaller the governing coalition, the more rewards for each party, faction, and individual.[36]

As previously noted, the maximum faction size has been about 30 to 40 seats, while the maximum party size had crept up from around 90 at the start of the 1980s to around 120 by the late 1990s, as both the parliament and government budgets grew. The faction has been the locus of allocation of rewards, through cabinet seats, with the cabinet seats as the primary site of corruption. This faction-based corruption, extensive as it was, had inherent limits of scale based on the small size and competitive nature of the factions.

The continuing relevance of the factions quickly became clear when the bargaining over positions in the new cabinet began. Each of the coalition partners faced problems as its factions jockeyed for positions. If anything, the struggle for cabinet positions may have been more intense than usual, as the new constitution limits the size of the cabinet to 36 members, 12 fewer than in the past, so that the necessary quota was about 8 to 9 parliamentary seats for each cabinet seat. The expansion of the size of the parliament thus diluted the power of the smallest factions, forcing them to join larger factions to obtain a share of patronage. Again the struggle over the Ministry of the Interior was particularly stormy, as Thai Rak Thai's Bangkok M.P.s gathered to show support of Sudarat Keyuraphan (about 36 M.P.s), and the northeastern M.P.s in support of Sanoh Thienthong (about 70 M.P.s).[37] In the end, however, Thaksin reserved the position for his own faction (about 100 M.P.s). Sudarat became the minister of public health, and members of the Sanoh faction became minister of agriculture and deputy minister of the interior.

While cabinet positions were contested along factional lines as in the past, Thai Rak Thai did employ a new strategy in making up its coalition government. It sought to create a grand coalition of factions and parties rather than a minimum winning coalition. The formation of a grand coalition divides the rewards into smaller shares, making it difficult to implement. However, it has the advantage of limiting the ability of any single faction to undermine the coalition, because the withdrawal of any single faction from the coalition does not bring down the government, but only eliminates access to rewards for the faction. So withdrawal of individual factions is not a viable option or an effective threat, and in the short term, barring a crisis, stability can be more easily maintained.

The grand coalition strategy only became possible in the wake of the 1997 financial crisis, and then only because Thai Rak Thai was built on the fortunes of some of Thailand's wealthiest concessionaires. In the past, wealthy tycoons have often supported several parties to maximize their chances of having allies in a coalition government. However, hurt by the crisis, many sought instead to back a winner. Thai Rak Thai looked like that winner. When Thai Rak Thai party leader Thaksin promised that local entrepreneurs would be given priority over foreign investors under his government, it sealed the deal. Meanwhile, Thaksin set out to recruit faction leaders. As momentum built, more and more former MPs decided that their best chances of reelection would come from joining Thai Rak Thai rather than competing with it. It won nearly twice as many seats as the next largest party, and was about twice the previous maximum size for any nonmilitary party. Under these unique circumstances, a grand coalition became possible. Once the size of the grand coalition became clear, Thai Rak Thai was able to coerce other parties to merge themselves with Thai Rak Thai to ensure their position in the coalition and in the cabinet. The alternative, as it has always been, was to lose access to patronage and the associated opportunities for growth.

Patronage

We can see the shift in patronage occasioned by the grand coalition strategy by briefly considering the telecommunications sector. Where previously telecommunications firms had links to different parties, and often each firm had links to multiple parties, when Thai Rak Thai came to power, nearly every major telecommunications concessionaire had financial links to the party or had contested seats for Thai Rak Thai.[38] Thai Rak Thai had to find a way to benefit groups that were in competition with each other. In its response, we see a new method of patronage that may be able to sustain the grand coalition. Nine months after taking office, the Thai Rak Thai government mooted a proposal to end mobile-phone concession payments early for all firms. It has been calculated that this would cost the government nearly 300 billion baht (about 700 million U.S. dollars) in revenues, while saving the concessionaires the same amount. The Thaksin family conglomerate would save over 100 billion baht of that amount, with much of the rest saved by other financial supporters of the Thai Rak Thai party. In addition, share prices for the firms involved would increase an estimated 43 to 225 percent, depending on the company.[39] The Shinawatra family conglomerate, and the other companies linked to Thai Rak Thai, would see a return on their investment in the party, ensuring their continued financial support. When this approach met with strong public opposition, the cabinet set the plan aside.

In early 2003, with little warning, the cabinet issued an executive decree designed to convert the concessions to an excise tax. An executive decree is intended for legislation that must be enacted rapidly in times of crisis and is not subject to debate in parliament. In this case, it was used in an attempt to prevent public controversy over the new plan. While the government insisted the new plan would not affect the revenues for the state or private operators, the telecommunications sector rose in reaction to the news, and the Telephone Organization of Thailand announced that, based on calculations for the previous year, it would have lost about one-third of its revenues compared to the concession system. The share of profits the telecoms firms would pay, it was estimated, would drop from 85 percent to 50 percent (*Bangkok Post*, 3 February 2003, B1; 25 January 2003, 1).

How this difference would be made up was left unclear. And with the Shinawatra family conglomerate controlling over 50 percent of the mobile-telephone market, it stood to benefit most. This new style of patronage is entirely legal. It is also on a scale that could never be matched by the old-style patronage of individual cabinet ministers.[40] And as Thaksin and some of his wealthiest supporters built their fortunes on monopoly concessions from the government, it is not surprising that his party has turned to such concessions for patronage.

At the same time, factions continue to employ patronage from cabinet seats and the parliament to fund themselves, yet the amounts they allocate cannot narrow the gap sufficiently for them to compete politically with the major financiers of the party, and especially the party leader. Indeed, the amounts they can allocate may not be sufficient to fully support their factions. In August–September of 2001, the frustrations of constituency M.P.s spilled over into the public arena, as they complained that some cabinet ministers were not doing enough to assist them in looking out for the needs of their financial supporters and constituents. The crisis (which was exacerbated by factional conflicts) was only eased when Thaksin stepped in to mediate.[41] Later the Thai Rak Thai party secretary-general was replaced by a much wealthier cabinet minister, better able to assist constituency M.P.s. However, this solution left the constituency M.P.s dependent on major party financiers, and over the long term this may perpetuate the relative financial weakness of the factions in the post-crisis period, even should the economy fully recover.

In the short term, this grand coalition strategy has worked remarkably well, because, as pointed out, no single faction can destabilize the government. However, the grand coalition remains a coalition of groups with divergent interests, and over the long term it will prove difficult—perhaps impossible, if Riker's (1962) formulation is correct—to hold it together. There may not be enough patronage to go around, even in the systematic form we find in the mobile-phone concessions.[42] Furthermore, this form of blatant but legal patronage risks alienating voters; it has already delayed the proposal to end concession fees on mobile telephones and ultimately led to an executive decree to avoid a parliamentary debate. The grand coalition strategy relies on both patronage and votes, and a dramatic fall in opinion polls due to excessive overt patronage or other policies could lead to defections from the party and the fall of the grand coalition. It is in this context that we should understand the pressure the government has brought to bear on poll takers and the attempts to influence press coverage (*Nation,* 1 March 2001, internet edition; *Nation,* 20 August 2001, internet edition; Case 2002:545). As the next election approaches, and the cost of abandoning the coalition is measured in months of access to resources rather than years, the difficulty of holding the coalition together will only increase. This is one reason why Thai Rak Thai has pressured coalition partners to accept mergers rather than continue as separate parties.

Thaksin and the Thai Rak Thai may succeed, given current dominance, their vast financial resources, and the weaknesses of other parties. Attempts to pressure both parties and individual M.P.s to join the Thai Rak Thai party to ensure participation in future governments began shortly after the coalition was formed, and continue. On the other hand, a single paradox may prove impossible to resolve. Thai Rak Thai put the coalition together because of the overwhelming financial superiority of its leaders in the wake of a devastating economic crisis. It came to power with a successful entrepreneur promising to revive the economy. If the party succeeds in reviving the economy, it will lose its overwhelming financial superiority; if it fails to revive the economy, it will lose its electoral support.[43] This paradox may eventually doom the grand coalition experiment to failure.

The striking success of the Thai Rak Thai party in the 2001 election seems to have resulted primarily from the impact of the financial crisis rather than the provisions of the new constitution. The crisis limited the financial resources available to faction leaders and financial backers, facilitating the ability of Thailand's wealthiest tycoon to recruit them to his new party. It also provided the basis for the nationalist and populist policy platform so successfully developed by the Thai Rak Thai party. Of course, taking advantage of the effects of the financial crisis required bold "new thinking," which Thai Rak Thai has displayed in abundance. Certainly it has changed the nature of politics, as policies have become much more important to voters.

The strength of the factions remains their control over electoral networks. For the 2001 election, parties again went to great lengths to recruit those with already existing electoral networks rather than build their own party-oriented networks. As long as the electoral networks remain in the hands of the factions, they will continue to hold considerable sway within parties. On the other hand, the Thai Rak Thai party was able to exert control over policy formulation, beginning with the formulation of its election platform, and then worked to implement those policies after gaining control of the parliament. Here Thai Rak Thai undermined the power of the provincial and local notables who comprise most faction leaders. By formulating party policies that appealed directly to rural people, Thai Rak Thai was able to take credit for improvements in the lives of villagers, at the expense of the provincial and local notables who had previously characterized such resource allocation as personal rather than party patronage. The shift here was not complete, however, as some programs, like the million baht revolving funds for every village, were subject to manipulation by provincial and local notables. To some degree, the support of Thai Rak Thai in rural Thailand will depend on the success of these policies.[44] At the same time, no other party has formulated alternatives with clear concrete appeal to rural voters.

While there is a precedent for the types of policies Thai Rak Thai promoted,[45] it is in coalition building that Thaksin's new thinking has had the greatest impact. If successful, the grand coalition strategy will limit the ability of any single faction to destabilize the government and so increase the power of the party over its factions. However, as we have seen, over the long term a grand coalition is actually less stable than a minimum winning coalition, and it will not be easy for Thaksin to hold it together. One means of doing so has been systematic and legal forms of patronage that have the potential to far outstrip the methods of individual cabinet ministers in the past. The economic resources he and his allies control, the promise of legal forms of patronage on a large scale, pressure on coalition partners to merge, and attempts to influence the press have thus far held the grand coalition together, despite occasional tensions.

Thaksin's new thinking has changed the political party system by changing the relationship between party and faction in some ways. However, the changes implemented thus far may not be sufficient or stable enough to become permanent. In order to effect lasting change in the political party system, the parties need either to develop their own electoral networks or to take over existing electoral networks. Otherwise, the faction leaders will remain powerful because they control the votes. Thaksin's ability to change the system depends on breaking this key link between factions and voters. It is not at all clear that he can do so. According to Election Commission statistics, Thai Rak Thai had nearly eleven million members as of June 2003, but just eight party branch offices. By contrast, each of the 294 M.P.s had a local office under his or her control, staffed by supporters, to reinforce their personal campaign networks.[46] There is thus a long way to go to bring electioneering under central control. At the same time, it may be possible to forge a link to voters outside of the party system. Indeed, Thaksin has clearly been attempting to do just that.

Thaksin's End Run

While Thaksin has brought change to the political party system and to the relationship between faction and party, we have also seen that there has been considerable continuity in the party system, and factions remain powerful. Thaksin is also seeking to circumvent the faction leaders and the party system in his attempts to consolidate power, taking his policies and personality to the people through the media. Thaksin as a telecommunications tycoon is both more aware of the power of the media and better positioned to employ it than any of his recent predecessors. Not since the days of Phibun—before the revival of the monarchy and the promotion of the monarch as the symbolic leader of the nation—has any Thai prime minister so effectively used the media to promote himself and his policies. And of course the media has expanded its reach and influence tremendously since the days of

Phibun. In particular, the 1990s saw a rapid rise in the number of rural households with a television set.[47] Thaksin's efforts to use the media to reach the people directly has taken place in three specific ways, which can be briefly outlined.

The most controversial way the coalition government has sought to influence the media in reaching out to the people has been through attempts to prevent them from criticizing him or his policies. These attempts, his opponents allege, amount to intimidation and censorship. Shortly after Shinawatra Corporation took over ITV, some reporters there charged the new ownership with interference with their reports on the election and the trial of Thaksin over his alleged failure to properly declare his assets. They subsequently lost their jobs (Nation, 20 August 2001). Later it was revealed that some media personalities were under investigation by the Anti–Money Laundering Organization. A number of political talk shows considered critical of the government have been canceled, and in some cases, live broadcasts of parliamentary debates and other political events have been curtailed (ibid.; Bangkok Post, 6 March 2002). More subtly, but perhaps more importantly, according to Senator Chirmsak Pinthong, state firms and the firms of the Shinawatra family conglomerate have withdrawn advertising from newspapers deemed overly critical, while those that report positively have received favorable treatment, using state assets (Bangkok Post, 30 April 2002; see also Nation, 10 April 2002). In addition, critical reports have provoked warnings from the police Special Branch or led to threats of libel suits (Nation, 20 August 2001). In these ways, the government has sought to rein in criticism and shape the way people perceive the government and the prime minister.

In reaching out directly to the people, circumventing provincial notables, Thaksin's efforts to promote positive portrayals of himself and his policies may have been even more consequential than his attempts to control negative publicity. The media relations effort was in high gear during the election campaign and has remained in place, albeit in different ways. The Thaksin government has launched a series of high-profile campaigns to great fanfare and seemingly shaped those campaigns to strengthen its popularity. The social order campaign of then Interior Minister Purachai Piemsomboon, ostensibly designed to impose order on Bangkok nightlife, such as discos, pubs, bars, and clubs, is but one example. Frequent high-profile raids by the minister, which received considerable attention in the media, were at the center of the campaign, rather than any detailed long-term plan for implementing the policy—similarly, with the anti-drug campaign, led by Thaksin himself, which, it was announced, would rid Thailand of narcotics within three months. The initially popular campaign did not include detailed long-term plans, but rather focused on short-term gains that brought positive publicity. When there were signs of discontent over the high number of deaths associated with the campaign, the government first decided that it would no longer announce the number of suspects killed, then shifted its focus away from the deaths to other aspects of the campaign. When one campaign has lost public and media attention, another has emerged to take its place.[48] And yet, in some ways even more influential than these high-profile campaigns have been Thaksin's Saturday afternoon speeches, broadcast live over the radio. It is through these speeches that Thaksin has taken his policies directly to the people, largely circumventing the party apparatus and the provincial notables. Of course, the reach of the weekly radio broadcasts are not limited to radio audiences; the speeches are widely reported in the press and in television news. But the live radio speech allows Thaksin to present his policies personally. In the process, the policies have become more closely associated with Thaksin himself than with the party as a whole.

Last, Thaksin's success in influencing the media has been in part due to influence over and ownership of media and media-related companies.[49] The Shinawatra family conglomerate is generally considered a telecommunications conglomerate, but it is also a media conglomerate. Investments run the gamut from an advertising company (Matchbox) to a television station (ITV) to an internet provider to satellite television to satellite concessions. Prior to the 2001 election, Thaksin had already moved to secure a controlling interest in ITV, the only privately owned television station in Thailand. He also made use of his satellite technology to broadcast rallies from one location to others throughout the country. These broadcasts became not only channels for disseminating policies but became policy, as Thaksin used them to demonstrate his technological expertise and promised progress in this area. In addition to his ITV holdings, Thaksin's close ally, Thai Rak Thai party-list candidate Pracha Maleenond controlled television channel 3. And after taking over the government, Thaksin added the government-controlled channels 9 and 11 and the military-controlled channel 5 to those he could influence, at least indirectly. Most radio channels are also in the hands of the government, or are let out on short-term concessions, so that concessionaires are highly vulnerable to pressure from the government.[50] Only part of the press lies largely outside the control of Thaksin's political allies.

So, through his use of the media to convey his policies directly to the people, Thaksin has also, to some degree, managed to circumvent the power of the powerful provincial notables who control party factions. In the process, he has also circumvented the party system. Policies have become associated with individual cabinet ministers, and especially with Thaksin himself. Thus, like the changes to the party system, it is not yet clear whether the policies will change the nature of politics permanently, to the benefit of the Thai Rak Thai party, or will be primarily associated with Thaksin personally. Furthermore, the new constitution envisions the privatization of the media, removing them from government control and making it more difficult in the future for a prime minister to so dominate them. The use of the media as an alternative route to promote policy will remain for other political leaders in the future, although perhaps in more competitive fashion. For better or worse, not only were the provincial notables and their factions weakened, but also the entire party system and its role in politics, even as the new constitution sought to strengthen them.

Thai Political Parties and Political Leadership

It is indeed the political parties, and particularly the factions within them, that have connected Western-style parliamentary institutions to Thai society. The way in which political parties have developed historically has been connected to the changing patterns of leadership in Thai society. When the absolute monarchy was overthrown in 1932, there was a legitimacy gap at the top of the political system. Rather than allow organized political competition, the new leadership banned political parties and effectively devolved political organization to powerful local leaders who thus retained their legitimacy and transferred it to the new parliamentary system. The decentralized party system, which may well have eventuated in any case, was entrenched by this decision. At least by the time of the later transition to strongly authoritarian patterns of leadership after 1957, political parties were convinced that it was better not to centralize assets, which could then be easily confiscated. Instead, organizations and finances were left to the local notables, who developed the intricate *hua khanaen* system and in turn became the leaders of the powerful factions. It is tempting to say that the factions and the *hua khanaen* system preserve the patron–client ties of the past. We have seen, however, that patron–client ties have been distorted rather than preserved. Instead of reciprocal relations of mutual benefit, increasingly weakened patron–client ties are a channel for distributing payments in cash or goods for votes. Indeed, in some cases, patron–client ties are missing entirely and the transaction is purely financial.

Thus far, most of the efforts to change the system have focused on the symptoms rather than the underlying causes. A Counter Corruption Commission and various organizations, including an official body, were established to monitor elections. More recently, a new constitution was written that attempts to solve the problem through legal mechanisms.[51] Cabinet members are no longer allowed to sit in the parliament, an attempt to separate elections and access to political patronage. Of course, this means no M.P. representing a constituency will be a cabinet minister. Given the ability of powerful patrons to win seats for friends and family members, this is unlikely to prove effective. Some of these policies will be beneficial, particularly the development of access to education. Yet none of this will eliminate the need the poor have for patronage, and none of it necessarily leads political parties to promote policies that attract the support of those who sell their votes. It took the financial crisis to place such policies on the Thai Rak Thai agenda, where they may—or may not—prove successful.

The causes may be more difficult to address than the symptoms. Most important, the gaps between rich and poor, between city and village, and between national politics and local concerns, have to be addressed. This would mean policies benefiting those in rural areas and the poor, rather than policies benefiting the rich and the middle class. The 2001 election indicated both the popularity of such measures and the difficulties that must be overcome. The Thai Rak Thai party promised a debt moratorium for farmers and the establishment of one million baht revolving funds for every village. Both policies proved very popular, and helped deliver an unprecedented victory to Thai Rak Thai. However, the party complemented those policies with one relieving the rich of their bad debts, a more costly policy than those aimed at the poor. Furthermore, neither debt relief for farmers nor the revolving funds is aimed at structural change; both are patronage-oriented. Wresting control over policy away from local patrons who wish to seem personally responsible for benefits to their constituents has proven a difficult task. Nevertheless, Thaksin has succeeded in putting clear and specific policies firmly on the political agenda. Some, such as the popular national health insurance plan, are centrally administered. No longer will parties be able to promote the kind of vague superficial policies seen so often in the past.

CHAPTER 3

■ ■ ■ ■ ■ ■ ■ ■ ■ ■

Women and Leadership

 Cultural differences between the palace and the village in premodern Thailand were evident in gender relations. In palace culture, women were considered the chattels of kings and male nobility (Darunee and Pandey 1987). Only men were admitted to royal service, and women could participate only as "appendages" of men in their role of wives of officials (Juree 1994). At the same time, it has long been reported that women in Thailand (and in Southeast Asia in general) have been better off than women elsewhere in Asia (see, for example, Winzeler 1982). As Anthony Reid (1988) pointed out, in precolonial Southeast Asia at least some women were able to succeed in trade, or as diplomats, warriors, and rulers, although they were rare exceptions. In contrast, women outside the palace, and especially at the village level, have routinely been able to play important roles, particularly in the economy. One early observer, Simon De La Loubere, wrote that, at the time of his visit in 1687, "The Women plough the Land, they sell and buy in the Cities" (De La Loubere 1986:50), asserting this was because men were subject to corvée labor, so women of necessity had to be the traders. However, this prominence in economic matters away from the palace did not extend to the political sphere in urban or rural areas: government officials, village headmen, and *nakleng*, with few exceptions, were male.

This pattern of participation outside the palace persisted after the 1932 overthrow of the absolute monarchy and the turmoil of war, as Skinner (1957:300–305), Kirsch (1975:172–196), and others have noted, women fulfilling economic roles and men the political and bureaucratic professions. This meant that, in many households, women participated in decision making, controlled finances, and safeguarded the family's wealth and status (Van Esterik 1996:6).[1]

With women involved in both the economy and agriculture, participation in the workforce outside the home has also been relatively high. By the end of 2000, women comprised over 44 percent of the labor force. They outnumbered men, not only in commerce, but also in the manufacturing and service sectors (National Statistical Office 2002). The high level of economic participation evident in the countryside transferred well to urban areas as the economy changed. Women were active in manufacturing, particularly in textile and electronics factories, where in many cases they outnumbered men. Consequently, women of rural- and lower-class origins became leaders in many labor unions, where their horizons expanded. Support from students and more recently from nongovernmental organizations helped to organize unions and put their leaders in contact with each other, and with unions in other parts of the world.

These advances in business and labor, of course, do not mean that the status of women is equal to that of men. As in earlier eras, the presence of women in these sectors is matched by their absence from politics and the bureaucracy. By 2000, women comprised just 5.6 percent of the House of Representatives (rising slightly to 8.8 percent in the 2001 election); 10.5 percent of the Senate; 6.1 percent of the cabinet; 2.6 percent of provincial governors; and, in 1999, 2.4 percent of village heads. In 1998, just one of twenty-seven civil servants at the top level was a woman. Furthermore, within the bureaucracy, women were concentrated in certain ministries. In 1998, at the upper levels of the civil service (C9, C10, and C11), women were particularly underrepresented in the Ministry of the Interior (0 out of 36), the Ministry of Justice (1 out of 11), the Ministry of Public Health (1 out of 29), and the Ministry of Agriculture and Cooperatives (3 out of 50). Women were best represented in the Ministry of Science, Technology, and the Environment, where 8 of 27 officials at the upper levels were women, and at the Ministry of Commerce, where 8 of 32 were women (Information provided by the Gender and Development Research Institute, Bangkok).[2] At all levels, including in the villages, nearly all of those who make and execute the laws are men.

And yet, these figures do represent some progress. If we focus on women elected to the parliament, we see a gradual growth in the numbers of women M.P.s, and an increasing growth rate (see Table 3.1). Furthermore, the most rapid changes have occurred in elections when democratic change has been consolidated: from 8 to 15 in 1983, the second election under a new constitution; from 15 to 22 in 1995, the second election after the overthrow of a military government; and from 22 to 44 in 2001, the second national election (and the first for the House of Representatives) after the implementation of the 1997 constitution. Parliamentary rule has allowed for the participation of women, and in turn has benefited from their support. Much of the impetus for this rise in political participation for women has come from the educated middle class in urban areas through organizations designed to encourage participation (Darunee and Pandey 1991). Although the numbers are few, the percentage of representatives who have been women has historically been higher in Bangkok than in the provinces. Nevertheless, interaction with the different gender attitudes of lower-class and rural women has had an impact on the nature of this political participation. Here, as with participation and democratization more generally, migration has been particularly important in changing attitudes and in bringing diverse ideas into contact.[3]

Table 3.1. Women in Parliament

Parliament	Nation	Bangkok
1933–1947	0	0
1949	1	0
1952	4	0
1957	1	0
1957	4[a]	0
1969	6	1
1975	3	1
1976	8	1
1979	8	2
1983	13	2
1986	12	2
1988	10	3
1992	15	3
1992	15	3
1995	24	5
1996	22	4
2001	44	5

Source: Data is drawn from parliamentary, Election Commission, and Ministry of the Interior records. See also Supatra 1991.

[a] One more woman, Oraphim Chaiyakan, was elected in a by-election in 1958.

The ways in which ideas are communicated to villages through temporary migration in Thailand have been analyzed by Mills (1999). She observed that such migration, aimed at bringing economic benefits back to the family, introduced tensions into the traditional gender relations of the countryside. "Employment in the city not only provides young women with access to cash income but also to an experience of independence and self-sufficiency that no previous generation of rural women has ever shared" (Mills 1999:18). This forces both the migrants and the family members who remained behind in the villages to confront new ideas. The most powerful of these, according to Mills, is modernity *(than samay):* the desire to consume modern goods, to act in modern ways, and participate in national progress. She concluded that the result of such migration is "deep personal transformation" "yet retaining a fundamental attachment to rural identity and village-based morality" (Mills 1999:165).[4]

Mills' conclusions indicated two tendencies. On the one hand, the pattern of urban migration and the desire to consume modern goods tended to reproduce existing relations of power, particularly in regard to capitalist consumption. On the other, individual women were able to increase their autonomy and capacity to maneuver within these relations of power. It is this tendency toward greater autonomy and the ability of young women to propagate those ideas of modernity in their villages that concern us here. Mills paid less attention to the propagation of rural ideas in the cities. In observing some successful women leaders I shall explore whether differences persist between urban and rural styles, or between upper- and lower-class styles.

Women and Political Leadership

The emergence of women leaders at the top levels of government in Asia has been quite remarkable. In the Philippines, Corazon Aquino became president on a wave of "people's power"; Megawati Sukarnoputri became first vice president and then president in newly democratic Indonesia; and in Burma, Aung San Suu Kyi became the leader of the Burmese democracy movement. Benazir Bhutto of Pakistan, Indira Ghandi of India, Chandrika Kumaratunga of Sri Lanka, and Khaleda Zia and Sheikh Hasina Wajed of Bangladesh, and Gloria Arroyo have all become leaders of their respective countries. Thus far, women in Thailand have had considerably less success at the top level. A brief examination of some literature on regional trends to determine how women leaders in the region have succeeded may be revealing.

To explain the rising numbers of female leaders elsewhere in Asia, Linda Richter examined a number of women prime ministers, searching for attributes they might have in common (Richter 1989). She explored eight variables: patriarchy, family ties, class, female lifestyles, historical context, prison experience, and electoral arrangements (Richter 1990:525–526). She argued that, in Asia, the concept of public and private spheres was strong, and that women were largely confined to the private sphere unless they were "filling a political void created by the death or imprisonment of a male family member" (Richter 1990:526).[5] Thus family ties were crucial to breaking through the structures of patriarchy, and misfortune enhanced the opportunity. Class and lifestyles were also important. Richter held that only those from the upper social classes could succeed in politics, partly because participation was limited to upper classes in all the countries she examined, partly because women were only able to participate if their "duties" in the private sphere could be assumed by servants or female relatives. Women prime ministers were often single or had few children (Richter 1990:530). Interestingly,

Richter did not examine the paths to mobility in the chosen societies, apparently assuming that mobility either did not exist, or that it came from the male or, perhaps, through the family. In terms of historical context, she focused on participation in independence movements, but historical context can include much more, and, like patriarchy, requires a careful consideration of culture and the way it changes. Finally, Richter argued that electoral arrangements may make a difference in the ability of women to succeed in politics.

If we look at the Thai parliament, we find some of these patterns are quite clear in Thailand as well. In Chapter 2, we noted that the factional structure of political parties and the personalized election networks often lead M.P.s to sponsor relatives, including wives and daughters, for additional seats in parliament. For a 1982 thesis, Rangson Prasertsri conducted a survey of members of parliament and included a question concerning family members who were also candidates for election. Of the women surveyed, fully 50 percent had another family member running for office. For men, only 19.5 percent had another family member as a candidate (Rangson 1982:132). Unfortunately, complete data on such relationships are unavailable. An examination of shared surnames in all the parliaments since 1932 reveals that 40 percent (39 out of 97) of women M.P.s have shared a surname with at least one other member of a parliament. This compares to about 20 percent of men.[6] Furthermore, if we look at some women cabinet ministers we see the same pattern. Former Prime Minister's Office Minister Suphatra Masadit is the daughter of Surin Masadit, a popular M.P. from Nakhon Sithammarat whose health declined after the 1976 massacre at Thammasat University. Suphatra took his place in the Democrat party. Former deputy minister of the interior Sudarat Keyuraphan is the daughter of a former M.P. Former deputy education minister Kanchana Silapa-acha is the daughter of former prime minister and sitting M.P. Banhan Silapa-acha. Other examples abound.[7] Martyrdom has not been as important in Thailand, nor has involvement in an independence movement, as the country was never colonized. Class and lifestyle are important factors for women as they are for men who win election in Thailand; all the women M.P.s have the means to employ maids.[8] In the Thai parliament, then, many of Richter's observations, especially concerning family, class, and lifestyle, hold true.

Richter's conclusions were less than optimistic. She argued that women in (South and Southeast) Asia had risen to power only in dramatic circumstances, that none had been able to develop power within institutional structures. In general, while women were considered public-spirited and incorruptible, they were also seen as weak and only temporary leaders. Thus, Richter concluded, the women who had succeeded were exceptional cases, and other women were not benefiting from their success. At the level of prime minister, this seems to be the case in Thailand as well. There are no women positioned to become prime minister in the near future.[9] Furthermore, not too long ago, the Thai Farmer's Bank research division polled the Bangkok electorate, perhaps the most liberal group in Thailand, on the question of a woman prime minister. The survey found that 40 percent thought that a woman could not be a good prime minister. Of those who thought a woman could be prime minister, twice as many were women as men (*Bangkok Post*, 26 October 1996, internet edition). As we saw in Table 3.1, in the parliament, progress has also been slow.

Mina Roces took a different approach in analyzing the role of women in politics in the Philippines. She suggested that we should not limit our analysis to traditional Western views of power and participation in politics. In Asia, she asserted, it is best to think, not in terms of the individual, but rather in terms of the family or kinship group. Thus we should not think, for example, of Ferdinand Marcos himself as politically powerful, but rather of the power of the Marcos family. In her view, it is erroneous to think of women as powerless simply because they do not hold positions. Within politically powerful families, Roces observed, there is a division of responsibility, with men holding the public positions of power, playing the formal roles, and women often in less formal and visible roles, as part of the "support system." She wrote:

> Since the dynamics of kinship politics assigns women to the category of support system, women become less likely to enter politics themselves . . . they generally are responsible for organising the campaigns, carrying out charity work, running civic organisations, and discoursing with electoral constituents. All these activities are essential for their husbands to gain re-election. Politicians' wives are often also more aggressive in gaining privileges for their own kin group and are therefore more successful practitioners of kinship politics than their husbands. (Roces 1994:17) [10]

To support her argument, Roces described the activities of Imelda Marcos as part of the Marcos dictatorship. She pointed out that Imelda was important in campaigning, as patron of the arts, as fund-raiser, as an unofficial ambassador, in civic projects, and in constituency work. Roces observed that Imelda's family became wealthier than Ferdinand's, which revealed Imelda's superior position in kinship politics, despite her inferior position as mayor of Metro Manila in national politics.[11] Finally, Roces (1998) noted that, like men, women can use gender stereotypes to their advantage. Whereas male politicians rely on masculinity, female politicians must rely on femininity, on beauty, grace, and elegance, or, alternatively, on the image of a religious wife, in seeking support.

The importance of family ties in gaining election has been discussed. But as Roces has pointed out, it should be recognized that it is not just women running for election who participate in politics; women play crucial support roles for male politicians. Again, this is a topic that has not yet been studied systematically. However, considerable anecdotal evidence exists. Former prime minister Chawalit Yongchaiyut said of his wife, Phankhrua, that he would probably lose the election if she were his rival: "She is very popular among the local people. She has extended her mercy to everyone from housewives to monks" (*Nation*, 28 November 1996, A7; see also *Nachun sutsapda*, 29 November 1996, 15–19). When there was a conflict over the allocation of cabinet seats, Phankhrua was sent to soothe the aggrieved M.P.s (*Nation*, 8 December 1996, A1). For Prime Minister Chuan Leekphai, his mother, Tuan, filled this role of meeting with constituents and keeping Chuan in touch with them (*Bangkok Post*, 13 April 1998, 3). Yaowapha Wongsawat, Prime Minister Thaksin's younger sister and an M.P. herself, has also played an important mediating role in Thaksin's personal faction of M.P.s. Maliwan Ngoenmuan, another political wife, lived in Ubon while her husband was a cabinet minister in Bangkok. There she was available to meet with his *hua khanaen* on a regular basis (*Bangkok Post*, 29 August 1988, 7). Phenphira Kanthawong, whose husband was also a cabinet minister, told of putting up campaign posters while pregnant. She also spent a lot of time with charitable organizations, attending social functions, and meeting with constituents (ibid.). Of course not all are so active in politics, but, as Roces observed for the Philippines, women often do play a crucial role, particularly because electoral networks are so highly personalized in Thailand.

As for femininity, Juree (1994:520) argued that the "beauty culture" has been a hindrance to the advancement of women in Thai society. Not only has it consumed large amounts of time and energy, it has also encouraged women to seek satisfaction by pleasing men. Yet some women have managed to overcome this beauty culture. They seem to have done so by using it to their advantage in ways similar to those outlined by Roces for the Philippines. Journalist and activist Sanitsuda Ekachai observed:

> One noticeable feature the women M.P.s share is their good looks. Yenchitr used to be a television star. Paveena Hongsakul's sister is the former Miss Universe Apasara Chirathiwat, and she herself did some modeling before joining the banking business. The stunning beauty of Srisakul Techapaibul makes people gape rather than listen to her. . . . (*Bangkok Post*, 29 August 1988, 31)

Another reporter wrote that the 1996 election was becoming a "political pageant":

> The election in Bangkok could become a mini-beauty pageant if political parties succeeded in their quests for women candidates. Prachakorn Thai deputy leader Chaipak Siriwat said yesterday his party has been wooing former Miss Thailand Araya Sirisopha, nicknamed Nong Pop, to contest the poll under its banner. Apart from Nong Pop, the name of Nanthida Kaewbuasai, a popular singer,

has also been floated. . . . Meanwhile, Palang Dharma has named Miss Piyathida Angsuphan . . . as its candidate . . . against Chart Pattana's Paveena Hongsakul, sister of former Miss Universe Apasara Hongsakul. Miss Piyathida is a younger sister of Palang Dharma secretary-general Sudarat Keyuraphan and is said to be second to none in terms of beauty. (*Bangkok Post,* 16 October 1996:3)

A reporter on the campaign trail with Major Sirilak Simuang, married to former Bangkok governor Chamlong Simuang, reported that residents reacted to her visits by saying, "So she's our *Khun-nai Poo-wa* (madame governor)? Oh, isn't she beautiful!" (*Bangkok Post,* 21 July 1988, 29). While some candidates have been former movie stars and models, most have not. Roces' point was that, not just beauty, but all stereotypes associated with femininity are an asset, and that perhaps adhering to some of them is a necessity. Of course this is not enough to ensure election. As cabinet minister Sudarat has observed: "Beauty alone is not a factor. A successful woman politician has to have a good personality" (*Bangkok Post,* "Outlook," 27 November 1996:1). In politics, then, demonstrating femininity may be important; however, in other endeavors, femininity plays less of a role, and in some cases may even be a hindrance.

This focus on femininity has made women candidates vulnerable to mud slinging in political campaigning. One of the most common charges has been promiscuity and adultery (see, for example, *Bangkok Post,* 28 February 1997; 27 November 1996). With so much attention paid to beauty, this is hardly surprising. Other charges include involvement in corruption and indecisiveness or weakness. These attacks are effective because they play on stereotypes of the very femininity that can be advantageous in winning election.

Roces' observations are important because they focus our attention not on position but on power, which can often be two very different things. Yet this tells us little about those women who do gain prominent positions in society. If women are generally part of the "support system," what characteristics and circumstances allow some to break out of that role and assume power? Richter's argument provided a partial answer in regard to circumstances, but as it focused only on prime ministers, and largely on exceptional circumstances, it can only be a partial answer. It does not explain the slowly rising numbers of women in Thai parliaments, where they have been able to win election by participating in traditional political institutions.

One possible answer here is that pursued in Chapter 1, which looked to changes in political culture to explain the rise of different types of leaders. I argued there that leaders emerge who fit the prevailing political culture, and because the political culture in Thailand has changed, new types of leaders have emerged. A change that makes political culture somewhat more conducive to women could account for the slow rise in the numbers of female M.P.s.[12] Such a change has been brought about both by contact with the West and modernization, or *than samay* to use Mills' term, and by interaction with village attitudes concerning leadership and participation. Democratization is closely connected to both these changes in attitudes regarding gender roles as well.

Democratization opened up the way for new types of leaders, including women. Under the absolute monarchy, the succession had been limited to males, at least during the Chakri era. Later, after the coup that overthrew the absolute monarchy, top political positions remained largely in the hands of the military, except for a few brief civilian interregnums. Since women could not attain top positions in the military, they were also shut out of top political positions. Democratization allowed civilians to compete on more equal grounds. Along with this change came one in political culture. Whereas in the past, strong, powerful, decisive figures were successful political leaders, in recent years successful leaders have been those able to assemble support through compromise. This change in attitudes may render greater female participation in politics more attainable.

It was with these ideas in mind that I conducted interviews. First, from Richter, I considered the importance of the background of successful leaders. Was there anything unusual in their background? What was it that first made them choose to pursue a leadership role? What structural barriers hindered their efforts? From Roces came the importance of family in their efforts, and the advantages and drawbacks of the stereotypes associated with femininity. Finally, I addressed the question of cultural change and continuity, particularly in regard to modernization and interaction with village culture.

I chose to interview women leaders from a variety of sectors: a labor leader who migrated to Bangkok, a Bangkok business leader, a slum community leader, a politician, and a provincial entrepreneur and village leader. My main purpose was to determine what the interviewees thought had made them successful where others had failed. Consequently, the interviews were loosely structured in order to allow the women to express their own concerns. Some spoke more about their upbringing, some, more about their opinions. What follows is simply a presentation of the results of these interviews. As they were conducted in Thai and have been reconstructed from notes, they are not presented verbatim; thus I have not made much use of direct quotations. I have nevertheless tried to convey as accurately as possible the sense and tone of the responses to my questions. To assist in comparisons, I have structured some of the answers around theoretical concerns and have added a few biographical details, mainly at the beginning of each interview; but for the most part, the responses appear as given to me.[13] Naturally the interviewees portrayed themselves in positive terms; however, the purpose here is not critical biography but rather to present the opinions of these leaders about the reasons for their successes, so this should not be unduly problematic.

CHODCHOY SOPHONPANICH, ENTREPRENEUR, SOCIAL ACTIVIST, AND ENVIRONMENTALIST

The daughter of the founder of Bangkok Bank, Chodchoy Sophonpanich[14] also chose banking and finance as her career, and became a successful entrepreneur in her own right. After completing her degree in Australia, she interned with the London branch of Bangkok Bank in 1966 and then went to work for the next three years for Siam Intercontinental Hotel, in public relations and sales. In 1969, she set up her own business; she received the franchise rights for and established Diner's Club in Thailand, also becoming the managing director of the company. This comprised her primary business until 1980, when she left it to work in charitable foundations. For part of the time while she was managing director of Diner's Club, she also held positions at the Bangkok Bank and as director of a finance company. She is now a member of the senate.

Life Experiences. In the interview, Chodchoy Sophonpanich said that the strongest influence in her life has been her family background. Her father, Chin Sophonpanich, was an ethnic Chinese entrepreneur who founded the Bangkok Bank. Her mother also worked outside the home. Chodchoy claimed that when she was young she did not know of the family's wealth or status. (It seems more likely that she simply took her lifestyle for granted, since the family was among the wealthiest in Thailand at the time.) Her parents were very strict with money, in order to teach her its value. She was taught to respect her elders and had a warm relationship with her parents. Perhaps particularly important, she believed, was the amount of independence she was given. She was encouraged to meet with adults while still young, and learned to associate with them and participate in their meetings and conversations. This gave her a sense of self-assurance. Chodchoy's father often worked at home, scheduling meetings there in his study, and Chodchoy was allowed to enter to greet her father and meet his visitors.

Chodchoy was an only daughter, with three older brothers and one younger, all very close in age. When growing up she never felt she was being treated as a female, but rather as a person. She was not told that "girls can't do this" when young, and she was expected to study and work from the time she was a child. The only time she felt she was treated differently was when it came to sports. Because light skin is admired in Thailand, she was not allowed to play outdoor sports, to prevent getting tanned. That was the only time she was made to feel like "a girl" (rather than "a person"). When she became interested in tennis, her mother refused to buy a racket, to prevent her from playing, so she borrowed rackets and played anyway. Eventually, she became good enough to make the tennis team, and then the coach called her mother and asked about a racket. This embarrassed her mother into buying one. Apparently it was also an early lesson in overcoming difficulties.

Chodchoy felt like she had no special traits or abilities when she was growing up in Bangkok. She started school at an early age, and was always younger than her classmates. Her academic rank was only around thirtieth in a class of fifty. Since her brothers all excelled academically, she was often asked why she did not do better. At age twelve she went to Australia to study. When she arrived, she spoke no English and had to learn by means of gestures and pictures. She learned quickly, however, and before long was in the top three in her class. There she also found that she had a talent for sports. She played many, and was regularly chosen team captain. In fifth form (equivalent to a junior in an American high school), she was chosen captain of the school sports program, a position that she said had always gone to sixth-formers; she was chosen again as a sixth-former. Chodchoy was accepted at Sydney University, and although she wanted to study interior design instead, her father encouraged her to enroll, telling her she could always study interior design afterward. So she went. By the time she finished university, she was tired of studying and decided to go into business instead of studying interior design. She then embarked on her business career.

Chodchoy first became active in social projects when she returned from Australia. Rather than the traditional activities, she wanted to do something new and different. When she learned about the activities of Khru Pratheep, she decided she wanted to help, and donated 4,000 baht a month (about 200 U.S. dollars at the time) to help pay the teachers at Pratheep's school. In addition, she would take her children to Khlong Toei community to give away things to the poor people there. She also got involved in the international service club Zonta. Since that time she has been active in one sort of service or another.

Around 1983, newly divorced Chodchoy sold the Diner's Club and a finance company and decided to make a new beginning. She admits to being a workaholic who often worked until 10 P.M. at her finance company, and she wanted to do something that would allow her to keep busy without feeling the need to work such long hours. So she joined the Chin Sophonpanich Foundation, a family-based charity organization established by her father. The foundation is mostly involved in promoting educational activities, such as scholarships and new school buildings, but it also donates to Buddhist temples. About a year later, Chodchoy established a foundation of her own, the Sangsan Thai Foundation. Her particular interest was environmental activism. She initiated a campaign called "Ta wiset," or Magic Eyes, which became the best known and probably the most effective environmentalist campaign in Bangkok.

Chodchoy's environmental activism began with her own children. She had tried to teach them the importance of taking care of the environment, and Magic Eyes drew on that experience, and on her experience in advertising and public relations. The campaign was designed for an audience with only upper primary school level education (po. 6), which then was the mean level of education in Thailand, and began with children. Chodchoy was able to call on her friends in business circles, mostly mid-level managers with advertising budgets, to help promote the campaign.

Political Activities. Chodchoy claimed that she initially wished to avoid politics, as she did not like the party system and the way it functioned. However, her social activities led her to take an interest in politics. In order to facilitate environmental concerns effectively, it was necessary to deal with politicians. She chose to work from the outside, promoting particular policies and programs with those who were politicians. She also used techniques available to any (wealthy) citizen— for example, bringing a lawsuit against the sky train over its environmental impact or writing to politicians on important issues. In addition, the NGO community in Thailand was small enough that Chodchoy came to know many of its leaders. She became involved with the Women's Council of Thailand as an adviser on environmental issues and was soon drawn into issues concerning the status of women and the low levels of participation of women in politics. Chodchoy's own foray into politics came as a result of this issue. In 1996, constitutional reform had made its way onto the political agenda in Thailand. As part of the process, elections were held to choose a constitution drafting assembly. Chodchoy was asked to spearhead a campaign to increase the participation of women in the election, with the hope of ensuring that women and women's issues would be part of the agenda. The most important thing at that stage, according to Chodchoy, was to get women's issues on the agenda, to raise awareness, as a first step. Since many of the obstacles to participation seemed small, too many failed to understand the underlying issues, she believed, and so the most important need at the time was to educate people.[15] Women's rights did make it onto the constitutional agenda, and a provision banning sexual discrimination was included.

It might be useful to interject an observation and a brief update here. When the new constitution allowed for a senate free of political parties, Chodchoy apparently found the opportunity to fulfill her expressed desire to make a difference in politics without becoming involved in the party system.[16] Chodchoy, encouraged by the NGO community, decided to run for the senate, winning a seat in Bangkok. It is interesting that Chodchoy claims she was reluctantly drawn into politics by her desire to do good. This allows her to portray herself as a nonpolitical politician, in line with traditional gender stereotypes for her class.

Opinions on Leadership, Gender, and Change. Chodchoy said that in the private sector there were no obstacles to participation by women.[17] She did believe, however, that obstacles were greater in the public sector and in particular in parts of the bureaucracy, such as the Ministry of the Interior. She believed that the relative equality in the private sector could be traced back to matrilineal inheritance: this tradition meant that parents were protective of daughters and taught them carefully so that they could look after the inheritance; men were given more freedom, and were spoiled and so less responsible. As for old-boy networks, Chodchoy never saw them as a problem. She found that in school and at university, networking was strong and not gender-oriented, so connections were not male-oriented.[18] Despite her belief that in the private sector there are few obstacles, Chodchoy does believe that women have to be committed, loyal, and work twice as hard as men to succeed.

In terms of leadership styles, Chodchoy thought that women are often more emotional and form closer relationships to their employees than do men in Thailand; women have a more participatory style of leadership. However, she said that leadership styles vary considerably among women and men, and depend more on the individual than on gender. Women can be aggressive, but in a Thai woman's way, which is a difficult balance to maintain. This is because men do not like to be threatened or dominated. Women must be able to make decisions, even if it sometimes seems they are being abrupt.

As for femininity, according to Chodchoy, a leader cannot be feminine in the stereotypical way. She cannot be "soft" like a (stereotypical) housewife. And yet, society will not accept a woman who is too masculine; gender differences are important. A woman should know how to dress in the proper style for the office. She should be *riaproy* (well-mannered, proper) and do the right thing on the right occasion. Ultimately, however, a woman cannot succeed and be perceived by male employees as "a woman"; the relationship cannot be a gender issue. A woman leader needs to be seen, not as a woman, but as a person.

Chodchoy believed that things are changing for the better. She pointed out that the public is more aware of inequalities and the importance of equal opportunity. Both men and women accept the need for equality; men accept the value of women and their work. However, men do not help out in the home, and so women still bear multiple responsibilities. Divorce has become more common as women are no longer willing to tolerate their husbands' minor wives and have the financial independence to allow them to choose divorce. Women no longer feel the need to be responsible for keeping the family together. These factors have improved the status of women, although Chodchoy pointed out that much remains to be done.

SUPHATRA MASADIT, SEVEN-TIME M.P. DEMOCRAT PARTY, NAKHON SITHAMMARAT

Suphatra Masadit[19] was first elected to parliament in 1979, representing the Democrat party. Despite taking time off from politics on two separate occasions, she has been elected a total of seven times. She advanced steadily in the Democrat party, serving in the parliament on the foreign relations and parliamentary affairs committees, and eventually becoming a cabinet minister attached to the prime minister's office in several different cabinets, beginning in 1986. She left politics and took up a fellowship at the Center for International Affairs at Harvard in

1995–1996, then later returned to Thailand and again won a seat in parliament, becoming a minister attached to the Prime Minister's Office. Her most important assignment in that position has been supervision of the Public Relations Department, including the government television and radio stations. She has also been a member of the National Commission on Women's Affairs and was a delegate to the Fourth World Conference on Women held in Beijing in 1995. Suphatra chose not to contest the parliamentary election in January 2001.

Life Experiences. Suphatra was born in Nakhon Sithammarat province, in southern Thailand, in 1950. She has an older brother who is also a politician and a younger brother who is in business. Her father and mother separated when she was young, and she stayed with her father, a journalist and publisher of *Siangrat*, a provincial newspaper. So she was closer to her father than to her mother, and he was an early role model for her. She planned to follow in his footsteps and become a journalist herself. However, her father later entered politics, first at the local level and then, in 1969, after Suphatra had already left home to study in Bangkok, at the national level. So Suphatra did follow in her father's footsteps—but not as a journalist.

Suphatra studied in Nakhon Sithammarat through upper secondary school (the equivalent of American high school). In her final year, she campaigned for the presidency of the student assembly and won. She then went to Bangkok to study for university entrance exams and gained entrance to the prestigious Chulalongkorn University's Department of Mass Communications and Public Relations. Again, she was involved in student politics, as the public relations director of the student union. Everything seemed to be in place for her to enter her father's profession as a journalist. However, during her studies at Chulalongkorn another path opened up.

During the break between terms, Suphatra joined a student volunteer group that was seeking to promote community development. The group would go to a village and camp there, working with the villagers on a development project. She so enjoyed this activity that after graduation she began working with Pui Ungkapakon of Thammasat University in his community development program. Professor Pui became her second role model. After working for him for about two years, Suphatra won a graduate scholarship to the East–West Center at the University of Hawai'i, which she attended for her M.A. degree. She was in Hawaii during the 1976 massacre of students at Thammasat University that marked the end of democracy for a brief period. It also proved to be the end of her father's political career, as his health deteriorated thereafter. Suphatra graduated in 1978 and returned to Thailand to take up a position as a lecturer in mass communications at Thammasat. She taught there for just eight months before leaving to contest a seat in the newly restored parliament.

Suphatra Masadit first ran for parliament in 1979 when the Democrat party asked her to contest her father's Nakhon Sithammarat parliamentary seat. She won one of the thirty seats that went to the Democrat party, in large part due to the respect people had for her father, and for the party. While she certainly benefited from the reputation of her father in her first election, she also built up a reputation of her own in her constituency, won seven times, and has never yet lost an election. Later, with her assistance, her brother also won election to parliament.

Opinions on Gender, Leadership, and Change. Suphatra, like Chodchoy, believed that women must work harder than men to succeed, three times as hard as men. But while Chodchoy thought that the old boy network *(phakphuak)* was not important, Suphatra believed that it was important in politics, though less so in the Democrat party than in other parties. In her own party, she claimed that those who were diligent would advance. She also pointed out that women are generally assigned to "suitable" work, rather than given positions of responsibility, and that they often receive less help and cooperation than do men. On the other hand, she believed that women have some advantages. In particular, trust comes easier for women than for men. This, and the increasing attention paid to "women's issues" have benefited women in elections.

In terms of leadership styles, Suphatra said that, in order to be leaders, women must add male traits to their style. In particular, they must be *jai nakleng*—have the heart of a *nakleng* in order to succeed. They must not speak too much, but must be decisive. Women can warn men when they make mistakes but cannot tattle on them. Women, on the other hand, are more polite and caring. As for femininity, *phuying jing jing* (true women) can succeed as leaders, but only if they work much harder than men. The best leaders, Suphatra said, are those who have both male and female characteristics.

Suphatra believed that differences between men and women were important in campaigning as well. In the south, gender made less difference, as most of the campaigning consisted of making speeches, which men and women can do equally well. Women have some advantage in communicating with other women, and with the elderly. In other regions, where *hua khanaen* (vote canvassers) are more important, gender matters more. While men are dominant in the *hua khanaen* system, women are more trustworthy as *hua khanaen* than men; they are less likely to change bosses or to spend campaign funds on alcohol. Nevertheless, women *hua khanaen* are still relatively few, and mostly at the lower levels.[20] Finances and vote buying are handled by men.

Suphatra agreed that politics is often a family affair. She pointed out that when she first ran for office most women M.P.s were replacing male family members in the parliament. Wives of M.P.s often do most of the constituency work and build up a rapport with the voters, especially in the provinces. Sometimes voters will even vote for an M.P. they dislike, because of the efforts of a wife. In some cases, wives of M.P.s participate actively in campaigning and even speak at rallies in support of their husbands.

Suphatra also believed that Thai society was changing, becoming more receptive to women leaders. In the past, she said, it was quite common for people to characterize a successful woman as *kaeng muan phuchai* (talented, like a man). Now such comments are heard less frequently, as attitudes change. She attributed these changes to several factors. First is the influence from overseas. Second is the presence of role models in Thailand; the opportunities and successes at the national level have changed attitudes at the local level, she believed. Third, opportunities have opened up. For example, before 1980, according to Suphatra, women were not allowed to be *phuyaiban* or *kamnan*. Now this has changed. Fourth, she pointed out, is the influence of democracy on views of women and politics in Thailand. In the past, "a leader had to be strong, like a soldier." Democracy has changed that perception. Finally, more women are willing to get involved. Taken together, these factors have led to an increase in successful women politicians in Thailand.

Although attitudes are changing, Suphatra felt that obstacles remain. In particular, she thought it unlikely that a woman would become prime minister in the near future. In order to overcome these obstacles, she emphasized the importance of preparing oneself, then encouraging other women to participate, and finally, ensuring that those who are willing to participate obtain the training they need to succeed. So a training program was established, with the help of NGOs, to prepare them to participate in the parliament. Suphatra was also involved in the attempts to have more women chosen for the Constitutional Drafting Assembly, and during the late 1990s, for the then appointed senate. Suphatra, like Chodchoy, claimed to be a reluctant politician. She said that she would have preferred not to be a minister, but that the Democrat party wanted to appoint a woman as a role model. She pointed out that she cannot encourage others to participate if she is not willing to do so herself.

PRATHEEP UNGSONGTHAM, SLUM COMMUNITY ACTIVIST, MAGSAYSAY AWARD WINNER

Born in Khlong Toei slum community near the Bangkok port, Pratheep Ungsongtham[21] became a representative of Khlong Toei slum dwellers, first with the government, and later with other organizations involved in development work. Her successes brought renown, and she was asked for assistance by other communities. Eventually she became one of the leaders of slum dwellers in Bangkok more generally. In 1978, she received important recognition from abroad when she was awarded the Magsaysay prize by the Ramon Magsaysay Foundation of the Philippines. This international recognition, and the 400,000-odd baht (then 20,000 U.S. dollars) that went with it, allowed Pratheep to establish the Duang Pratheep

Foundation to assist the poor in Thailand, which she has expanded from an NGO helping slum dwellers to an organization that also helps the poor of Thailand in the countryside. In 2000, she was elected to the senate.

Life Experiences. Pratheep Ungsongtham was born in 1951 in the Khlong Toei slums of Bangkok. She was the only female child at home at the time, and her mother often said that she was like a boy, exhibiting many male behaviors. In particular, she always loved justice and was a fighter in its cause. She did not have a sole role model, but several, both male and female. She would admire a particular characteristic and try to emulate it. As a child, Pratheep received only four years of primary education, then had to withdraw to help support her family. At age twelve, she began saving part of her salary to pay for night school. She enrolled at fifteen, then at age seventeen went on to a teacher's college, where she found her primary vocation. Her teaching career began soon after she enrolled in college. In 1968, at the age of seventeen, Pratheep noticed the large number of children playing in the streets and pathways of Khlong Toei because they lacked proper birth certificates and the other documentation necessary to enroll in government schools. Concerned for their welfare, she made the area under her home available for the children to play. Eventually she began teaching the children, and the school grew to include seven buildings. By 1971, Pratheep had assumed the responsibility of trying to obtain the proper documentation for the children so that they could continue their studies. In 1976 the municipal government granted the school formal recognition. This cause marked the beginning of her social activism, bringing her into contact with bureaucrats, politicians, and politics. Consequently, when the Port Authority of Thailand decided to evict the residents of Khlong Toei, the residents held a meeting and chose Pratheep to represent them in their efforts to resist. Pratheep and the community eventually convinced (or perhaps forced) the Port Authority to compromise by letting them settle on another nearby plot of Port Authority land.

The struggle to assist the poor of Bangkok is inherently political. However, Pratheep did not participate directly in politics until the May 1992 uprising against military rule. She felt she owed a personal debt to hunger striker Chalat Worachat, and so went to visit him and show her support by presenting him with a lei. From that beginning, Pratheep became one of the key leaders in subsequent events. Since that time Pratheep has been more involved in politics. For instance, when one large political party advocated policies she deemed detrimental to slum dwellers, she encouraged her supporters to vote against that party. Like Chodchoy and Suphatra, Pratheep was also involved in the effort to promote participation of women in the Constitution Drafting Assembly and ran herself, though she said she did it to raise awareness, not with any expectation of victory.

Opinions on Gender, Leadership, and Change.[22] According to Pratheep, the reason there were fewer women leaders than men could be found in three broad areas: time, interest, and *klum phuak* (networks of friends). In terms of time, Pratheep pointed out that, when men come home from work, their time is generally their own, they seldom do housework; women, even when employed outside the home, take care of the housework and the children, so that half their efforts are spent at home. This allows men more time to network and develop the friendships that are so crucial for elections. So, she believed, even if a man and a woman have equal abilities, the man wins; only if a woman is much more qualified does she win. Second, men tend to be generalists, while women tend to focus on a single issue and pour all their efforts into it. Men get involved in many issues and leave the details to women. (Consequently?) men do not understand society and social welfare as well as women.[23] Also, among women there is a propensity to help—to serve rather than lead—and the willingness of women to accept male leadership contributes to a large degree to the predominance of men in leadership positions. Finally, Pratheep said, *klum phuak* are stronger among men. Women can join those networks, but only within limits. For example, when a woman is present, men do not use rough language. This alters the usual dynamics of the group.

As for more specific obstacles, again Pratheep pointed to three. First, women leaders do not receive acceptance in the same way as men do. Second, sometimes people *du thuk* (look down on) women leaders, saying that they *mai khao thung ruang* (don't get it). Finally, she reiterated here the problem of a lack of time for women who face the burdens of housework and children.

In terms of styles of leadership, Pratheep thought that many women prefer to work behind the scenes. (Others, she said, only want to be leaders; otherwise, they are unwilling to participate at all.) Women, she believed, are good at searching out facts but do not like being in front of people. As for herself, Pratheep said that she prefers to work behind the scenes, but is willing to move to the forefront if necessary, and characterized herself as a fighter. She tries to be strategic, letting minor issues go in order to focus on larger ones, which sometimes leaves her vulnerable to attack. She is not forceful in meetings, but prefers to let the group decide.

Pratheep believed that women at different levels of society have different leadership characteristics. At the "higher" level, most women leaders have had to rely on money or their family backgrounds for their start. That does not mean they lacked talent, but is an indication of the obstacles to women leaders at the higher level. Only a few have broken through and succeeded solely due to their own expertise. At the community level, few come from influential families. Rather, they emerge when there is a problem in the community and there is no one else to step forward. A woman leader at this level must be active, speak well, and have some particular talent, such as an ability to research facts or to investigate problems. Many women community leaders are *jai nakleng*, brave, honest, willing to take risks, admit their errors, and back up their words with action. Indeed, in community action, women often take the lead in battles with the police to prevent possible police violence. Society, by way of contrast, likes women to be polite and refined, and beauty does matter in the media and in high society.

As for change, Pratheep said that changes have been very slow. Nevertheless, some important changes have taken place: war is less prevalent, and rape less common. She believed that it might be possible for a woman to become prime minister, and pointed in particular to Suphatra and to Sudarat Keyuraphan, a Thai Rak Thai party cabinet minister.

ARUNEE SITO, LABOR LEADER

Arunee Sito[24] worked her way up from the factory floor to become head of the union at the Thai Krieng textile factory. In that capacity, she gained considerable prominence in labor circles and has become an influential voice for labor in negotiations with the government, in interactions with NGOs, and in academic settings.

Life Experiences. Arunee Sito was born in 1953 in Nonthaburi, now a suburb of Bangkok but then still rural, to a farming family. She was the only daughter and so grew up among boys. When she was young, her father was the *phuyaiban* and would often take her along on his visits to the villagers. From these experiences she learned to socialize and learned independence. Arunee had only four years of schooling, and when she was seventeen a relative helped her get a job at the Thai Krieng textile factory, across the river from central Bangkok.[25] She was the first worker from Nonthaburi in the factory, so she had to learn to get along well with people from other places from the beginning. Since there was then a shortage of workers, she was able to begin work right away. At that time, there was no union, and workers were paid only 10 baht per day (then about 50 U.S. cents), in addition to their room and board. In fact, it would be nearly ten years after her arrival before workers at Thai Krieng managed to form a union.

Although there was no union until 1980, there were protests, especially after the student-led demonstrations of 1973 brought about democracy. The particular issue that activated Arunee was the bonuses paid to workers, which were always smaller for women than for men. So for Arunee, labor activism and gender were associated from the beginning. Later, students from Thammasat University came to instruct workers. The owner of the factory opposed the teach-ins, and to demonstrate his displeasure, fired about half of his employees. Arunee was involved in the protests that followed, and then helped to found the union at Thai Krieng. In learning about organizing labor, she also studied the unions formed at some of the state enterprises.

When the union held elections to choose its leaders, Arunee decided to seek election to the leadership committee. However, in the early elections, workers were reluctant to choose women, as there were no examples of successful women labor leaders. She lost in that first election, but continued to help in union activities. In the second election she won, becoming the first woman member of the leadership committee of the union—but only by a few votes, and was given only low-level positions, such as treasurer, registrar, and public relations officer.[26] Four or five years later, workers, especially women workers (who outnumbered men by about five to one at Thai Krieng), realized that women could lead. Furthermore, they came to believe that men leave their positions more easily and are more susceptible to bribery, whereas women leaders *mai thing khonngan* (do not abandon the workers). More and more women were elected to the union leadership committee, so that by 1997 only one union leader was a man.

Opinions on Gender, Leadership, and Change. Arunee believed that women are more likely to consider the group rather than themselves, and consequently are less easily bought off or coopted than are men. She also believed that, where men are quick to join a cause, they are also quick to leave it, while women are more determined. She listed a number of specific characteristics that she believed were necessary for a woman to become a successful leader. First, a woman must be dedicated to her work. Second, it is important to speak convincingly, and well. Third, it is crucial that a woman be bold enough to make decisions; she cannot act indecisively. Fourth, a woman must be honest. Fifth, a woman must be able to make big problems smaller, and small problems disappear. And finally, to be successful, a woman must have the proper demeanor; she must be calm and collected and able to get along with all. Women who would lead cannot be stereotypical polite ladies, but must be bold. Those who are independent from a young age are more likely to become leaders.

According to Arunee, the greatest difficulty for women who would be leaders in the workplace is longevity. After marriage, women seldom receive support from their families in their work. Even before marriage parents may not be supportive. Arunee said that her mother worried about her returning home late, worried about her safety, and thought that union work was not women's work. However, her brothers supported her and helped her convince their mother of the importance of her union work. Related to this, women often had responsibilities, such as child care, that prevent them from devoting long hours to union work. To make matters worse, those involved in union work have to spend more of their own time studying in order to lead well. The income from the work itself is already low, and all the time devoted to union work leaves less time for the overtime work that would supplement wages. Consequently, few women have persisted long enough to become important leaders in the workplace.

Arunee also believed that society has become more accepting of women leaders. However, she said, many men still resist the change. Male leaders do not understand women's problems, such as maternity leave, and fail to provide support, or even oppose prioritizing such demands. Men often try to channel women who do become leaders into concentrating on "women's issues" while men take overall responsibility. Women have to work twice as hard as men to gain acceptance; very few can overcome all the obstacles facing them.

KIM HAW, PROVINCIAL ENTREPRENEUR AND *KAMNAN* OF BAN PHE

Kim Haw [27] has risen from a market trader to a powerful entrepreneur and politician. She owns a large fishing fleet in her village on the eastern seaboard and real estate in a number of provinces. She is the *kamnan*, or commune leader, of Ban Phe and has successfully supported her brother for a seat in parliament. She has also supported other family members in local elections.

Kim Haw's life is described in detail in Chapter 5, and can be summarized very briefly here. She was born in 1941 in Ban Phe, a seaside province on the eastern seaboard, to a poor Chinese immigrant father and a Ban Phe mother. She was the eldest of sixteen children. As the eldest child, Kim Haw was forced to leave school after the fourth grade and work to support her family. She worked at a variety of jobs as she grew older: she climbed trees to pick fruit, washed clothes, carried water, and sold fried bananas. Her father taught her to be thrifty, and she managed to save some money from these activities.

Kim Haw then began selling food at festivals and outdoor activities. She saw that those who were selling fish made more money, so she saved and studied until she too could break into the trade. From selling fish, she moved up to fishing and eventually saved enough to buy a boat of her own. She joined a convoy of boats, and there made many friends. When she had saved enough, she bought a motor for her boat and towed others out to deeper waters for a share of the catch. This solidified her ties, and her leadership, with her convoy. Success followed upon success as she built fish traps, then a pier, and eventually expanded into tourism, real estate, and a fleet of fishing boats.

Kim Haw's economic activities led her into politics. She began as a *hua khan-aen* by supporting other candidates for office, including two brothers—one later an M.P., the other a provincial councilor. Another brother was planning to run for the city council at the time of this interview. Kim Haw herself is *kamnan*, and also *phuyaiban*. Thus she is involved in every level of politics, from local to national, and has been successful at all.

In short, Kim Haw fit the *nakleng* style of leadership well and attributed her success to those characteristics. She also believed that she has succeeded because she is particularly adept at compromise and discussion, and at persuading others to provide assistance. Kim Haw said that she calls in all her new employees and explains to them that they must act like family. She apparently has not had trouble fitting into the *klum phuak;* indeed, along with her entrepreneurial ability, it seems to be an important strength.

Kim Haw believed that women, in order to succeed as leaders, have to be responsible, diligent, and good at details. She said that, generally speaking, women are more responsible and more caring than men. For example, they do not leave their duties to go and drink. She believed that a woman could be prime minister, although society might be slow to accept this at first. Women, she said, must work harder than men in order to be accepted.

Concluding Observations

Women leaders seem to be subject both to the same criticisms as men and to additional ones common to women leaders in other parts of the world. As an example of censure similar to that encountered by male politicians, Suphatra, who has been a politician for the longest period of time, has elicited the most criticism. She has been accused of using her status to advance her spouse's career, of seeking personal gain from political office, and of being inefficient.[28] There are those who have also claimed that she lacks commitment because she has left the field of politics twice. Chodchoy, Suphatra, and Pratheep have all been accused of being self-interested rather than representing their constituents.[29] Kim Haw has been called a *jaomae* (godmother). These are the same criticisms often leveled at male politicians, although they may be more effective if women are held to a different moral standard.

A second form of criticism leveled at women leaders is also commonly found in other parts of the world. Women in the legislature, including Suphatra who, it will be recalled, represented Thailand at the Fourth World Conference on Women in Beijing, have been rebuked for failing to do enough to support women and women's issues. Representing women's issues places women in a double bind. On the one hand, Suphatra and others have claimed that women are more easily trusted than men, that they are better able to sympathize with other women and the elderly, and that they best understand what are often referred to as "women's issues." These assumptions can be useful in winning elections and have benefited women, particularly as "women's issues" have become a greater part of the political agenda in recent years. However, the same stereotypical assumptions often serve to confine women to those "women's issues" after they are elected. As Pratheep put it, women become specialists, while men become generalists; thus, for the most part, women have not yet been able to gain the cabinet positions necessary for later becoming prime minister. Yet, failure to focus on women's issues leads to criticism: Marilee (1995:62–63) noted that only two women (Prime Minister Gro Harlem Brundtland of Norway and President Mary Robinson of Ireland) who have been closely involved with women's issues and women's movements have become leaders of their countries. Davis (1997:20–21) pointed out, regarding specialization in women's issues: "Concentrating or specializing within parliaments, for example, on a set of issues that are traditionally accorded less parliamentary time and prestige may contribute to women's invisibility within legislatures. Being visible . . . plays a critical role in being tapped for government leadership." This double bind clearly presents a dilemma for women legislators who wish to advance within their parties, a dilemma men do not face.

The most striking characteristic that emerges from these interviews with successful women leaders is the strong relationship they had with fathers and brothers. They stated that they were socialized differently from many other women because they were treated more like boys when they were young. The facts that they were encouraged to be independent and be involved in their fathers' activities, they believed, were crucial to their success.

It is also interesting to note that all these women considered beauty, politeness, and femininity important factors. But they were divided on how they thought these traits were relevant. Suphatra and Chodchoy thought it useful to overtly demonstate these traits, though both considered other characteristics more efficacious. Kim Haw, judging from her leadership style, and Arunee believed that women leaders cannot act in such stereotypically feminine ways. I believe that Pratheep provided a resolution to this puzzle when she divided female leadership styles into two types: community-level leadership and "higher"-level leadership. At the community level, the characteristics of effective leaders that she has identified do not include femininity or any of the traditional stereotypes; they are closer to those categorized by Arunee and exemplified by Kim Haw. At the higher level, she mentioned femininity, beauty, and politeness as being important. Here, the "higher" level seems to reflect the interaction of modernization and elite culture, or at least urban culture, which, as Juree (1993:179–180; see also above, Chap. 1) pointed out, assimilated many of the characteristics of elite culture. Both Suphatra and Chodchoy sought to align themselves more closely with gender stereotypes by claiming that they had no interest in political offices, but only pursued them to do good.[30] At the community level, the village patterns of leadership and participation seem to be combining, so that satisfying stereotypical images of leaders is more important than meeting (urban) gender stereotypes. Mills (1999) and Juree (1994) have previously noted the tendency to retain aspects of village life, and that may be what is occurring here. Some sort of merging of these two types of female leadership may eventually occur as women like Pratheep bridge the gap.

As for the family, leadership, and power, it is worth noting that three of the five women interviewed followed their fathers' careers: Chodchoy went into business, more specifically, into banking and finance; Suphatra entered politics; and Kim Haw also followed her father into business, though she quickly surpassed him, indeed, he worked alongside her in the business. In a sense, Arunee has also emulated her father: both became community leaders, although Arunee's community consists of coworkers rather than villagers. The two high-society women, Chodchoy and Suphatra, assuredly benefited from the influence of their families, whereas the community-based leaders, Pratheep, Arunee, and Kim Haw, succeeded largely on their own. Pratheep has been able to make the transition from community leader to societal leader, indicating that it is possible to become such a leader without family support, although several interviewees, Pratheep included, maintained that this had been very difficult in the past. Finally, we have from Suphatra concrete support for the contention that women are very important to men's political power. In Thailand, according to Suphatra, wives do much of the constituency work, and people sometimes vote for a male candidate because they like his wife. Kim Haw is an example of this, having put her brothers into office.

All the women interviewed believe that the situation is changing for the better. The hypothesis I have advanced in this chapter is similar to that expressed by former cabinet minister Suphatra Masadit, who argued both that change has been effected by forces outside Thailand and that democratic structures have helped to create a transformation in attitudes toward the ability of women to be political leaders. In her interview, she also noted that the transition to democracy opened up the path for women to become national leaders, even as she emphasized the importance of change in attitudes. All the women agreed that women still have to work much harder than men to gain societal acceptance. While each mentioned more than one obstacle to women's participation, each of them focused on different problems. For Chodchoy, the wealthy entrepreneur, there were no obstacles to her career. Instead, she thought what needed to be worked toward was equality under the law, especially in issues involving marriage and divorce. Suphatra thought that the key was to encourage greater political participation, and to ensure that those who were willing to participate could obtain the knowledge they needed. Pratheep believed that acceptance is still a major problem in Thai society. Arunee was concerned about longevity, the ability of women to continue in their careers after marriage and family. Kim Haw, like Pratheep, thought that acceptance remains a problem. All the interviewees considered the dual burden carried by women in Thai society a formidable obstacle. All the women felt that education would help to overcome obstacles.

One last obstacle must be mentioned here. In chapter 1, I pointed out that one would expect the transition from *nakleng-* to *phudi-*style leadership to benefit women; yet the low numbers of women in parliament indicate that women are only slowly benefiting from this change. Several of my interviewees pointed out that it is necessary to possess characteristics of the *nakleng* style of leadership in order to succeed in politics. They specifically mentioned boldness and decisiveness, stating that it was good to be *jai nakleng*—have the heart of a *nakleng*. The reason women have not yet derived as much benefit from this leadership style as men can be attributed to the nature and the strength of gender stereotypes in Thailand. *Phudi*-style leaders, while generally more acceptable than *nakleng*-style leaders, are also often seen as weak and indecisive. And because women are generally stereotyped as being weak and indecisive, they are automatically encumbered with all the negative images of the *phudi* style and have to struggle to dispel those assumptions. Gender stereotypes are discussed further in Chapter 5.

CHAPTER 4

■ ■ ■ ■ ■ ■ ■ ■ ■ ■

From *Nakleng* to *Jaopho*
Traditional and Modern Patrons

We have already seen that one of the impediments to the development of democratic leadership has been the distortion of patron-client ties and consequent prevalence of patronage politics. The persistence of patronage politics was partly ascribed to the wide gaps between rich and poor, city and countryside, national politics and local politics, and to the lack of policies to provide a social security net for the poor.[1] Although such patronage is often characterized as traditional, it has undergone considerable change in recent years and is, at most, quasi-traditional. This chapter examines more closely the changes that have come about with the rise of powerful *hua khanaen* who have developed political influence based on their ability to control votes, focusing on the rise of a new type of patron who has become extremely influential in Thai politics, the *jaopho,* or godfather.

Origins

The term *jaopho* seems to have entered into general use during the 1970s—probably as a direct translation of the English word "godfather" from the movie *The Godfather*—as a result of the rising influence of this group upon the economic and political changes of that decade.[2] The *jaopho* have cultural roots in two earlier figures in Thai history: the *nakleng,* from mainstream Thai culture; and the *sia,* from Sino-Thai culture. Some of the traits of both the *nakleng* and the *sia* are evident in the behavior of the modern *jaopho.*

Although I have already briefly discussed the *nakleng,* in order to see the ways in which the traditional patron has evolved, it will be helpful to provide more details. The traditional *nakleng* has been described as "noted for his 'manly bearing and courage, readiness to fight in single combat or in a riot, fidelity to friends, deep loyalty and respect towards feudal lords and parents.' Dressed in his dashing best, the *nakleng* frequented market centers and gambling houses . . . 'to meet friends or make foes in the hope of adding to his prowess . . .'" (Johnston 1980:91).[3] The *nakleng* developed at least partly as a result of the distance between the village and the governmental authority, and came to play an important role not only in crime but in protection of the village (Johnston 1980:passim; Sombat 1992:120). The *nakleng* would protect the property of the villagers from theft, prevent other *nakleng* from coming into the village, and himself refrain from stealing from the village.[4] At the same time, he would engage in raids on other villages, on the rich, and at times even on his own village. The *nakleng* would then help resolve the crime by playing the role of mediator, arranging the return of the stolen goods—perhaps taken by his own followers—in exchange for a reward (Johnston 1980:91–92; Trocki, unpublished paper). In some cases, the *nakleng* and his followers would gain protection from officials in return for a share of the spoils (Rujaya 1984:92–105). The *nakleng* was respected, admired, and necessary to village life. In some cases, the young *nakleng* would go on to become the village headman *(phuyaiban);* in others the *nakleng* was the headman (Johnston 1980:91; Bunnag 1977:23). He then would be the source of political patronage, and in some cases may also have distributed some of the financial rewards of banditry to the villagers.[5] Through a combination of threats and rewards,[6] the *nakleng* exercised considerable power and commanded respect within the village.

The Teochiu word *sia*, which translates roughly as "tycoon," has become widely used to refer to important *jaopho*. In fact many, perhaps most, of the *jaopho* are Sino-Thai. We can also discover some of the origins of the *jaopho* in criminal activity in Sino-Thai culture. The most important contributor to the later values of the *jaopho* was probably the secret society.[7] The Hungmen society began to form in Thailand at least by the early eighteenth century (Skinner 1957:139).[8] These societies, like those formed in China, had as their stated objective the overthrow of the Qing dynasty and the restoration of the Ming. They originally performed many of the functions of government, providing help to other members of the community and serving as a type of social security net; however, as with the societies in China, they turned from their political and social goals in search of profit through illegal activities.

Administration under the absolute monarchy during this period was, for the most part, indirect; the monarchy recognized the authority of local rulers in each community. In many areas, the Chinese community was administered separately, with its own leaders approved by the king to govern the community, in order to ensure fairness in disputes where Thai community leaders might side against the Chinese. Often those chosen as leaders of the Chinese communities were secret society members. Although the government banned the secret societies between 1824 and 1857, after 1857 the ban proved unenforceable. The societies were legalized, required to register, and ordered to cooperate with the government (Supharat 1981:chap. 6).

The Chinese community during this period was comprised largely of two classes, workers and entrepreneurs. Equally important, the community was made up almost entirely of males, with the businessmen seeking opportunities to benefit not only from the work of their fellow immigrants but also from their pleasures: gambling, liquor, prostitution, and opium became commonplace. Both the secret societies and the government cooperated to share in the profits. This cooperation became manifest in the tax farms created to benefit both the government and entrepreneurs, who contracted to collect the taxes from these activities. As the secret societies increasingly turned to crime, they took control of these tax farms, fixing the bids and applying violence and coercion to collection (Hong 1984:103).[9]

Secret societies flourished both in the provinces and in the capital, and by 1906, there were at least thirty such societies operating in Bangkok alone (Supharat 1981:58).[10] While the government had tolerated and even worked with these groups because of their usefulness in controlling disputes in the Chinese community, riots in Bangkok in 1869, 1883, and 1889, as well as a number of lesser disturbances, eroded this tolerance, and after the riot of 1889, secret societies were banned, this time with a more effective administration to enforce the ban (Supharat 1981:212–213; Skinner 1957:144).[11] The role of the secret societies had gradually evolved from being mutual assistance groups to organized crime, and now, with the ban in place, other types of organizations expanded to fill the traditional assistance services formerly performed by the secret societies.

Secret societies, like *nakleng,* played both positive and negative roles in society and were accepted, perhaps grudgingly, by both the Sino-Thai community and the government. They provided welfare services both to members and to the larger community. Leaders were often made representatives of the government. As with the *nakleng,* the secret society leader was a respected member of the community and an important patron as well as a protector. After the decline of the societies, much of the patronage moved into dialect and lineage associations. However, helping members of one's own group and building up the reputation of one's family remained important values.

The Transition to *Jaopho*

After the overthrow of the absolute monarchy, the Promoters found that in order to maintain their political sway, they needed to develop economic power. That meant forging links of their own with the Sino-Thai business community: in some cases, with the same powerful families that had cooperated with the absolute monarchy as tax farmers and in other roles; in others, with newly emerging families (see Sungsidh 1983). As part of this process of exerting control and developing economic power, the new government cracked down on organized crime. Police Chief Adun Detcharat, who was appointed to monitor political enemies (Stowe 1991:86), was responsible for this operation. Perhaps due to this crackdown, other than a brief revival of the secret societies during World War II to support Nationalist China (Skinner, 1957:254–255, 264–265), there was little visible role for the *nakleng* and *sia* during this period.

It was during the lead-up to the Sarit coup that organized crime again became heavily enmeshed in politics. During the mid-1950s, a power struggle was under way between army commander Sarit Thanarat and police chief Phao Siyanon that would determine who would succeed Prime Minister Phibun (for details, see Thak 1979). Both Sarit and Phao built up extensive networks of supporters, not just in the army and police but in society as a whole. Each developed a business network and media outlet, and sought to extend their ties into politics and foreign affairs. Phao, as police chief, was in a position to cultivate criminals, who proved to be important allies in carrying out illegal activities. Within the police force, Phao had his own *asawin* (knights) [12] who would compete for the favor of the boss by performing his errands, up to and including killing his opponents, many of whom were killed while "resisting arrest" while others simply disappeared. [13] Phao had police forces for every purpose: from the railroads to the oceans, from horseback to airborne. The *asawin* specialized in crime. They were given special treatment and bonuses for their services, and were heavily involved in the illegal opium trade.

Under the leadership of Phao and his *asawin,* and at their direction, cooperation between police and the underworld became systematic. This association reached its political height in the 1957 election, when Phao made a bid for power in his role as secretary-general of the government political party. He used the *nakleng* and *sia* to break up the rallies of other parties, extort money for the use of his own party, intimidate and generally harass other candidates, and to get out the vote. In return, the gangsters were issued cards declaring them *phukwangkhwang* (prominent people) and reading, "the holder of this card is a close associate and servant of the director-general of the police. If there is a problem, please contact me" (Suriyan, n.d.:9). This card in effect made them immune from arrest. Phao (and Phibun's) political party won the election, widely believed to be the most fraudulent in Thai history, and Phao was appointed minister of the interior. The dirty election, with its fraud and tactics of intimidation, however, provided the pretext for the Sarit faction to stage a coup later that same year, forcing Phao into exile. Phao was the first to use criminal elements in political elections in a systematic way. As head of the police and secretary-general of the government political party, he was able to hold a virtual monopoly on the use of such persons in the election of February 1957. No other government has been able to so monopolize the support of the *nakleng* and *sia*. Later democratization brought about competition between political parties for the assistance of these criminal groups (Anderson 1990).

While Sarit agreed to elections after the coup, he soon began the moves that would lead to a new system of government, "despotic paternalism," his form of centralized authoritarian rule. Among the first moves toward dictatorship was the elimination of those gangsters who had cooperated with his enemy, Phao. Sarit implemented a new law allowing the arrest of *anthaphan* (gangsters)—in most cases, the same individuals Phao had designated *phukwangkhwang*—without evidence or trial, and imprisoned nearly all the most powerful figures in organized crime. However, Sarit did not really intend to wipe out crime; he simply wanted to bring it under his control, and new leadership gradually emerged. When the old leadership got out of prison, organized crime, infused with both new and old blood, and with the influx of cash from the beginning of the Vietnam War, became more prevalent than ever.

Current *jaopho* come from the combination of the *nakleng* and *sia* traditions, modified by the rapid growth of the provincial economy and the emergence of democracy.[14] Thus, to describe the rise of *jaopho*, it is necessary to examine the interconnections among *nakleng, sia,* economic growth, and democracy.

After the coup of 1957, the Sarit Thanarat government, on the advice of the World Bank, began to promote private-sector-led economic development. This marked a change to the state-enterprise-led development pursued earlier and allowed the rise of powerful, often newly rich provincial notables. Much of the money flooding into the provinces during this period came by way of development and counterinsurgency funds, and those who had close relations to the government were often in the best position to benefit financially. Political influence thus became even more closely tied to economic wealth. Many of these relationships involved corruption, and *nakleng* and *sia* were well positioned to profit from the new wealth. Furthermore, narcotics, smuggling, and especially gambling all allowed *nakleng/sia* now becoming *jaopho* to enjoy particularly high profits during this period, which could then be invested in legitimate, profitable businesses.

The establishment of democracy during the seventies further enhanced the political power of the *jaopho*. When democracy was revived after the student-led uprising of 1973, there were no political organizations in the provinces capable of mobilizing votes. In the past, government parties had used the bureaucracy to win elections; however, government parties disappeared after the 1973 demonstrations that overthrew the military government. As parties scrambled to form organizations (see Chapter 3), they found that some of the most effective already existing ones belonged to the rising *jaopho. Jaopho* employed numerous young men who often had time on their hands. They had networks for selling tickets for the underground lottery. And they often had construction companies that could build roads or bridges in exchange for votes. As coercion and patronage, often in the form of vote buying, soon proved crucial to winning elections, *jaopho* became valuable political allies.

By the end of the 1970s, *jaopho* realized that success in delivering votes meant they could elect their own *candidates,* or even contest the elections themselves. By winning elections and becoming members of parliament and even cabinet ministers, *jaopho* became national figures, increased their access to government resources, and placed themselves beyond the reach of the local police. All these factors have made the *jaopho* the most powerful individuals in many provinces (Ockey 1992:chap. 4, 5); and the resulting power has enhanced their capabilities to act as criminals and benefactors within their own provinces, and even to extend their influence to other provinces and to Bangkok.

While the *jaopho* have their origins in the *nakleng* and *sia,* and in fact invariably refer to themselves as either *nakleng* or *sia,* they have obviously gone well beyond those origins. Pino Arlacchi (1987) has traced a similar process for the Sicilian mafia in Italy that may be useful in understanding this evolution from *nakleng/sia* to *jaopho.* Arlacchi argues that the Sicilian mafia went through a period of crisis during the 1950s and 1960s as the state took back powers that had been abrogated to the mafia at the time of the Second World War (Arlacchi 1987:xiii–xiv). The new mafia that emerged from the crisis, according to Arlacchi, "have ceased to play the role of *mediators,* and have devoted themselves to *capital accumulation"*—have, in effect, abandoned many of the elements of the traditional mafia to become mafia entrepreneurs (Arlacchi 1987:xiv–xv). Two other factors, stated Arlacchi, influenced the development of this new mafia: preeminence in the international drug trade and political autonomy from the state (Arlacchi 1987:xiv). This new mafia is more ruthless, more preoccupied with profit, and less concerned about community or family.[15]

Similar events, though in a milder form, have taken place in Thailand and help to explain the difference between the *jaopho* and the *nakleng/sia.* Police General Phao Siyanon had used the *nakleng/sia* as a part of his political and economic organization. When Sarit came to power, Phao went into exile and Sarit cracked down on crime in an attempt to eliminate Phao's allies. This crackdown was of limited duration and scope, but it did reduce some of the power and influence of the *nakleng* that had developed under Phao. Also, as in Sicily, highly profitable construction contracts with the government became a reality during this period, as counterinsurgency and development projects focused on building up infrastructure. As in Sicily, Thailand and the golden triangle became a major player in the international narcotics trade during the 1960s and 1970s. And finally, as in Sicily, the rise of parliamentary rule allowed the *nakleng* who had now become *jaopho* to develop considerable autonomy by winning elective offices in their own areas, at the village, *tambon,* city, provincial, and national levels. And also as in Sicily, these developments created a new, more ruthless, and less "honorable" *nakleng,* now called a *jaopho,*[16] interested in capital accumulation rather than in the community, power, and prestige.

The transition to a more ruthless form has been less abrupt and complete in Thailand; nevertheless, the *jaopho* of today is far more concerned with capital accumulation than was his predecessor. The role of patron is still important for most *jaopho*, perhaps partly because political influence and autonomy depend on the ability to win elections: both coercion and patronage are useful in earning votes. Patronage can be seen as a means of buying protection, either through elected office or more simply through information concerning police officers. In the *jaopho* of today, then, we can identify both criminal and benefactor, mafia entrepreneur and mediator. This contradiction partly explains why the *jaopho* is both accepted and resisted by the people and the government. Only when we come to a better understanding of the role of benefactor can we disentangle the part of the criminal. Only in looking at the development of the entrepreneurial role can we determine the changes in the relationship between benefactor and recipient.

I shall now turn to the social-welfare types of activities of three *jaopho:* one relatively unassimilated Sino-Thai, who more nearly resembles the traditional *sia;* one Thai, a *jaopho* direct from the *nakleng* tradition; and one highly assimilated Sino-Thai, a modern *jaopho* entrepreneur. Two are in the provinces and one in Bangkok. All are involved in illegal activities, although one, the traditional *sia,* is perhaps more inclined toward corruption than violent crime. All are wealthy, respected, and feared in their own communities, and known as *jaopho* by those who read the national press. All are also active in politics, if not directly, then behind the scenes. And all have legitimate business activities in addition to their lucrative illegal activities.

Kamnan W., Phichit Province

Kamnan W. was *kamnan* of Hua Dong, a *tambon* in Muang district, Phichit province.[17] He served as a village headman for just one month before becoming *kamnan,* and a month later was elected the head of the Kamnan and Phuyaiban Association. His enemies claim that he uses threats, violence, and killing to maintain control over the press in Phichit and that his close ties to police in the province allow him to flaunt the law at will.[18] Kamnan W. lives, not in Hua Dong, but in the nearby provincial capital, Phichit, in a compound that occupies the middle of a downtown block. On one side is a building housing the offices of his finance company. On the other side of the block is a high metal gate with a guard at the entrance to the home of the *kamnan.* Entry is difficult; the guard says he only admits visitors on the personal authorization of the *"sia."* Upon passing the guard and the gate, the visitor is confronted with a traditional Chinese-style residence, with the *kamnan*'s office on the right and the house directly in front. The *kamnan* served Chinese dishes, ate with chopsticks, and discussed Chinese and Thai politics. He retained many Chinese traditions and bore a strong resemblance to the old-style *sia.*

Kamnan W. and his family have long been powerful in Phichit. Their influence also extends to Bangkok. In Phichit and nearby provinces, the family businesses, managed by Kamnan W., included three rice mills; a finance company with four branch offices, including one in Bangkok; at least one sawmill; and the concession to produce and distribute liquor in twelve nearby provinces. In Bangkok, the family businesses, managed by Kamnan W.'s younger brother, included major shareholdings in one of the banks and in one of the largest and most successful department store chains.

Financial success has also been accompanied by political participation. Kamnan W.'s older brother was a *kamnan* for sixteen years before resigning to run for parliament, where he served two terms before his death.[19] Kamnan W. himself was not eligible to run for parliament; he lacked the education required of candidates whose fathers were not born in Thailand. However, he had been *kamnan* of Hua Dong for more than ten years.[20] Furthermore, his enemies claim that no member of parliament in his election district could win a seat without his support.[21] Kamnan W. admitted to supporting candidates for parliament but downplayed his influence on the results. Given his financial resources, his position in the Kamnan and Phuyaiban Association, and the resources and organizational networks of his businesses, his support as a *hua khanaen* in an election would be crucial, perhaps decisive.

Kamnan W. took his role as *kamnan* very seriously. He had been named the Outstanding Kamnan of the Year once and, he claimed, was recommended for the award a second time by a neutral committee in 1989. The governor gave the award to another kamnan that year in the midst of a series of demonstrations against the governor led by the Kamnan and Phuyaiban Association. Kamnan W. was so angry when he did not win that award that he stepped up efforts to have the governor transferred; after numerous demonstrations by his supporters and much lobbying, he was ultimately successful, despite strong support for the governor in Bangkok. After the new governor arrived, among the first issues he faced was a petition to withdraw the award from the recipient and give it to Kamnan W.[22] Kamnan W. saw this award as a means of expanding the reputation of his *trakun* or *sae*.[23] This desire to build up the family reputation is crucial to understanding his motivations.

Kamnan W. believed that the rich have a responsibility to serve as patrons for the poor. As a corollary to this view, he believed that all *kamnan* should be rich business leaders who have the means to donate money to development efforts in their own *tambon*. According to Kamnan W., he often spent his own money to help, not only the people of Hua Dong, but of the entire district. Specific types of assistance included money for schools and schoolchildren and donations for road construction. While the amount of money he gained through the influence he could wield from his position may have dwarfed the amount he contributed to these causes, only the money he bestowed was evident to villagers. The money gained through influence came from business or the government; only when it was reported in the national press did it become visible, and then more visible to

Bangkokians than to those in Hua Dong. For the villagers, the nearly 400,000 baht (15,000 U.S. dollars) Kamnan W. donated in the year he pushed for the outstanding *kamnan* award was a result of his largesse, and was more than they could otherwise have expected for development. It is important to keep in mind that Kamnan W. did not donate this money to ensure reelection: at that time, once elected, *kamnan* served until retirement at age sixty. Nor did he live among his constituents. His willingness to spend money for their benefit, then, should be viewed in the tradition of *sia*, of building up prestige, and of helping his own. On the other hand, reinforcing patron–client ties helped to ensure his influence in soliciting votes for his candidates in parliamentary elections. And many of the demonstrators who helped to expel Kamnan W.'s rival, the governor, must have benefited from his past generosity.

The case of Kamnan W. shows that the traditional *sia* have not disappeared entirely. Interestingly, Kamnan W.'s business interests included rice mills and a finance company, two arenas where rural patrons have always dominated.[24] Yet, even this relatively traditional *sia* showed signs of the modern *jaopho*. The finance company is a modern institution and the move to expand to Bangkok was certainly aimed at capital accumulation. These changes in legitimate business were accompanied by increased reliance on government contracts. In the sawmill, the whisky concession, and the reported fixing of construction bids, Kamnan W. had begun to look to the state for income and away from agriculture. And by taking control of politics in the *tambon,* and expanding influence in the district and the parliament, Kamnan W. had managed to carve out some autonomy. However, Phichit is not located on a route for smuggling narcotics or weapons, and so internationalization was not likely to take place. Finally, although Kamnan W. was always present when one of the projects he sponsored was completed, he distanced himself from his clients. The house in Phichit complete with gate and high walls, the intimidating finance company office, and especially the second home in Bangkok were all aspects of this distancing, which correlated with the new source of income—the state rather than agriculture—and the need to buy votes rather than just request them. As for social welfare, the new focus seemed to be on visible donations—not surprising as Kamnan W. himself was not in the community. The patron–client ties he employed had been developed by other members of his family; his own ties were not very personalized. This hastened the process of patron–client-style personal ties being replaced by economic transactions. Many of these trends are even more marked in the other cases presented here.

Mr. C.K., "Business Leader"

Mr. C.K. is one of the few ethnic Thai *jaopho* in Bangkok.[25] He was born and raised near a market in the northern part of the city and still lives there. From the time he was very young, Mr. C.K., though poor, had at least two important patrons: Ngiap, the local *nakleng,* and Khukrit Pramot, an important politician (*Khao krong,* 21 June 1990, 15).[26] C.K. grew up as a *nakleng,* facing his first trial while still a juvenile for knifing a schoolmate while fighting on behalf of a friend. He has admitted his guilt, explaining that the schoolmate refused to testify against him, and since that time they have been friends (*Khao krong,* 21 June 1990, 16; *Matuphum raisapda,* 24 June 1991, 8). This fight gave him a reputation as a *nakleng,* and by age eighteen or nineteen he had become leader of his group of friends (*Bangkok Post,* 14 April 1991, 9). He began his career as a *nakleng* by taking control over a minibus queue near his home (*Kotfathoe...* 1989, 13). During this period, he also tried his luck as a professional singer, a controller for some of the city's garbage trucks, and a clerk at a pawnshop (*Matuphum raisapda,* 24 June 1991, 8). However, he liked gambling and was drawn to gambling dens. At age twenty-one he was asked to provide protection for a small gambling den, and from this beginning he expanded his influence in gambling circles until he had enough capital to establish his own den not far from the market where he grew up; he later moved it into the market during floods that affected the original den (*Bangkok Post,* 14 April 1991, 9; *Matuphum raisapda,* 24 June 1991, 45). Eventually that gambling house grew to be one of the largest in Bangkok, and Mr. C.K. became one of the top *jao-pho* in the capital.[27]

C.K. became involved in politics when his patron, Khukrit Pramot, ran for office in 1975. Together with his other patron, Ngiap, he helped manage Khukrit's campaign in his own and nearby neighborhoods. Khukrit won the election and went on to become prime minister. Mr. C.K. was rewarded with a house (*Matichon sutsapda,* 21 August 1988, 5; *Khao krong,* 21 June 1990, 15). The next year, in a new election, the military, which has a number of bases in the area, voted as a block against Khukrit; he lost in a close election. After that time, C.K. looked to Khukrit for advice on whom to support in every election, up until Khukrit quit politics. He later transferred his allegiance to Samak Suntharawet of the Thai Citizen party, and then he began to consider standing for election himself (*Khao krong,* 21 June 1990, 14–15). C.K. believed, like Kamnan W., that in order to serve the nation one had to be rich, and planned to build up his business interests before entering politics (*Khao krong,* 21 June 1990, 14–16). In 2000, C.K. won election to the senate in Bangkok. In the first round he was disqualified by the Election Commission for suspected vote buying. He ran in the subsequent election to replace those disqualified and won by an even greater margin, whereupon he was allowed to take his seat.

Mr. C.K.'s record of charity is even more impressive than that of Kamnan W. His success at gambling has been shared with friends and neighbors. In return, they warn him of police raids and vote as he asks. He said that if the people of his neighborhood need something—for example, dredging of water culverts—they do not go to the M.P. or the government but come to him (*Khao phiset*, 13 July 1988, 20). He claimed to have built over a hundred rooms for those who live in the slums around his gambling den (*Khao phiset*, 13 July 1988, 21). He also said he had supported the education of many young people, had provided money for medicines and loans to start businesses, and had served as a mediator in disputes. C.K. told of a time when a large group of women who sold goods at a nearby market, located on land owned by the State Railway of Thailand (SRT), arrived at his door early one morning. An ambitious entrepreneur had gone to the SRT and offered to rent the land to build a market. He then charged high rents on all the stalls. Naturally, the peddlers had simply moved across the tracks. The entrepreneur then went to the SRT and asked for help in forcing the peddlers to move back into the marketplace. The SRT called in the police, and the peddlers came to C.K. He called in the entrepreneur and worked out an agreement (*Khao phiset*, 13 July 1988, 20).[28] As his reputation spread, people from nearby communities, and eventually people from as far away as Prachinburi province on the Cambodian border came to ask him for help (*Khao krong*, 21 June 1990, 16). Although these appeals expanded the amount of assistance C.K. offered and his scope of influence, it also shifted his help from welfare based on personal ties to money given to those in need. By making him a benefactor on a larger scale, it may have reduced the special relationship he had once had with his own community. "If I can do anything for the poor, I will do it immediately, because I was born into poverty," he said (*Matuphum raisapda*, 24 June 1991, 45; see also *Bangkok Post* (Perspective), 17 December 2000, 6).

Although Mr. C.K. has stated over and over again that he is a *lukphuchai*, a "man," and claimed to exemplify the traits of the traditional *nakleng*,[29] his relationship with his people has also been changing. As part of an attempt to rehabilitate his *jaopho* image, and to increase his wealth, Mr. C.K. became a business leader. He is a major shareholder in several companies, including a construction company and a real-estate development company. Significantly, the real-estate company built a condominium on the site of some of the slums C.K. had long protected (see also Chapter 7). When asked about this, he replied, "If we are to help others, we must have [money] first" (*Khao krong*, 21 June 1990, 12). The condominiums were aimed at people with middle-class-level incomes rather than the poor. Where C.K. the *nakleng* looked after his own, and they looked after him, C.K. the business leader had to look after his business.

While C.K.'s involvement in the narcotics trade, if any, is not clear, he is certainly not a major player internationally.[30] However, like Kamnan W., he has turned increasingly to capital accumulation, especially in his new role as legitimate business leader. The new companies are positioned to take advantage of both government contracts and distribution of products from abroad.[31] Among them is a publishing company, founded by C.K.'s mentor, the late Khukrit Pramot. It produces a major daily newspaper *(Siamrat)* and a political weekly magazine *(Siamrat sapda wijan)*, so that C.K. has a forum to shape public opinion, especially regarding himself. In addition, the companies are a mechanism for employing many of his followers—over two hundred and growing *(Khao krong,* 21 June 1990, 14). Again, though, the new relationship is employer to employee, a formal economic relationship characterized by contracts and interchangeable workers.

Like Kamnan W., Mr. C.K. is gradually becoming more distant from many of his clients. C.K. has been transformed, albeit never completely, from local *nakleng,* to powerful *jaopho,* to business leader. Each step, while providing him with more resources to help, distanced him further from members of his own community and brought him into loose contact with needy members of a wider one. Here too, we see economics breaking down the old patron-based personalistic welfare practices, replacing them, in many cases, with more direct economic transactions, the dispensing of cash to any able to convince the godfather of sufficient need. And since he has become a politician himself, C.K. will continue to build his ties with as many clients as possible, especially in Bangkok, which comprises a single election district for the senate. In the senate, he may have further resources available from the state in developing ties, albeit mostly financially generated rather than personal ones.

Mayor S., Saensuk Municipality

Mayor S., like C.K. and Kamnan W., has denied being a *jaopho.*[32] He has claimed, however, that he can give orders to the *nakleng* along the eastern seaboard *(Prachachat Thurakit,* 20 April 1988, 31), and while he does not control the entire network of *nakleng/jaopho* in the area, he is certainly the most powerful. Mayor S. rose to power upon the death of the old *jaopho* of Chonburi, Sia Jiew, in 1981. Prior to that time, he had been preeminent in his own *tambon* but chose to cooperate with and defer to the power of Sia Jiew. He reportedly had interests in construction and helped out in Sia Jiew's gambling den *(Lak thai,* 24 April 1989, 17).[33] The killing of Sia Jiew led to a power struggle in which his son and a key assistant also died. The mayor, then a *kamnan,* emerged on top, taking over from Sia Jiew the distribution of whisky, smuggling activities, and the underground lottery, among other operations.[34] He has been accused of involvement in everything from smuggling drugs, to smuggling refugees out of Cambodia for a price, to running guns to the Burmese insurgencies, to murdering his rivals.[35] Mayor S., along with the *jaopho* from Phetburi and perhaps a few other provinces, is most like the new mafia described by Arlacchi. And yet he has also retained many of the characteristics of the traditional *nakleng.*

Mayor S. also took over the political role of Sia Jiew. The mayor, while still a *kamnan,* had been the head of the local association of *kamnan* and *phuyaiban,* and after the death of Sia Jiew, he took over the distribution of whisky in much of the region. These two groups formed the basis for his *hua khanaen* network to solicit votes for his favored candidates for the parliament. He has supported numerous members of parliament, including some who became cabinet ministers. When he threw a party to celebrate his election as mayor (he ran unopposed), an estimated (and probably somewhat exaggerated) fifty thousand people came, including the minister of foreign affairs, the deputy minister of the interior, the deputy minister of education, and the provincial governor (*Matichon sutsapda,* 30 April 1989, 10). In the 1992 election, two of his sons won election to the parliament in Chonburi; one later became a cabinet minister. A third son, Itthiphon (literally "influence") was elected in 2001.

While Mayor S. has been ruthless in his business and criminal activities, like C.K. and Kamnan W. he has been popular in his home *tambon.* Following the large victory celebration when he was elected mayor, he organized a group of villagers to voluntarily clean up the beach. Some five hundred villagers showed up.

> [Mayor S.] worked shoulder-to-shoulder with his villagers, with only a wide-rimmed straw hat to shield him from the scorching heat. It seemed like he knew just about everybody there, chatting amicably and calling people by their names. "Except for the young people, I know most of the villagers. They often come to my house to seek help or advice about just anything," he explained. (*Bangkok Post,* 4 May 1989, 31)

While his efforts on the beach were certainly aimed at improving his image, the attendance at the party and at the beach reveals Mayor S.'s popularity with many local villagers. Like C.K., he has spent considerable sums on those who have come to ask his help. In the two years after he was elected mayor, he claimed to have spent 20 million baht (then U.S. $800,000) of his own money on the municipality and to have donated another 10 million baht to monasteries (*Matuphum raisapda,* 18 August 1991, 7). He claimed that individuals and groups come about twenty-five days each month, seeking assistance ranging up into the hundreds of thousands of baht, with most asking for 2–5,000 baht (then U.S. $100–200). Although he knew most of these supplicants, like C.K., he received visitors from distant provinces as well (*Prachachat thurakit,* 20 April 1988, 30). "This house is like a place where the villagers come to make complaints about officials . . . some days as many as 100 people, and when there is a festival there have been as many as a thousand. Ordinarily there are at least 20 people" (Suriyan 1993:44). The mayor not only provided money for those in need, but also acted as a mediator between those who came to him and government officials.

Mayor S. admitted that one of the key reasons for his acts of charity is to maintain his influence over elections.[36] He also dispensed his largesse on government officials to win their support, thereby convincing them to ignore his illegal activities. According to a former Chonburi chief of police:

> It was only at the front of my office that I was the chief in Chonburi. . . . Under the commander, all were the people of [Mayor S.]. Whenever they had a problem, they would go to the *jaopho*. When their children would enter a new term at school and they had no money, they would go see [Mayor S.] . . . and would get the money. If their wives were pregnant, about to enter the hospital to give birth and they didn't have any money, they would go to see him. He would give them money. . . . And it wasn't just the police who were under his control. Other government officials who could benefit his interests all came under his protection. (Seri Temeyawet in Phasuk and Sangsit 1992:147)

By providing these welfare services to government officials, the mayor enhanced his ability to serve as a mediator between the officials and the people, and ensured that his own illegal activities would be protected.

Mayor S. has also used his political position to great advantage in obtaining funds from the central government to benefit his community—and his own interests. "I spoke with Phi [elder] Banhan [Silapa-acha, then a cabinet minister] for 10 minutes and obtained 20 million baht [then U.S. $800,000], I went another time and got 35 million baht [then U.S. $1,400,000]. We can get money from the center to develop our village" (*Matichon sutsapda,* 30 April 1989, 10). He said that he had obtained over 70 million baht while working through Banhan, and that at one point, he got 6 million baht from the Tourist Authority of Thailand that he could not spend and had to return (*Matichon sutsapda,* 30 April 1989, 10–12). In addition, the city budget is under the control of the mayor and can be dispensed as patronage—through jobs, construction contracts, and similar means. This allowed the mayor to continue to provide social welfare without spending his own money. In fact, he became the distributor of patronage for the state, usurping the credit and the power that the state might otherwise have had itself. He both received and dispensed state patronage, convincing the state, and particularly the politicians who depended on him for reelection, to cooperate with him for mutual benefit.

In addition to his alleged smuggling, gambling, and other illicit activities, Mayor S. became heavily involved in legitimate businesses. These businesses included hotels, the whisky distribution already mentioned, construction, a fleet of ten-wheel trucks, adviser to a number of Japanese companies where he helped solve problems—that is, acted as a mediator—and real-estate development (*Prachachat thurakit,* 20 April 1988, 30). A former chief of police in the province described his real-estate transactions: "If he wants to buy land, he sends someone to buy it cheaply; those who are afraid sell, those who aren't afraid die. . . . Therefore, he takes that business, takes this business, all of which he shares with his followers. His followers have it easy with him because they get a share."[37] Certainly the followers of the mayor benefited, as did the villagers who lived near him. However, his relations with the wider community tended to be based on economic transactions, such as people coming from afar to ask for money or vote buying, or on physical violence, such as those who were forced to sell him land cheaply. Again we see the personalistic-style patron–client ties of the past increasingly replaced by other methods. For close followers, shared work, shared influence, and shared economic benefits; for others, threats, dependency, or occasional gifts.

Conclusions

We have seen that the *nakleng* and the *sia* have long been used by rulers in Thailand in administration: the *nakleng* as village heads and informal police; the *sia* as tax collectors and leaders of the Sino-Thai community. After the overthrow of the absolute monarchy in 1932, the new government naturally moved to take control over the *nakleng* and *sia* to consolidate its control. The real change for *nakleng* and *sia*, and even for straight criminals, came in the mid-1950s, when police chief Phao Siyanon brought them directly into politics and the election system. No longer were they mere administrators, but suddenly they were deeply involved in determining who gained power. He also effected a dramatic increase in the use of *nakleng, sia,* and criminals to accumulate capital for individual government leaders rather than for the government as a whole. In this sense, Phao privatized the use of these individuals and paved the way for later competition. This competition came about in the 1970s with the demise of the government political party, as all political parties turned to the former *nakleng* and *sia,* then becoming *jaopho,* to secure election. This enhanced the power and autonomy of individual *jaopho;* though, arguably, by making them available to all sides, it also made them, and the system, more democratic (see Anderson 1990).

Meanwhile, beginning primarily during the Sarit era, processes similar to those which had transformed the Sicilian mafia also occurred in Thailand, turning the traditional *nakleng* and *sia* into *jaopho.* The economic growth of the last thirty years and the integration of the rural economy into the international economy have borne higher stakes, more corruption, and more violence in their wake. Just as development and internationalization have been uneven, so has the transition from traditional *nakleng* and *sia* to modern forms of *jaopho,* with some areas and some *jaopho* being transformed more rapidly and more completely than others. This unevenness is clear in the contrast between Kamnan W., who strongly resembles the traditional *sia,* and Mayor S., who is the most prominent example of the *jaopho*. But even in areas where the transformation has been less complete, significant changes have taken place in the character of the *nakleng* and the *sia* that are reminiscent of the Sicilian mafia.

Nevertheless, the *nakleng* and the *sia* are not like the mafia. *Jaopho* and their *phakphuak* are not as formalized, institutionalized, or acculturated as the Sicilian mafia, and have little structure above the local level. Consequently, the results have been different. Two distinct tensions have been created: one that involves perceptions of power in Thai society, and a second that involves the decline of traditional patron–client ties and the rise of market ties.

Niels Mulder (1992a:chap. 2) contended that power in Thailand is amoral.[38] This amoral power, according to Mulder, is

> in everything that has mysterious qualities. This power is both potentially beneficent and harmful. . . . People have to come to an accommodation with this sphere of power and must approach it on its own terms, in accordance with the laws that guide it. . . . [It] can be tapped for personal purposes, its protection may be sought, and its vengeful manifestations can be neutralized. (Mulder 1992a:12)

Jaopho exemplify many of these characteristics. Their activities are often hidden and mysterious; consequently they become an object of fascination. They are capable of bestowing both benefits and punishments, and if treated respectfully can be a great advantage to the community or the individual in dealings with other powers. And they must be treated carefully, respectfully, and according to established customs.

As power is essentially amoral, the illegal activities of the *jaopho* are not a serious handicap to their legitimacy—as long as this legitimacy is based on traditional notions of power. However, alternative notions of power are incorporated into the legal code, according to which wealth and power are obtained either legally or illegally. Thus where the activities of a *jaopho* may be acceptable according to traditional notions of power, according to the law they are not. The legitimacy afforded by traditional notions of power may, along with the economic and political power, explain how *jaopho* are able to flaunt the law, seemingly at will. However, the fact that they are acting illegally—and this is repeated frequently in the media—partly erodes legitimacy based on the traditional notion of power.

Jaopho have resisted this erosion of legitimacy in two closely related ways, one aimed at shoring up their standing within traditional norms, the other aimed at increasing their standing with respect to the law.[39] Mulder pointed out that a leader is also expected to exhibit virtue *(khunna)*. To the extent that the *jaopho* wishes to become a community leader, he must convince his constituents that he is benevolent. In return, "benevolence engenders a moral debt that should be acknowledged;

it is the fountain-head from which moral obligation arises" (Mulder 1992a:19). By exhibiting virtue, or to be more accurate, by substituting generosity for it, at least within their own constituencies, *jaopho* reinforce their legitimacy through appeals to traditional norms.[40] At the same time, the moral obligation is repaid in votes that provide the *jaopho* with political influence. As a politician, or the ally of a politician, the *jaopho* enhances his legitimacy in the eyes of the law. A mayor or member of parliament *makes* laws, has greater status than a police officer, and is therefore difficult to arrest.

By exhibiting generosity, the *jaopho* is also appealing to the same patron–client ties that long sustained the legitimacy of the *sia* and the *nakleng*. However, the steady encroachment of the market has subverted those ties and forced the *jaopho* to rely on a less dependable combination of primarily economic ties.[41] Where in the past, the *nakleng* may have been the only source of protection for a village and the *sia* the only connection to the market, today the *jaopho* has numerous competitors: the state, private enterprise, and other *jaopho*. For the traditional patron, such as Kamnan W., the old ties to community weakened as he turned to capital accumulation in order to compete with other *jaopho* and with legitimate businessmen in a wider world.[42] For the newly emergent *jaopho*, such as Mayor S., the old ties never existed and had to be formed within a new context: many of the aspects of personalistic ties were replaced by direct financial transactions; votes were bought rather than earned through loyalty. Where the transformation from *sia/nakleng* to *jaopho* has been most complete—as for example, with Mayor S.— the buying of loyalty and of entrance into politics have become most salient.

Another factor in the transformation of patron–client ties between the *jaopho* and the villagers is the expansion of the territory under the control of *jaopho*. As some *jaopho* have expanded their reputations and their operations to cover entire provinces, and even entire regions, it has become impossible to maintain personal ties with this enlarged community. Thus cash contributions to the needy connect Mr. C.K. and Mayor S. to people from distant provinces. Although the traditional personalistic ties were far from benign, the new economic ties are often equally exploitative, and much more fragile. A hierarchy of relationships may develop, with personal relations being maintained with nearby villagers, and economic transactions and violence employed for those at a greater distance. In other cases, as with Kamnan W., the *jaopho* may not live in the community, creating distance even from his core constituents. And business interests may come into conflict with personal ties, as happened when C.K. decided to build a condominium in the middle of his slum community, or when Mayor S. used threats and violence to buy land. This more distant, sometimes conflictual relationship has meant a greater need for visible donations and public relations. Interviews in the newspapers with known *jaopho* have become quite common, as they seek to influence public opinion.[43]

Significant changes have also taken place in the relationships between the state, the *jaopho,* and the villager. In the past, the *sia/nakleng* often looked to the villagers as the source of wealth; now the *jaopho* often looks to the state—with its construction contracts, concessions, and assistance—and to the wider economy, centered at Bangkok and connected to the outside world. In other areas, the *jaopho,* like Mayor S. in his capacity as adviser to Japanese firms, as well as in his smuggling activities, has direct access to the international market. The community is then a source of legitimacy and protection, but not necessarily an economic base.[44]

Further complicating the transition from the traditional *sia* or *nakleng* to the *jaopho* is the advent of democracy and the participation of the *jaopho* in the democratic system. This has allowed him to gain a measure of autonomy in his own area. Participation in politics allows the *jaopho* to widen the scope of his operations, particularly through contracts and concessions from the state. It also offers protection in the forms of a patron at the center and an official position, and the associated respectability. *Kamnan* and mayors are partly responsible for police work in their communities and are much more difficult to arrest than typical criminals. And since *jaopho* are in competition with each other and with legitimate business leaders for contracts and concessions, the participation of one in politics requires others to follow suit.[45]

Participation in politics and business gives the *jaopho* a dual nature. Where the *jaopho* as business leader might be inclined toward capital accumulation, the *jaopho* as politician is inclined toward generosity; where the *jaopho* as business leader might be inclined toward violence, the *jaopho* as politician is inclined toward mediation. Sometimes even in elections violence reigns, as supporters of the political opposition are murdered or citizens are coerced to vote for a candidate. More often, we find a combination of violence and generosity: voters are paid for their votes and threatened if they fail to deliver. The need to retain electoral support mediates the violence and guarantees at least some generosity. Thus while the relationship has become less personal and more of an economic exchange, the need to participate in politics and, to a lesser extent, to gain protection through the support of the community, ensures that at least some degree of social welfare activity on the part of most *jaopho* will continue.

Participation in politics has also preserved another aspect of the traditional *sia/nakleng:* cooperation between the state and the *jaopho* for the mutual economic benefit of both. Politicians support *jaopho* in conflicts with the police or other government officials and in their attempts to win government contracts and concessions; in return, the *jaopho* supplies finances and organization for the election campaigns of the politicians. The *jaopho* shares profits with government officials, in effect buying protection. And the *jaopho* may even help suppress crime in his region—at least the crime not under his protection.[46]

Although the importance of the *jaopho* in the current electoral system is likely to prevent decisive state action against them, other factors might weaken the support base of the *jaopho* without direct action by the state. First, the economy and the social security net may develop to the point where whole communities are no longer in need; if only individuals are in need, the *jaopho* may lose the protection of the community. Second, many of the lucrative activities of the *jaopho* are disappearing. For example, narcotics routes now frequently go through China and Indochina. Import duties on many commodities, including alcohol and cigarettes, have been lowered, making smuggling less profitable. The war, and along with it the black market, in Cambodia is over. However, perhaps inevitably, new lucrative opportunities, such as the domestic narcotics trade, have emerged. Third, many *jaopho*, having made their fortunes and seeing the opportunities available in business, are seeking to legitimize themselves and their children. And finally, the new constitution was designed, at least in part, in the belief that it would reduce corruption. If it is ultimately successful, *jaopho* may find their influence weakened.

The participation of the *jaopho* in politics presents one further crucial dilemma. Patronage from the state to the people passes through the hands of the *jaopho* who are *kamnan*, mayors, provincial councilors, or even M.P.s and cabinet ministers. This allows a *jaopho* to skim from the development and welfare efforts of the state, while portraying himself as the source of the patronage and usurping the credit. The *jaopho* thus justifies his position in politics and enhances his ability to win votes while reducing the total amount of state money that actually reaches the villagers. For any particular village, however, the *jaopho* will often obtain more development money—even after skimming—than villagers could otherwise expect. It is then perfectly reasonable for the community to elect that *jaopho* for the benefit of the community, allow him to skim, and net more development money than it would under a more scrupulous politician. Thus the gap between national politics and its Bangkok-oriented policies perpetuates the ability of the *jaopho* to maintain control. Rather than weaning the villagers away from the patronage of the *jaopho* by providing for their welfare, the national budget actually increases the amount of patronage the *jaopho* can dispense. Consequently, as long as welfare efforts to the poor and the rural population continue to be funneled through the *jaopho*, the *jaopho* will likely remain powerful.

Before popular support for the *jaopho* can be weakened, the role of patron must be disentangled from the role of criminal. Only when the welfare needs of villagers and slum dwellers are met directly can such support be expected to disappear. Of course the *jaopho* are fully aware of the need to maintain this dependency. The policy platform of the Thai Rak Thai party in the 2001 election was potentially a step in the right direction, but it also demonstrates the scope of the problem. Thai Rak Thai promised a three-year debt moratorium for farmers and a one million baht "revolving fund" for every *tambon* in Thailand. These policies were easily explained and very popular, and earned the party many votes, suggesting that the poor do vote for parties with policies that help them when given the chance. However, both policies are patronage-oriented, do nothing to change structural problems, and in some areas may increase dependency on powerful local figures who will likely control these "revolving funds." Forging links between local and national politics and encouraging rural participation in national politics might prove more successful.

■ ■ ■ ■ ■ ■ ■ ■ ■ ■

CHAPTER 5

God Mothers, Good Mothers, Good Lovers, Godmothers
Changing Stereotypes and Leadership in Thailand

The details of the hit were not unusual. A gunman fired a nine-millimeter pistol into the car of Mass Communications Organization of Thailand chief Saengchai Sunthonwat, then fled with the driver on a waiting motorcycle. Two other members of the gang who had identified the victim also escaped. Due to the prominence of the widely respected Saengchai, the police devoted a great deal of time and resources to solving the crime. Ultimately, they traced the gunmen, who led them to the alleged mastermind. The assassination, according to police, was the result of a conflict of interests in the granting of concessions for provincial radio stations. When the accused mastermind had offered Saengchai a gift of an expensive gold chain and a valuable image of the Buddha to smooth relations, Saengchai had refused the offer. He further insulted the mastermind by saying that the gift was good enough only for his dog. This insult, as much as the loss of income, lay behind the killing. Although the hit was typical in many ways, two facts—beyond the tragic death of a good man—make this killing academically interesting: first, the alleged mastermind was not a godfather but a godmother; second, the press drew no particular attention to the fact that the culprit was a woman. In almost every reference, the word "godfather" could have been substituted for "godmother" with no change in meaning or inference.

Gendered Criminals

In examining the status of women in a society, the focus is usually on their positions of leadership in business or politics, or, alternatively, on the roles they play at the village level. However, interesting aspects of changing perceptions of gender and gender stereotypes may be found by looking at the most male-dominated sectors of society. These stereotypes, as we have seen, remain a barrier to women in the political arena. Considerable attention has been lavished on *jaopho*, or "godfathers," in Thailand (e.g., Anderson 1990; Pasuk and Sungsidh 1994; Pasuk and

Sungsidh 1992; Ockey 1993; and Ockey 1992). However, up to this point, little has been written of *jaomae*, or "godmothers."[1] Here I shall attempt to begin to fill that gap, while also examining *jaopho* and especially *jaomae* in the context of gender roles. I do not mean to imply that it is desirable for more women to engage in crime. Rather, given the important role of *jaopho* in the political system, and the opportunities this path offers for social mobility, it is worth examining the nature of *jaomae* and the perceptions of them more closely.

Before considering *jaomae*, let us contextualize godmothers within the literature on the status of women in Thailand. As we have observed, women have long been active in business in Thailand, perhaps due to the nature of corvée labor. Nowhere is this more true than in the typical marketplace, where women can be seen hawking all sorts of commodities. These female market traders are called *mae kha* (mother who trades), which, Keyes (1984:229) argued, is related to the role of mother. There are, however, considerable differences between the images of the tough, tight-fisted, often rough-talking market trader and the mother stereotypes to be discussed.

To reiterate, the presence of women in business is matched by an absence in politics and the bureaucracy: at all levels those who make and execute the laws are men. The discrepancy between the roles of women in business and trade and the dearth of their participation in politics and the bureaucracy has been the subject of much of the literature on gender relations in Thailand. Many writers have looked to religion in search of answers. Anthropologist Thomas Kirsch argued that:

> Buddhist factors serve to rank various kinds of activities: religious highest, political next, economic lowest. Thai men have been so overwhelmingly committed to religious and political achievements that economic activities have been left up to non-Thai and to Thai women. Thai women are left with such economic roles because in religious belief, in the structure of religious roles and rituals, and in popular thought, they are deemed to be more deeply rooted in this-worldly activities and secular concerns than men. (Kirsch 1975:191)[2]

Darunee and Pandey (1987) further developed this theme, claiming that males receive merit directly by becoming monks, while females can only receive it indirectly through male monks. They argued that "At the societal level, males (monks) are the 'merit patrons' and females as a whole (and other non-clerical males) are the 'merit clients'" (Darunee and Pandey 1987:129). This "kept women in the economic cycle by forcing them to be content with their peripheral, service role to Buddhism" and led to the "marginalization of the status and value of daughters," who, like their mothers, would spend their lives "merit-deficient" (Darunee and Pandey 1987:130).

This argument that Buddhism has cast women as worldly, lacking virtue, and even as a temptation to the purity of the monastic order has not gone unchallenged. Other writers have pointed out that Thai Buddhism has adapted many beliefs from other religions, particularly Hinduism, Animism, and Mahayana Buddhism. Consequently, although women cannot become monks, they are often associated with virtue. Neils Mulder (1992) has argued that *khunna,* or "moral goodness" in the Thai worldview is exemplified by "the pure love a mother has for her children" and is associated, not only with Buddhism, but with "the home, the mother, and the female symbols of Mother Earth and Mother Rice." "The earth on which we depend for our living, the rice that feeds us, the water that sustains life, and the guardian angel that protects the young child are all represented as female" (Mulder 1992:25, 15, 26; cf. Anuman 1955:55–61). (Power, on the other hand, Mulder wrote, is associated with men.) Charles Keyes (1984) also noted the virtue associated with women. He argued that, although men and women follow different paths to salvation, neither is inherently superior. As for women:

> In her "natural" state, as it were, the mother proves to be inherently good because of her role as mother . . . such a quality must be cultivated by males. . . . While a man must reject his "nature" (that is, his sexuality) in order to pursue the Path, a woman must first realize her "nature" (becoming a mother) as a prerequisite to her traversing the Path. Moreover, by "nature" a woman is compassionate, whereas a man acquires compassion only through a discipline that entails the suppression of his nature. (Keyes 1984:228–229)

On the depiction of women as a sexual temptation, Keyes argued that this is a secondary image, of less importance.

However, this second image, whether of less importance or not, has also received considerable attention. In a rejoinder to Keyes, Thomas Kirsch (1985: 312–313) demonstrated that in Thailand there is a potent image of woman as oversexed temptress. This perception of woman as temptation can be found in the story of the enlightenment of the Buddha. Along the path to enlightenment, Siddartha abandoned all objects of desire. His wealth, his position, and his wife figure prominently in that abandonment—woman is placed alongside wealth and position as worldly temptations, as objects of desire. It is this image that implies women may be a threat to the purity of the monastic order. Khin Thitsa argues that this image also supported the spread of prostitution in Thailand, the idea being, perhaps, that if a beautiful woman is such a tremendous temptation for even a monk, laymen cannot be expected to resist her. In this prefiguration, a woman is an object of desire, never a subject.[3] In other words, a woman is either a subject, an actor, a mother, and virtuous, or she is an object, passive, a temptation, and worldly. Herein lies the importance of the image of the *jaomae:* she subverts this dichotomy in rather profound ways, appropriating the term "mother" and playing an active role, yet in many cases not a virtuous role, and one that has been clearly associated with "manliness" in the past. As Kirsch (1985) demonstrated, economic, religious, and social changes in Thailand have begun to affect cultural stereotypes. Jackson (1997) has identified one such change, pointing to the development of a new category, the masculine *kae* (gay) homosexual, in contrast to both the feminine *kratoey* homosexual and the masculine heterosexual images. Here I focus on the threat of destabilization to the traditional male and female stereotypes inherent in the existence of *jaomae.* This subversion of gender images may be the reason why "godmothers" are accepted so matter-of-factly yet have never been carefully studied. They are in some senses familiar; yet if considered too carefully, they create complex dissonances. So they become both visible and invisible, accepted but never contemplated.

Along with the military, politics, and the bureaucracy, the criminal world has traditionally been highly male-dominated. In the past, two types of criminals, the *sua* and the *nakleng,* captured public attention. *Sua,* or "tiger," was generally used to describe a lone bandit who survived outside of society, in areas that the law could not reach.[4] From his remote fastnesses, he would make forays against targets within society. He was perceived as brave and daring, but as a loner, not part of a larger group. As such, he is of less interest here. The *nakleng* (see Chapter 4), on the other hand, is invariably a part of a *phakphuak,* a group, and is associated with manliness. The *jaopho* of today draw heavily on this "manly" tradition. Masculinity is further reinforced by tales of sexual conquest and of minor wives, as opposed to tales of family life.[5] *Nakleng* is applied almost exclusively to men, although when asked most people will agree that a woman can be a *nakleng. Sua* is also applied only to men. Yet both words have been subverted in such a way that they can be used to describe women. *Mae sua,* literally "mother tiger" but meaning female tiger, has long been used to describe women who are "fierce." As for *nakleng,* the phrase *jai nakleng,* "heart of the *nakleng,*" has entered the language to describe those who are courageous, loyal, and decisive—who embody the positive traits of the *nakleng. Jai nakleng* is freed of both the connotations of crime and of maleness, and women also describe themselves in this way.[6] Nevertheless, although the vocabulary has been subverted, there are still distinct words to describe men and women, with the words used to describe women, such as *jai nakleng,* being stripped of the connotations of crime "boss."

We noted that, beginning in the 1970s, criminals began to be described by the word *jaopho,* or "godfather."[7] However, *jaopho* already existed in Thai with a different meaning and naturally took on some of the connotations of that earlier usage as well. *Jao pho* referred to a type of guardian spirit, a god father[8] that occupied a particular locality. The *jao pho* was neither good nor evil, but was powerful and had to be appeased. This was usually done by building a shrine and making offerings. In some cases, the *jao pho* was a known person who had died tragically and become associated with the place of death. This conflation of definitions meant that the word *jaopho* took on some ambiguous connotations, and a "godfather" gradually came to mean one who had great power and influence. Although *jaopho* is not used to describe men seen as unequivocally benevolent, it is used to describe powerful ministers, bureaucrats, and entrepreneurs who are not criminals.

The guardian spirits were not exclusively male. *Jao mae* (god mother) spirits also existed.[9] However, connotations differed somewhat. As Mulder and Keyes pointed out, "mother" has been associated with moral goodness, and this had an impact on the term *jao mae*, which has been used to describe not only the female version of this type of guardian spirit, but also more powerful and benevolent figures. The Mahayana Buddhist bodhisattva Kuan Yin is often referred to as *Jao mae Kuan Im*; the Princess Mother was sometimes referred to as *jao mae yalang* in the north (*Sayamrat sapda wijan*, 21 April 1968, 15–16, 35–37; this was before *jaopho* was used to describe criminals); and the Statue of Liberty has been called *Jao mae muang lungsaem* (*Matichon sutsapda*, 13 November 1983, 40). Nowadays, the older meaning of *jao mae* is more common than that of *jao pho*, especially with the resurgence of the Kuan Yin sect among women,[10] giving this term a wider range of connotations, from the sinister to the benevolent. Even environmentalist Chodchoy Sophonpanich has been called *jaomae ta wiset* or "Magic Eyes Godmother" in praise of her leading role in promoting an antilitter campaign (*Mae lae dek*, February 1990, 124). Sometimes, as will be seen in at least one case below, it is unclear where a *jaomae* fits in this wide range of meanings. More important than virtue, however, is the implication of power, a type of power formerly associated with men.

One final word that is frequently used to describe *jaopho*, many of whom are *lukjin* (Sino-Thai), is *sia*, a Teochiu Chinese word meaning tycoon. Here too there is a female equivalent, *Je*, from the Chinese word for older sister. However, *je* and *sia*, unlike *jaopho* and *jaomae*, are not male and female forms of the same word. "Older sister" certainly has more familiar connotations than "tycoon" and is not clearly associated with economic success, although "older" conveys respect.[11]

This exploration of the terminology of gendered criminals reveals the differences in the ways they have been perceived. The development of *jaopho* to describe criminal figures is particularly significant, as it ensured the development of *jaomae* as a female version, as these words were already paired in the earlier usage. In this way, the (criminal) *jaomae* could become visible for the first time, although space remained for different connotations.

Like women warriors, diplomats, and monarchs, women criminal leaders existed in the past.[12] However, they were certainly the exception rather than the rule. Up until the 1950s, the *nakleng* and the *sua* relied heavily on physical strength. Women were not encouraged to develop the necessary strength, or the skills of fighting, and were definitely discouraged from becoming violent criminals. Later, when the use of handguns—and eventually assault weapons and explosive devices —became more common, these skills were generally learned in the military or police forces, which were restricted to men. Although they are not unknown, hired women gun hands are still extremely scarce.[13] However, the *jaopho* differs from the *nakleng* in a way that is crucial here. The traditional *nakleng*, as Johnston pointed out, had to be a man of physical prowess; he had to have demonstrated his own "manly" strength in order to lead his *phakphuak*. The *jaopho*, however, generally does not do his own fighting and killing. He orders it done (or sometimes simply implies that it should be done) and then pays for it. This does not require "manliness," physical prowess, or even a knowledge of weapons, and since women have long participated in the economic system, opportunities for the development of *jaomae* expanded. Increasingly, the *jaopho* retained power not through physical prowess but through their ability to make enough money to support many clients. If the capacity of a *jaopho* to make money declined, his clients would be forced to find new patrons. Physical strength was thus replaced by entrepreneurial ability.

The second crucial change that opened the way for *jaomae* (and for the increasing influence of *jaopho*) was the transition to parliamentary rule in the late 1970s and the 1980s. Under military rule, those in positions of authority were soldiers. When military rule ended, opportunities arose for new types of leaders, both men and women. *Jaomae* might have found it easier to associate with these new types of leaders; more important, they could either support candidates for office or even run for office themselves. Again, the way to greater visibility and participation opened up for *jaomae*.

The Cocktail Lounge Godmother

Although *jaomae* have now become visible, and apparently more common, for the most part women remain heavily concentrated in certain types of activities, especially control over prostitution and gambling.[14] This should not be surprising, since women have long been prominent in entrepreneurial activities. One example of a woman who emerged as a force in control over prostitution during the 1980s was "Oi. B. M." Oi (her nickname) claims that she was abandoned as a baby and found on a garbage heap by a kindhearted prostitute (Thomyanti 1994:39). As a child, she collected oysters and recyclable refuse to help support the other orphans rescued by her "auntie." She had no formal schooling, teaching herself how to read, write, and do the arithmetic necessary to trade. Later, she went to work in a shop in Bangkok's Chinatown, and then moved on to a bar, initially as a cigarette girl and, when she was older, as a bartender and a "partner," talking and dancing with customers. Despite this admission, she insists she never sold herself (ibid., passim) or went out with customers. She also stayed for two years with former prime minister and army strongman Sarit Thanarat, but denies rumors that she was his mistress (*Khao sot*, 20 August 1997, 10). She fell in love with a boy from her neighborhood and got pregnant. However, she never married him because his mother objected, and, according to her story, he was too weak to stand up to her. Oi had the child and made the difficult decision to let the child's grandmother raise her, as Oi then had no means of support other than returning to work at the bar (Thomyanti 1994:chap. 9). The public depiction, then, is of a mother who loved her child, yet still a strong woman unencumbered by family. Later, Oi began to procure women for others, initially for those who wanted to go with her, and from this beginning she built up a business empire.

Oi. B. M., sometimes known as the *jaomae koktenlaon* (cocktail lounge godmother), has been described as the "'mother' of girls and boys numbering hundreds, even thousands, that have chosen to undertake the occupation of service" —a euphemism for prostitution (*Matichon sutsapda*, 21 July 1991, 50). Oi. B. M. has been active in the industry for more than thirty years. She is famous for encouraging her employees to become minor wives when given the chance. She taught them to serve their husbands well, for these husbands were doing them a great honor by ignoring their past. She went so far as to say that they should bow down to their husbands five times a day for giving them this chance at a new life. She also planned the creation of a "Sensuality Bank," or escort service, which would attract members from all over the world in order to bring them "true happiness" (ibid.). After an extended period out of the spotlight, Oi. B. M. again made headlines when a rival of newly appointed Education Minister Chingchai Mongkhontham suggested that reporters ask Oi. B. M. about him. Oi. B. M. admitted to being friends with Chingchai but denied any intimate relationship with him. She claimed that her Sensuality Bank brought in 500,000 baht (about U.S.$15,000) a month, and that customers had included a thousand members and former members of the legislature. She also named two prime ministers, a deputy prime minister, and a foreign minister as customers.[15]

While Oi. B. M.'s plan for an international Sensuality Bank seems rather grandiose, it demonstrates the ambition and entrepreneurial spirit associated with both *jaomae* and *jaopho* during the economic boom. Of course, it is not unimportant that the employees of these types of *jaomae* were mostly women. Nor is it surprising that this type of *jaomae* was visible relatively early. Oi. B. M.'s attitude toward gender relations may be unexpected, but on further consideration she was an entrepreneur who catered to a male clientele, and her profits depended on satisfying her customers. In this context, her publicly expressed attitudes support her economic interests.[16] More fascinating, however, is the way in which she appears as an actor, an entrepreneur, while her workers appear as objects; even after marriage, they are depicted as minor wives, not as mothers, and are taught to acknowledge their "debt" by remaining objects for their husbands.

The Godmother of the Oil Share Fund

The second area where *jaomae* appeared early on, and are still concentrated, is gambling in its many forms. During the 1980s and 1990s, *jaomae* such as "Je Daeng," "Je Nuan," and "Mu Thong," ran gambling dens. Many gambling operations have been run by women with powerful male figures behind the scenes: Je Nuan was said to be the wife of a member of parliament, himself a *jaopho,* and Mu Thong to be the minor wife of a senior police officer. While in such cases power may have resided in the male behind the scenes, management was the responsibility of the *jaomae.*[17] In other cases, the *jaomae* seems to have been the main force. One such woman, Chamoi Thipso, known as Mae Chamoi, or the *jaomae chae namman* (Godmother of the Oil Share Fund), became famous as the operator of a share scheme.[18]

Mae Chamoi was born in the provincial capital of Singburi, about two hours north of Bangkok. A classmate from the Provincial Women's School described her as an average student, polite, but with a taste for fancy dress.[19] She later studied at Rachanibon School, where one of her teachers described her as an honest and reliable child. Around 1961, she took a job with the predecessor of the Petroleum Authority of Thailand (PTT) in Bangkok as a clerk in the sales department and married a fellow employee. It was at this point that her involvement in share schemes apparently began. Mae Chamoi started by organizing small schemes among friends, usually groups of ten, taking three or four of the shares herself. Her share plans proved successful and popular because she always ensured that payments were made on schedule; soon she was the organizer of a large number of schemes. Although she apparently enjoyed organizing them and profited from them, she eventually reached the point where arranging all the bidding and the interest proved too much. At that point the idea occurred to her to pay a standard interest rate each month to everyone. The oil shares scheme, which would eventually grow to include some seventeen thousand people and a pool of some eight billion baht (U.S.$400 million), apparently originated from this innovation, and from an opportunity for profit that came her way as an employee of the PTT. The PTT controlled the import of petroleum into Thailand and thus controlled prices. The military, however, had its own quota, allowing it to purchase a certain amount each month to meet its own needs. Mae Chamoi reportedly bought up the excess from the military quota and sold it directly to service stations at a profit (*Nation,* 29 August 1984, 1; *Phujatkan rai duan,* August 1985, 35). Mae Chamoi had two relatives in the Air Force, one at a senior rank, and she exploited these ties.

Although Mae Chamoi's connections were essential to the expansion of her share scheme, her character played an equally important part. A coworker at the PTT said that Mae Chamoi was transferred to the accounting department, a more suitable position, because she was "hard." She was honest and reliable, and always paid on time. Apparently she was in a car accident one month yet still insisted on going to make the payments herself. She was also loyal to friends. Her coworker recounted that, even after Mae Chamoi went to prison, "when aristocratic women go to meet her, she refuses, she only agrees to meet with us, those who worked together at PTT. She loves friends very much" (*Phujatkan rai duan,* August 1985,

35). In other words, Mae Chamoi had the characteristics of *jai nakleng,* the heart of a *nakleng.* These characteristics meant that people trusted her, that she could associate easily with her coworkers, with shop owners, with bureaucrats, and even with soldiers. Yet she dressed and acted as an upper-middle-class woman and mother should.[20] Along with her entrepreneurial ability, her *jai nakleng* character and her image as an upper-middle-class woman allowed her to develop tremendous influence in Thai society.

Mae Chamoi also used her position at PTT to legitimize her share scheme. Shares were called "Oil Trucks" and sold for 160,800 baht per share (U.S.$8,000). The scheme soon expanded beyond the PTT to the Air Force, initially through her relatives, and as it became clear that the interest was always paid on time, extended up the ranks until generals and their wives had invested. From there it grew rapidly, as Mae Chamoi used their names to promote the scheme, and they did some recruiting of their own. As there were limits to the amount that could be made from the petroleum quota of the military, Mae Chamoi apparently began making short-term loans at high rates of interest to supplement the income from the burgeoning investments. However, again there were limits, and opportunities for such loans were irregular, so she was forced to use new investments to pay off the old. At that point, if not sooner, the share scheme became a pyramid scheme. Mae Chamoi could not let her old shareholders down; so she continued to promote the fund and to expand it. Eventually she developed a network of agents who sold shares at smaller amounts in the provinces, including Chiang Mai, Chonburi, Chanthaburi, Nakhon Sawan, Korat, and Lampang (*Nation,* 2 September 1984, 1).

Mae Chamoi's enterprise came under public scrutiny for the first time in November 1983. Rumors spread that she was investing the fund in oil, or smuggling, or narcotics, or weapons; she denied the rumors and refused to reveal her business investments, other than to say that it was going into short-term loans (*Nation,* 22 November 1983, 3; 30 November 1983, 1; 29 August 1984, 1; 12 September 1984, 1). The governor of the PTT insisted that she had no special knowledge of or influence over oil, as she was only a low-level official who shuffled papers, and opined that the only way she could be making enough money to pay the interest was through some illegal business (*Nation,* 22 November 1983, 3). Prominent aristocrat, opposition politician, and former prime minister Khukrit Pramot came to her defense, asserting that her business depended on trust and that trust was being eroded.[21] Mae Chamoi was placed on sick leave, but refused to quit until she could prove her innocence. The share scheme again disappeared from the pages of the newspapers. Eventually she did retire from the PTT to devote full time to running her Oil Share Fund. By September 1984, the government became convinced that Mae Chamoi was running a pyramid scheme, and that it was large enough to damage the Thai economy. This information was duly made known to the press; however, there was then no law against pyramid schemes.

Many entrepreneurs pulled out of the fund at that time, but civil servants and soldiers were convinced to continue by an informal public relations campaign. The campaign included rumors that the military had insisted on a large deposit at the Thai Military Bank to cover investments made by officers (officially denied by the bank); assurances from Mae Chamoi that the scheme was not illegal, that all interest would be paid, and that principal would be returned on request; and, finally, interviews on army television channels 5 and 7 by then Supreme Commander Athit Kamlang-ek in defense of Mae Chamoi. With no law in place, and this support for Mae Chamoi from the military, the government could do little more than issue warnings.[22]

Although the government was initially frustrated in its attempts to break up the share scheme of Mae Chamoi, it did manage to erode trust in it and slow its expansion. It also used the incident to support its efforts to put in place a law against pyramid share schemes. After an acrimonious debate in parliament, the government passed the law in November of that same year. With the law in place and growth of the fund slackening, Mae Chamoi was forced to try to bring the scheme to an end. She went into hiding in early 1985 for a three-month period, claiming that she needed to get finances in order to pay back investors. In June, she emerged at an air force base in Bangkok, where she was eventually taken into custody. The supreme commander himself signed the order, after she admitted that she would be able to pay back only about 3 percent of the investment. A search of her assets and properties ensued, with cash, gold, and documents turned up in safe deposit boxes, buried in her yard, and in the possession of her accomplices. The trial that followed took three years, mainly due to the number of participants who were called as witnesses. At the end of the trial Mae Chamoi was found guilty on two charges, with more than sixteen thousand counts of each, and sentenced to a total of 154,005 years in jail, limited to the maximum term of 20 years for the offenses in question. She was also ordered to return the money, along with 15 percent interest.[23]

A number of observations can be made about the case of Mae Chamoi. First, through her entrepreneurial ability, her skills, and her willingness to engage in this type of activity, Mae Chamoi was able to move from a position as a low-level bureaucrat at a state enterprise to high society, where she associated with some of the most powerful people in Thailand, and enjoyed tremendous wealth. Second, we find that even in this form of gambling, which is far more reputable than illegal gambling dens, for example, Mae Chamoi had to exhibit those character traits which are associated with *nakleng*: honesty, loyalty, toughness. Yet, because of being in the public eye and expected to act the part of a woman of high society, she had to walk a fine line between somehow appearing to be both a (manly!) *nakleng* and a "lady," depending on the situation. Her success came, in part, because she was able to portray herself as both. This was not only necessary but useful, as it allowed her to promote her business both with those who respect *jai nakleng* and those more likely to trust a woman entrepreneur.

Finally, it is worth noting that Chamoi was never designated *"nang"* (Mrs.), and though she was occasionally called simply Chamoi, usually she was called "Mae" Chamoi, or "Mother" Chamoi. She was described as a *mae kha,* a "mother trader," as an actor, and, until the end, as benevolent. She was never portrayed as beautiful or passive. However, when it became clear that she was running a pyramid scheme, the image of her as benevolent became increasingly dissonant. For the government, and for those investors who pulled out, she was transformed into a schemer, a crooked entrepreneur; she became, in effect, Chamoi Thipso rather than Mae Chamoi. The depiction of her personality changed, became less familiar, less personal, less like a mother. Even more interesting are the images invoked among those who continued to believe in her. She changed from subject to object, from benefactor to victim, first going into hiding with, went the rumors, military protection; then later, when she emerged from hiding, she claimed that the money had been stolen. According to one account, it was stolen by one of her agents, implying that she was faithful to her clients and friends but was betrayed by someone she had trusted. According to another account, it was taken by a *phuyai,* a large (in status) person, making Chamoi a victim in the same way as her clients and friends. In both these portrayals, Mae Chamoi remains *"mae,"* familiar and good, but in order to do so, she must become weak, discard her *nakleng* image, and become an object, a victim. In this way, the dissonances involved in *"mae,"* a virtuous subject acting as a criminal, worldly, and evil, could be eased.

The Godmother of Ban Phe

Whereas Oi. B. M. and Mae Chamoi operated in Bangkok in fairly traditional roles and in the spotlight, other women called *jaomae* have been able to follow paths to social mobility usually confined to men. With its ambiguous connotations, being labeled a *jaomae* can be politically damaging to such women. Kim Haw, often called the *Jaomae* of Ban Phe, has found herself in just such straits. She[24] was born in 1941 in Ban Phe, a seaside province on the eastern seaboard. Her father emigrated from China, married a Ban Phe resident, and she was the eldest of sixteen children. Her father had been very poor in China, and although he came to Thailand with nothing, he always told her that things were better in Ban Phe than they had been in China. He worked until he could afford a sewing machine, then made his living by sewing. He continued to save, and eventually managed to buy some small items to resell. As the oldest child, Kim Haw was forced to leave school after the fourth grade and work to support her family. She worked at a variety of jobs as she grew older: climbing trees to pick fruit, washing clothes, carrying water, and selling fried bananas. Her father taught her to be thrifty, and so she managed to save some money from these activities, which eventually enabled her to start buying and selling. She began to sell various types of food, carrying it on her shoulders to festivals, outdoor movies, and similar events. Then, still in her teens, she noticed that those who sold fish seemed to be better off, and she began to study the various types of fish, their uses, their prices, and the methods of fishing. Kim Haw eventually managed to save enough money to begin selling fish. She would buy baskets of fresh fish, clean it, and market it in smaller lots. She also dried some of the fish for sale to local farmers. Since farmers often lacked cash, she began to take raw rice in trade, carrying the rice to the mill for processing, then reselling it at a profit. In this gradual fashion, Kim Haw continued to build up her resources and her income. As her business expanded, her father became the buyer at the dock and arranged to rent a truck to carry the fish to the market at the provincial capital. Kim Haw would get up at 2:00 A.M. to walk more than twenty kilometers to the market so that she could make preparations to sell the fish.

Kim Haw decided that the way to expand her small business and increase her income was to catch the fish herself. She saved enough to buy a net and began to accumulate the equipment needed to enter the highly male-dominated fishing trade. The most difficult purchase was the boat itself. Kim Haw saved for some time and had to take out a loan before she could manage to buy the timber for a boat. As before, she learned everything she could about fishing as she saved and prepared for the new occupation, and even helped build the boat herself.[25] Once the boat was built, Kim Haw began fishing. She would row the boat out, often with other boats in a convoy, and in this way formed friendships. She also continued to put aside her profits, eventually saving up enough to buy a motor. This allowed her to fish deeper waters and catch more and bigger fish. She also towed the other boats in her convoy in return for a share of their catch. In this way, she expanded her business beyond her own family. She became an employer, a woman who was a boss in a world of fishing dominated by men.

Kim Haw, like Mae Chamoi, has been described in ways similar to the *nakleng*. In my interviews with her and her executive secretary, both explained that she is able to supervise the sometimes rough men of the fishing industry because she is *"detkhat,"* or bold, firm, and decisive. She said that even when her family was poor, her father taught her to "make merit" by helping others, and that she is generous with her wealth now, donating especially to hospitals and monasteries and assisting friends, family, and employees. She says that she helps those in financial difficulties by making loans without written contracts. Kim Haw also said that her father taught her that it is better to be cheated than to cheat someone else, and so she is honest and straightforward in her dealings with others. She is intensely loyal to her friends and says she treats her employees like family, telling them that they must act like family. Although she owns the largest home in Ban Phe, she does not bother to lock her house when she leaves because, said her executive secretary, no one would dare to steal from her. These, again, are the qualities of *jai nakleng*, the heart of a *nakleng*.

Kim Haw's real breakthrough in business came about when she began to build fish traps to concentrate the fish and increase the catch. She ultimately built five and began to increase her fleet of fishing boats and the number of her employees. She then built her own pier and started to buy fish from others. From that point on, her business expanded exponentially, and she now has an animal feed factory, various shops, a restaurant, a hotel, real estate, and other businesses in Ban Phe. Her fleet, which now numbers over a hundred ships, ranges from Phasae to Song-khla.[26] She also owns land as far away as Chiang Mai in the north. The original pier has fallen into disuse now, and has been replaced by another new pier and fish market. Kim Haw has also built another pier that is used primarily for tourist excursions.

Kim Haw's economic activities eventually led her into politics. As the daughter of an immigrant, under Thai law she had to complete primary school and some secondary school before she could run for office herself, and that slowed down her own entry into politics. Instead she supported other candidates for office, most notably two of her brothers. One brother became an M.P. for the district that includes Ban Phe. Kim Haw says she has supported his campaigns, and that she has insisted that he not take on any other career while in parliament but instead devote full time to serving his constituents. Her executive secretary claimed that, in fact, Kim Haw is the M.P. in all but name, as many voters elect her brother because of their respect for her.[27] Kim Haw also has another brother who is a member of the provincial council, and a third younger brother who is planning to run for the city council. Kim Haw completed enough schooling in recent years to qualify for local office and has become *kamnan* or commune head—she is also a village leader. If her brother wins election to the city council, she would have a voice and an ear at every level of government, from local to national. As *kamnan,* Kim Haw is responsible for some of the police work in her *tambon* and is authorized to carry a gun and make arrests, holding suspects until the police can arrive. I asked her if this responsibility entailed any difficulty for her as a woman, and she said that she has friends assist her in this duty. She relies on the village scouts, a sort of paramilitary group that she heads, and on friends who are police officers. She has enough influence locally that the provincial governor has called on her several times to speak to protestors, to convince them to disperse. Finally, as her executive secretary put it, even *nakleng* and M.P.s respect and fear her.

The ability to give orders to rough men, her *jai nakleng* character, and her economic and political influence won for Kim Haw the designation of *jaomae*. In addition, she still talks and acts not like an upper-middle-class "lady," but like others of her class background. Her speech is rough, and her dress is plain and sturdy rather than elegant. In a sense, she has "neutralized" her gender; in other ways, she has appropriated traditionally male characteristics. She acts like just another tough and important player in the fishing industry, where all the people with whom she associates happen to be male. She is, then, highly vulnerable to the more negative aspects of the word *jaomae,* those connotations usually associated with the men who play similar roles in other seaside towns. Her political opponents have played on the negative connotations of *jaomae,* and have spread rumors that she has used her fishing fleet for smuggling various goods, including marijuana. Interestingly, Kim Haw's publicly portrayed reaction to the accusations was to portray herself as a victim, a weeping female.[28] Because she often acts in masculine ways, she has become vulnerable to accusations of being evil in the same way as men. Where men could perhaps have shrugged off the accusations or retaliated with similar accusations, Kim Haw reacted, at least through the press, by reasserting her gender, and the connotations of virtue (and weakness) associated with it. Few in Thailand would associate a weeping woman with evil.

That the partial "neutralization" of her gender image, along with the appropriation of some typically male characteristics, has allowed Kim Haw to work in the male-dominated fisheries industry is evident in two more ways. First, although she is roughly the same age as Mae Chamoi, she is never called "Mae." She is addressed by her friends and refers to herself as "Pa" (or "Auntie"). This term, while still gender-specific, does not carry the same connotations as mother, in that it is not dependent on some other person: a mother is only "Mae" because she has a son. Any older woman can be called "Pa," regardless of her actual status. Second, Kim Haw is actually a mother, with two children. Yet when she tells her story, her family, and especially her husband, are surprisingly absent. Her daughter studied at Thammasat in accounting, drawing her out of Kim Haw's sphere, and while she has reentered it as her mother's accountant, she is from another world—Bangkok, and Thailand's most elite university. Kim Haw spoke only briefly of her son and told me that he is not (yet) quite dependable. Her husband does not work and spends most of his time around the house. Kim Haw never mentioned him to me in the long interview, and, although I spent much of the day with her executive secretary, he only spoke of Kim Haw's husband when I specifically asked, and then only briefly. He is not mentioned in the news articles that were given to me, nor in the profile of Kim Haw as "Outstanding Entrepreneur." In these ways too, Kim Haw not only deemphasizes her gender but avoids the thorny problem of bossing men at work without seeming to break social mores at home. It also places the emphasis on her role as leader of a *phakphuak* rather than as wife and mother.

The Radio Station Godmother

Kim Haw provided a fascinating example of social mobility in a male-dominated industry as well as a *jaomae* who had to fight against the connotations of crime and evil often associated with that term. Another image of a *jaomae* emerged from the circumstances of the killing of Saengchai Sunthonwat in 1996. In the latter case, too, we see both social mobility and political activity. Yet whereas the image we have of Kim Haw is ambiguous, that of the alleged mastermind behind the Saengchai hit, Ubon Bunyachalothon, is not. She has been depicted as a typical *jaopho* who just happens to be a woman—a view, it will become evident, that has important implications for the stereotypical concepts of women in Thai society.

Ubon Bunyachalothon is also known as *jaomae Ubon, jaomae withayu* (Radio Godmother), and *jaomae Yasothon* (Yasothon Province Godmother). She was born in the Samsuk district of Suphanburi province, located about three hours north of Bangkok, in 1939. Ubon was the second of nine children; her Chinese name was Je Hui. Her father, who had immigrated to Thailand from China with his parents when he was just three years old, had a small trucking business in Samsuk, transporting rice from the fields and charcoal from the jungle.[29] Ubon also worked to help support the family, carrying water in her village, which did not yet have indoor plumbing. The family business was not very profitable. In 1952, when Ubon was thirteen, her father came to the decision that the business could not be saved; he packed up his family and moved to Bangkok, fleeing his debts and abandoning his home.[30] Ubon's father, who remains unnamed in both her press interview and in other biographical accounts, settled his family in Phrakhanong slum, behind the market, and began to repair watches for a jewelery store. Ubon also worked, although other than that she carried water and worked in a clothing factory, which may have come later, no details of this period in her life are available. Ubon only tells of riding on a bus, looking out at the cars, and thinking to herself that someday she would have a car and a house and wealth (*Thansetthakit*, 22 May 1996, 16). It is as if she had tried to escape her past, seldom talking about it even with close friends.

When Ubon was nineteen, she married a man eleven years her senior who poured cement for a living, and a year later she had her first child. (She later had two more children—in all, two daughters and one son.) At that time, she claimed, she sold all her gold and a silver belt for 8,000 baht (U.S.$400 at the time) and became a moneylender.[31] In order to ensure repayment, she had her debtors sign over a check. If payments were not made, she could then call in the police and have her debtors arrested. Ubon admits that she had "many" people jailed during the period she was a moneylender. After three years, she claims, she could not bear to see them imprisoned and began to let debts go. Shortly thereafter, her money was gone (*Phujatkan rai sapda*, 26 August 1996, 33). The interest on her money-lending activities amounted to 1,600 baht a month, which was not enough for her family. So she also bought shrimp in the market at Paknam and walked through the neighborhood selling it. In the evenings, she sewed for a clothing shop.

According to Ubon, the turning point in her life came when she decided to take on construction contracts, relying on her husband's ability. She obtained a loan of 80,000 baht, she claims, from a local moneylender,[32] secured a ten-year lease on a piece of property, and put up some shop houses. The rent on these shop houses produced a profit of 30,000 baht. Ubon claims that she spent the entire profit to "make merit," donating it to various charities to compensate for her earlier "sins," such as having had many people put in jail (*Phujatkan rai sapda*, 26 August 1996, 33).

From this beginning, Ubon entered two of the most lucrative businesses of Thailand's economic boom, construction and property development, both of which have also drawn people into politics in order to secure government contracts and permits. She admitted that she had to bribe civil servants regularly and became quite proficient at it. Nevertheless, she said, such payments are also difficult due to rivalries, jealousies, and the vagaries of amounts and methods (*Phujatkan rai sapda*, 26 August 1996, 34). Through engaging in these activities, she also learned how to develop connections to politicians, including strongman Praphat Charusathian, the minister of the interior at the time of her first major government contract. It was these activities, and the emergence of democracy after the 1973 popular uprising, that drew Ubon into politics.

But before discussing her entry into politics, it is worth mentioning two other changes in Ubon's life during this period. In 1973, she got a divorce, giving her husband 10 million baht in the settlement (then U.S.$400,000). She claims that this was good for her business as he had never been any help. Furthermore: "It was good to be divorced. It made business easier, because—a woman all alone in the construction business—everyone sympathized" (*Phujatkan rai sapda*, 26 August 1996, 34). The second major change in her life came when she went to a monastery in Lamphun to become a "disciple" of a well-known monk. Afterward, Ubon spent one month out of every year at the monastery, and the monk became a sort of counselor to her. In her version of events, when she began to consider political involvement, he advised against it. She did not listen to his advice, and suffered the consequences (*Phujatkan rai sapda*, 26 August 1996, 34).

Although most sources locate Ubon's earliest political activity in the late 1980s, according to her own account she first became involved in politics in the 1970s, when she joined the Phalang Mai party and began to provide electoral and financial support.[33] She also ran as a candidate for the party in Suphanburi and returned with her father to her home village, where the old debts were finally repaid. Ubon lost the election, but apparently continued to support the party financially. Her next foray into politics came in 1984, in Yasothon province. She began by supporting candidates for the municipal council. According to her own account, this took place after the mayor—the head of the council—thwarted her in a property deal for a hotel she had decided to build. He also offended her when she threatened to support his opposition, saying that having her as an opponent would be like having no competition at all. She poured her resources into the election and won fourteen of the eighteen seats on the municipal council (*Phujatkan rai sapda,* 26 August 1996, 34). Ubon thus became a provincial politician, securing the political base that would lead to the designation *jaomae Yasothon.* She also expanded her economic interests in the province, completing the hotel—Yasothon's only first-class one—and won the concession for the provincial radio station from the Mass Communications Organization of Thailand (MCOT). It was her use of the radio station in election campaigns that would lead to her clash with Saengchai.

In the 1986 national election, General Chawalit Yongchaiyut, an old acquaintance of Ubon, asked her to support the leader of the promilitary Puang Chon Chao Thai party in Yasothon; she agreed. The candidate, General Rawi Wanphen, failed to win a seat.[34] By 1988, Ubon was ready to run again for election herself. She joined the Ruam Thai party of Narong Wongwan[35] and began campaigning for a seat in Yasothon. In this first attempt, she came in fourth in the three-member electorate, receiving 36,140 votes, some 10,000 less than necessary to win election (Krasuang mahatthai n.d. [1988]:191). Press reports of one particular campaign incident reveal something of her tactics, which resemble those of *jaopho* in other parts of Thailand. One of Ubon's most important *hua khanaen* (campaigners) apparently kept the money he was given to buy votes for himself. "In the end, the *hua khanaen* did not have a chance to spend a single baht of the money." This story, according to the press, is known to everyone in Yasothon.[36]

The succeeding election, in 1992, took place after the military had seized power in a coup in 1991 and written a new constitution to secure it. Ubon again ran for parliament, following Narong Wongwan into the promilitary Sammakkhitham party. This time she succeeded in winning election, placing third. Unfortunately for her, the term of this parliament lasted just a few months. A popular uprising in May overthrew the military prime minister and forced constitutional amendments and new elections. In the midst of the uprising, however, Ubon managed to attain national prominence. At one point, a prodemocracy activist decided he would fast until the constitution was changed or until death. After several days of his fast, Ubon sent him a coffin. Although she would later claim that she sent it to bring him to his senses, this ensured her reputation as a hard woman. Of her support for General Suchinda, she said, "The government of Thailand must be firm and strong."[37] In the second election, after the removal of Suchinda, Ubon lost her seat. She then decided to strengthen her provincial base, and in the 1995 provincial elections both her daughters won seats. Ubon had enough supporters in the provincial council to have one of them elected president of the council.

By the 1990s, Ubon's business interests had expanded both in Bangkok and in the provinces. In addition to her construction and property-development companies, she held the concessions for radio stations in five provinces, owned a shopping center on the outskirts of Bangkok, and a supermarket. Her most lucrative business was property development, which she pursued both in Bangkok and in the provinces. One report (*Thairat*, 18 May 1996, 1, 17) describes the unscrupulous side of this business for the northern province of Chiang Rai, reputedly a place where the influence of *jaopho* is quite strong. There Ubon cooperated closely with Thawi Phutchan, her former son-in-law and once an M.P. from Chiang Rai. Thawi was also a lawyer for one of Ubon's companies.[38] According to the report, Ubon and Thawi would buy up properties at a low price, sometimes resorting to extortion. Oftentimes the land was in forest reserves, with limits on ownership and usage, so they enlisted the assistance of an official in the forestry department who could clear title. Once the title was clear, the land could be sold at a large profit, or further developed and then sold. Ubon and Thawi reportedly used this method (quite typical of the techniques of *jaopho*) to reap substantial profits; with these profits, they financed their costly election campaigns.

The decision to have Saengchai killed reportedly stemmed both from a conflict of interest and a perceived slight. Problems with the radio concessions had begun even before Saengchai took over the MCOT, when Ubon was accused of using the radio station in Ubonratchathani province to support her campaign. After an investigation, MCOT decided to withdraw the concession. Ubon took the matter to court, initiating a series of lawsuits between her and MCOT. When Saengchai took over, Ubon gradually lost her other concessions—partly because Saengchai believed she was falsifying accounts, partly because he had decided that MCOT should manage the provincial stations. By the time Saengchai was murdered, Ubon had only a single concession, in Kanchanaburi, and only a year left on that one. Ubon and Thawi both claimed that the radio stations brought in only small profits, that some of them were running at a loss, and that they had no plans to renew the concessions. In any case, they claimed, concessions were only a small part of her business empire, estimated by Thawi at five billion baht (U.S.$200 million; *Thansetthakit*, 22 May 1996, 16). The financial loss from the withdrawal of these concessions has been estimated by others at 45 million baht (U.S.$1.8 million), which Ubon denied, challenging those who had made the statement to swear to its truthfulness before the sacred Buddha image at Wat Phra Kaeo.[39] Saengchai, we recall, had added insult to financial injury when Ubon had given him the Buddhist amulet and expensive gold chain,[40] and he had publicly declared it fit only for his dog. Ubon claimed that she was not angry but shocked and *noijai* (slighted) because he had not respected her (*Matichon*, 17 May 1996, 2).

According to police investigators, Ubon and Thawi began to plot to have Saengchai killed as early as 1994 and tried to hire gunmen on four occasions. Police traced the gunmen, who confessed and identified Thawi as the one who had hired them. Police also claimed to have a record of a bank transaction that linked Ubon to the killing. However, when the case went to the prosecutors, they decided that there was insufficient evidence against her, and after forty-five days in jail she was released. Thawi and the four gunmen were all convicted.

Like Kim Haw and Mae Chamoi, Ubon had many of the characteristics of *jai nakleng*. She was generous, firm, resolute, and concerned with honor. Like them, she was also very upwardly mobile—once having had to flee debtors with her family as a child, later owning a billion-baht business empire. Like Mae Chamoi, Ubon left her class background behind; she studied part-time and earned a degree in accounting from Ramkhamhaeng University, and often acted like an upper-middle-class matron for the public. Her image in the press, at least after the killing of Saengchai, was quite different. Throughout the investigation, even before she was named, she was designated a *jaomae* by the police and the press. In all the press reports, the word *"jaopho"* could have been substituted for *jaomae* with no change in connotation or meaning. I found only one highly revealing passage that treats her gender, in *Thairat*, which has the largest circulation of any Thai newspaper, partly because of its heavy focus on crime.

> This *jaomae*, although she is a woman, lives her life like a broad-chested man, a real he-man. Her work is always carefully planned, whether it is [for example] establishing a provincial newspaper in order to smooth her path to politics— unlike ordinary women—and along with it, entering into a role with MCOT by renting time on MCOT radio stations, with many stations all over the country. From that point, she used the MCOT radio stations to build herself a foundation, and as a means of making money. . . . (*Thairat*, 12 May 1996, 17)

During this time, Ubon was painted as irremediably evil by the press. She had not yet had the opportunity to defend herself. She was acting as a *jaopho*, and, as a wholly evil *jaopho*, she must therefore have been not an ordinary woman but a man in disguise, a broad-chested he-man in a woman's body. Otherwise how could the contradiction be resolved? A woman acting, but not as a virtuous mother. So *Thairat* put it, and so the rest of the newspapers covered it, using the word *jaomae* exactly as if they meant *jaopho*. Equally interesting, only with Ubon does a male partner appear in the depiction. One widely reported rumor (which she denied) had her seducing her former son-in-law, Thawi, who was convicted of arranging the killing. So, the associations of goodness connected with the mother image were dually subverted as she became the temptress who seduced her own daughter's husband.

After her arrest, Ubon made several attempts to defend herself through interviews with the press. Her defense is a fascinating confirmation of her own acceptance of this image. Although she occasionally refered to herself as *mae*, according to reporters, in every case where she was quoted, she used the word *"pa,"* auntie.[41] She did not cry, but called for justice, threatening to sue police for damage to her reputation.[42] She also lumped *jaopho* and *jaomae* together, declaring, "I am not a *jaomae jaopho* anywhere" (*Thairat*, 14 May 1996, 23). She spoke openly about events, providing a defense but not blaming anyone and not evading difficult issues, like the gift to Saengchai. Of her rumored intimate relationship with her son-in-law, she accused the press of being insensitive for hurting her daughter. No mention of herself. Perhaps most interesting of all, however, is the reason Ubon gave that she could not have been guilty: "I did not do anything wrong . . . I am a religious woman, and I have been observing the precepts since 1973" (*Bangkok Post*, 25 June 1996, Internet edition), claiming that the reason police had been unable to find her was because she had been in seclusion at a monastery. Like many men, but few women, she entered the monastery periodically to make merit, in her case for one month each year. She also wore amulets, which are primarily seen as male-oriented receptacles of power—until recently, exclusively so. And when asked what she would do if she were forced to spend time in jail, she responded that she would meditate (*Thairat*, 14 May 1996, 23). In other words, Ubon also claimed to be virtuous, but she did so by appealing to the mainstream masculine side of Buddhism. When asked about the possible guilt of her son-in-law, she defended him in the same way, saying: "When he was elected in 1992, villagers asked him to kill a cow by way of celebration. He said no, it would be a sin. I don't think he'd do anything like that [have Saengchai killed]" (*Bangkok Post*, 17 May 1996, Internet edition). The argument for the *jaopho* Thawi is the same as for the *jaomae* Ubon: he is a good Buddhist; he could not have done it.

Conclusions

Although I have been able to deal with only a few godmothers here, some tentative conclusions can be drawn concerning both godmothers and gender images in Thailand. First, godmothers have become more visible. The arrests of Mae Chamoi and Ubon raised the profile of *jaomae*, landing them on the front pages of the press for extended periods. Obviously, it is impossible to determine the actual numbers of either *jaomae* or *jaopho*, yet there seem to be more *jaomae* than in the past. Although police sources would not admit that there were more of any type of criminal, they did estimate that perhaps 5 percent of such characters were women. They also estimated that perhaps 90 percent of those in gambling and 50 percent of those controlling prostitution are women. They said that some are involved in the narcotics trade, especially along the border.[43] Those I consulted in the academic community and the press who follow *jaopho* and crime agree that there are more *jaomae* than before, especially in gambling, where, they say, many front for powerful male figures behind the scenes.[44] More concretely, prison records show that the number of women prisoners rose from 1,074 in 1970 to 3,524 in 1990 to 5,624 in 1994. Over this time period, the ratio of male to female convicted prisoners dropped from 37:1 in 1970 to 15:1 in 1990 to 11:1 in 1994 (Wilson 1983:292; *Statistical Booklet on Thai Women* 1995:78). Taken together, this admittedly sketchy evidence provides some support for the contention that there are more *jaomae* today than in the past.

As with *jaopho,* there is a wide range of types of *jaomae.* In fact, the range is even wider for *jaomae,* as not just powerful individuals but also positive role models are sometimes called *jaomae.* Otherwise, *jaomae,* like *jaopho,* may come from old established families or poor struggling families; may engage primarily in entrepreneurial activities, perhaps gaining advantages through corruption; or may engage in violent crime such as murder and extortion in pursuit of wealth. Like *jaopho, jaomae* may enter politics to seek protection, to gain access to inside information on contracts and concessions, and to gain influence over government officials. They also build up political machines in the provinces and strive to take over municipal and provincial politics to support their efforts at the national level. They work through the same types of electoral organizations. To prosper in this male-dominated world, they must take on at least some of the characteristics of *nakleng,* like the men around them.

There is, however, an important qualification to be made. *Jaomae* do not come from the *nakleng* tradition. They come instead from the entrepreneurial tradition, as do many *jaopho,* a tradition that is based, not on strength and fighting ability, but on organizational skills, on the ability to make money, and on the kind of charisma necessary to hold together a successful organization of usually rough, mostly male characters. Michael Montesano has labeled this tradition "market society," arguing that it originated in post–World War II Sino-Thai culture. This "market society," he argues, "afforded both great opportunity for social mobility to the commercially ambitious and access to extensive commercial and social networks through which such successful merchants could move" (Montesano 2000: 99).[45] "Fluid, competitive, wide open to those who refused to see obstacles to their ambition, that society . . . conditioned them to attend carefully to their status in the *talat* [market] and among people of their own kind but not at all to the standards of the wider society" (Montesano 2000:115). It is this tradition that accounts for the *jaomae.* Ambitious and talented entrepreneurs, they need to conform to the standards of those around them—whether *nakleng,* tough young fishermen, or society women—but not necessarily to the standards of the law, the press, or the wider society. This helps to explain the ability of Mae Chamoi to portray herself as *nakleng* in one set of relationships and as high-society "lady" and investment genius in another, without subscribing to the norms of either. *Jaopho,* of course, also portray themselves in various ways, but the range seems to be narrower and more firmly based on characteristics of the *nakleng.*

Despite this wide range of meanings, the *jaomae* studied here have a number of common characteristics. Most noteworthy is the tremendous social mobility each achieved. With the exception of Mae Chamoi, described as "average," all came from very underprivileged backgrounds and all became wealthy and prominent. It seems unlikely that a woman from a privileged background would want or need to follow this path to success, though it may be that in some cases daughters of *jaomae* or *jaopho* will continue in their parents' footsteps. Second, all these women are Sino-Thai but were not themselves immigrants. Rather, they are the children of immigrants who failed to become wealthy. Perhaps this endowed them with a willingness to work harder and take greater risks to win the fame and fortune that had eluded their families. Third, it is worth noting that all these women were middle-aged when they achieved their fame and fortune. While this may be because such a career path takes time, it may also be because younger women must overcome the "sexual object" stereotype. This seems most obvious in the case of Oi. B. M. Finally, it is clear that all these women see themselves as highly moral, within the moral code of the *nakleng:* all see themselves as honest, generous, daring, and loyal to their *phakphuak.*

The rise of *jaomae* has affected gender in Thailand especially at the intersection between stereotypes. On the one hand, we find that when the stereotypes of femaleness mix with the stereotypes of *jaopho,* the result seems to be a softening and expansion of the meanings of *jaopho,* so that even those seen to be powerful and good can be described as *jaomae.* The most prominent Buddhist bodhisattva, Kuan Yin, is described as a *jaomae,* but the Buddha would never be described in such terms. *Jaomae* of the less savory type can and do take advantage of the intersection of the two stereotypes, describing themselves as victims or publicly shedding tears. The combining of stereotypes has had an impact on Thai society in other ways. Because women are seen as soft, it has been difficult for the Thai military or police department to conceive of women generals, and only in 1996 did it become possible. Still, women are confined to noncombative roles. Women politicians worry that they may be seen as too weak to make difficult decisions, and therefore as not good candidates for prime minister, a worry that was borne out in a Thai Farmers Bank Research Division survey. The survey found that 40 percent thought that a woman could not be a good prime minister, and this was in Bangkok, not the provinces. Furthermore, of those who thought a woman could be prime minister, twice as many were women as men. According to the survey, "Their ideal female M.P. would be witty, sharp, sincere and *dare to make big decisions,*" and, in another indication of the prevailing stereotypes, "The respondents said they wanted female MPs to focus on at least five areas—social issues, women's and children's rights, education and the traffic problem" (*Bangkok Post,* 26 October 1996, Internet edition; italics added). Conspicuously absent from the responsibilities they selected for women M.P.s are crime, defense, and the economy.

Perhaps even more interesting is the reverse image, the evil *jaomae* and the implications it has for changing stereotypes of women. When a *jaomae* is portrayed as evil, as has been the case with Ubon, her gender is ignored, almost erased. This indicates just how much dissonance can be created between the good, if weak, stereotype generally associated with women and the evil of this type of *jaomae*. The second image of women, that of temptress, also emerges in connection with Ubon, in a particularly nasty rumor; yet it appears rather uneasily, as gossip of an order even lower than the mostly hearsay reported as news. Since the dissonance cannot be easily resolved, it is diminished as far as possible by largely removing gender from the depiction. This also hints at the strength of these stereotypes, and the difficulties in breaking them down. And yet, gender cannot be erased from the picture entirely, for *jaomae* are clearly women, as is evident every time the word appears. In the end, depicting them as males in female form breaks down gender images in more fundamental if more subtle ways. In this reading, some women are just like men, on the inside at least. They are as ruthless, as cunning, as violent; they can be treated as men. This is possible in part because there is a related image where women and men are fairly equal, that of entrepreneur, and a *jaomae* is, after all, a type of entrepreneur. But if a male-in-female-form can be a ruthless and vicious entrepreneur, of course a male-in-female-form can also be a general or a prime minister.[46] A male-in-female-form is indistinguishable from a woman except through her actions. Thus this depiction of the *jaomae* holds tremendous potential to subtly break down the stereotypes inherent in gender images in Thailand.[47]

Epilogue

On 27 February 1999, Ubon Bunyachalothon was assassinated in front of her home in Yasothon. Police believed the most likely motive was a conflict in provincial politics; other possibilities included a disagreement over Ubon's role in national politics, a debtor unwilling to pay her, or even a revenge killing for her alleged role in the murder of Saengchai (*Bangkok Post*, 1 March 1999, Internet edition). In the wake of the assassination, various rumors of scandals concerning Ubon made their way into the media. As with many a deceased *jaopho*, Ubon's love life became a favorite topic.[48] Such amatory rumors could not help but restore to Ubon her long-lost gender, even though the media continued to treat her as a typical *jaopho*. Thus the exposé of her love life revived the dissonances between mother and temptress, subject and object, good and evil. But then again, in death Ubon was no longer a good mother, no longer a godmother, no longer a good lover, but only a dead body: no longer a subject, but only an object of rumor, of scandal, and of pity.

■ ■ ■ ■ ■ ■ ■ ■ ■ ■

CHAPTER 6

Eviction and Changing Patterns of Leadership in Bangkok Slum Communities

In my opening chapters I pointed out that in Thailand, and much of Southeast Asia, village governments were generally participatory prior to the time the European powers brought powerful centralized bureaucracies to the region, and that, even after the centralization of administration allowed authoritarianism to infringe directly on village life, the legacy of participation remained. Yet, in the last two chapters we have seen how the *hua khanaen* system has subverted the ethic of participation, at least in national politics, developing in place of political party organizations as a distortion of patron–client ties, in order to connect national politics to the villages. In this chapter I shall return to the the ethic of participation.

I will examine how participation in national politics has sometimes developed despite the prevalence of the *hua khanaen*, the *jaopho*, and the political party system. I shall focus on urban poor communities, although the same processes are taking place in some rural areas, often with assistance from the Assembly of the Poor[1] and other nongovernmental organizations. In tracing the development from *nakleng* to new forms of leadership, however, here the focus will shift to the development and expansion of horizontal ties rather than vertical patron–client ties. Different tactics are also necessary, as participation is taking place in different ways. These are tactics available to those with few resources and no strong patron —in other words, the weapons of the weak. The horizontal ties and the utilization of these weapons of the weak necessitate different styles of leadership that are more suited to democratic politics. This can be seen in resistance to eviction by congested communities, as eviction often forces them to become involved in politics in clearly visible ways.

In his pathbreaking work on the peasantry, James Scott (1985; 1986; 1989) focused our attention on the types of resistance that can be found in the countryside on an everyday basis. Everyday resistance, he argued, consists of such low-risk pragmatic strategies for resisting the unjust demands of those in power as dissimulation, false compliance, foot dragging, and sabotage. These efforts, according to Scott, are unorganized, uncoordinated, essentially leaderless, yet class-based and pervasive. He uses the example of squatting to describe everyday resistance:

Thus in one sphere lies the quiet, piecemeal process by which peasant squatters or poachers have often encroached on plantation and state forest lands; in the other a public invasion of property that openly challenges property relations. Each action aims at a redistribution of control over property; the former aims at tacit, de facto gains while the latter aims at formal, de jure recognition of those gains. (Scott 1989:5–6)

Scott, then, considers squatting to be a good example of everyday resistance when it does not "openly challenge property relations."

Scott is not clear about the mechanism whereby everyday resistance may become less passive and lead to confrontation. When the evicted refuse to leave, they move out of the realm of everyday resistance and less passive forms of resistance come into play. Andrew Turton has identified "a middle-ground in-between everyday and exceptional forms of resistance . . . a terrain of struggle, on which practices may possibly serve to link the other two terms" (Turton 1986:36). This middle ground is entered when everyday resistance is no longer sufficient to protect the de facto gains made. Whereas everyday resistance to a particular policy is often general rather than specific, on the middle ground, the tactics of eviction must often be resisted quite directly, or the struggle is lost. This direct resistance requires organization, leadership, and careful consideration of tactics, especially if it is to remain close to the everyday sphere and minimize confrontation. The new tactics and types of leadership that emerge when resistance reaches the middle ground are the primary foci of this chapter.

While the specific techniques Scott outlines describe the countryside, the general phenomenon can be applied to urban communities as well. If there is an urban equivalent of the everyday forms of resistance he outlines, we should find it in slum communities. First, many slums, at least in Bangkok, are indeed communities, places where people interact frequently in a fairly developed social structure. Many of them have been in existence for decades, and some were actually semi-rural communities on the outskirts of Bangkok when originally settled. Second, residents of slum communities are frequently migrants from the countryside, or the children of migrants: one study shows that by the mid-1980s, 60 percent of residents in Bangkok's slums were born in the capital (Sopon 1992:30), while most (59 percent) of the heads of households were born in rural areas outside of Bangkok (Yap 1992:34).[2] Many of the attitudes and values of rural society may thus be present in slum communities, modified by the exigencies of life in the city. Third, everyday resistance is characterized as a form of class warfare (Scott 1989): it is in the slums that we would expect class warfare to be most salient.

Over a million people in Bangkok live in slums, officially and more accurately designated "congested communities." This amounts to about 14 percent of the population of the city (Kankheha 1997:27; Yap 1992:31).[3] There is tremendous variety in this official category of congested communities: while some communities are small, temporary, new, and built underneath bridges or overpasses, others are large, old, with homes built of permanent materials, and occupy blocks of valuable land.[4] Many of the houses in older slum communities are well-constructed if crowded homes, complete with electricity, running water, and consumer goods such as refrigerators and television sets. In these older communities, a few children have become educated and moved into middle-class occupations. Yet this decades-long occupancy of the land does not change the inhabitants' status as squatters, sometimes renters, who own the houses but not the land. It is these older communities, where the sense of community is stronger and patron–client ties and leadership have had time to develop, upon which I shall concentrate.

Of the million-odd people living in congested communities, somewhat less than half have rental agreements. Nearly a quarter are squatters, with no formal or informal agreement to occupy the land.[5] Simply by living on the land illegally, they are engaged in a form of everyday resistance. The same is the case for renters who stay on after their contract is terminated, or who simply refuse to pay rent. Tens of thousands of families in various congested communities are threatened with eviction, many of them in the near future. In the face of this threat, many slum dwellers will have to choose between accepting eviction or challenging property rights, particularly the right of formal ownership versus long-term occupation of the land. They must either press for recognition of their gains or surrender their de facto possession. It is this transition to more confrontational forms of resistance, and the leadership and organization it entails, that we shall see in the subsequent case studies.

Although urban weapons of the weak differ from those of their rural counterparts, in both cases there is considerable uniformity in tactics over widespread areas. An explanation for this uniformity can be found in the work of Charles Tilly. Tilly (1975, 1979, 1983) argued that any given society has a "repertoire of contention" that is familiar and standardized. He argued that the repertoire changes over time, but only very slowly.[6] In contrast, in Bangkok, the standard repertoire changed quite rapidly. This rapid change can be explained, as was Tilly's slow change, by reference to the political structure.

Herbert Kitschelt (1986) maintained that "political opportunity structures" (those aspects of the political environment that determine the range of actions possible, including resources, institutions, and precedents) largely determine both strategic decisions and the societal impact of protests. He identified two important dimensions of political opportunity structures: the openness of political input structures, that is, the possibility of influencing decision making; and the strength of political output structures, or the ability of the state to enforce its decisions. The strategy of a protest movement would depend on whether it could more effectively influence decision making, resist implementation, both, or neither. The Thai political input structures remain largely closed to the poor, at least at the crucial policy formation stage; however, the output structures changed markedly in the 1970s as Thailand moved from military authoritarianism to unstable parliamentary government. This has altered the tactics of resistance to eviction in congested communities in Bangkok.

Finally, the ethnicity, gender, age, level of education, occupation, and class of the protestors may affect their choice of tactics: a schoolteacher will likely choose different tactics than a gangster. This may be either because of differences in disposition or in the likelihood of success. Even among the weapons of the weak, a large repertoire is available, and many of those weapons are best employed by those perceived as weak: women, the old, and the very young.[7]

Looking at the middle ground also allows examination of the relationship between class-based everyday resistance and patron–client ties. In Bangkok slum communities, I also find that the erosion of patron–client ties is crucial to the development of everyday resistance. As those ties have become less efficacious, class-based horizontal ties have sometimes replaced them. New types of leadership have emerged to take advantage of this new style of resistance. Ultimately, however, the remnants of patron–client ties have caused this class-based resistance to be generally aimed not at the rich—the former patrons—but at the state. And this resistance to the state has important implications for the development of democracy.

Eviction and Authoritarian Patterns of Leadership: Trok Tai

Trok Tai community is located along Khlong (Canal) Krung Kasem, approximately halfway between the old Grand Palace and the new Chitlada Palace.[8] The community was first settled some 125 years ago by captured Vietnamese soldiers. By the late 1950s, it had become crowded, occupying a narrow strip of land with row houses along one side and the canal along the other. Until 1970, ownership of the land was disputed between the absentee landlords of the row houses—descendants of the original Vietnamese settlers who had no land-title deeds—the Crown Property Bureau, and an adjacent Buddhist temple. That year, the dispute was settled when the Crown Property Bureau and the temple agreed to divide the land, thus turning all the slum dwellers, including those in the row houses, into illegal squatters (Akin 1978:4–11).

Leadership in Trok Tai was based on patron–client ties and on the exemplification of the traits of the *nakleng*. Nate, the leader in the struggle against eviction that followed, was one of the most important patrons in the community and also a leading *nakleng*, living by their code and benefiting from the associated social status.[9] He was not, however, the richest member of the community; in fact, Akin (1978:21) has pointed out that the pursuit of riches and the qualities of a *nakleng* are incompatible, as the *nakleng* must place friends ahead of profit.[10] Nate was a tile layer by trade who taught his craft to others in the community and established a business that subcontracted tile work. Thus he was able to provide work for members of the community and become their patron. Nate also organized the share scheme in the community, a scheme that allowed participants to invest money in a fund each month, then bid for the right to use the entire fund that month until all investors had had a turn at the money (described in more detail in Chapter 5). As the organizer, Nate had the responsibility of making sure that payments were made to the fund. By providing this service, he became a patron to all participants in the scheme.

Nate also benefited from his relationship with the local authorities. Akin points out that the slum dwellers always sought an intermediary when they needed to go to government officials, someone with personal ties to those officials (Akin 1975:174, 222–223). Nate had personal ties with police and a member of the nobility who lived nearby for whom he had worked during his youth. In the elections of 1957, part of a brief attempt at parliamentary rule, Nate worked as a *hua khan-aen* for Trok Tai, thus developing contacts with politicians. He met the head of the local police station when one of his police friends came to him and asked him to watch for signs of communist activity among the local Vietnamese community. Nate used the resulting relationship to help villagers who got into trouble with the law, thus enlarging the number of his clients and enhancing his reputation as a *nakleng*.

The first conflict over eviction came in the early fifties when the city government decided to fine residents who had built too close to the canal, and to raze their homes. The residents went to Nate for help and he led them to the municipal offices to see the mayor, where he succeeded in having the fines lifted. Only houses built completely above the canal were demolished, and the city agreed to provide low-rent rooms to those affected. Nate was charged with allocating those rooms (Akin 1978:24–25). This outcome solidified his position of leadership and ensured he would be the leader against later eviction attempts.

In 1967, when the government decided to hold elections for a committee to represent the community, Nate was elected head, making his leadership official (Akin 1978:25).

The second attempt at eviction occurred at the end of 1968. Everyday resistance at Trok Tai as discussed in Akin's work consisted of several elements. First, and partly speculative, was the organization of a watch. Shortly before the fire of 1968, there was widespread gossip about incidents of eviction by arson in other communities. Subsequently, a list of duty hours for sentries was posted in the community. Although there is no suggestion of arson in the press or in Akin's work, after the fire the list disappeared. When Akin asked, he was told that it was "off" (1975:187). Although Akin speculates that the purpose of the watch was to protect the community's small gambling den, gambling continued after the fire; the watch did not. Nevertheless, there is no clear evidence that arson was threatened or feared.

A second element of everyday resistance was the ongoing attempt to forge patron–client ties with those in authority. Where in the case of landlord–tenant relations these ties can be seen to deepen dependency and weaken resistance, when it comes to resisting the state, the situation is somewhat different. The patron–client ties are not with the state as institution but to members of the state. Developing personal ties to those in authority (or in a position to influence those in authority) is an attempt to resist the laws of the state by appealing to the individual members who make it up. Throughout the period, Nate sought to extend those connections.

The first foray onto the middle ground occurred when a fire destroyed some eighty homes, including Nate's (Akin 1978:26). Immediately after the fire, both the city and the temple came and put up signs banning the construction of new houses. There followed a week of homelessness and rejection of an offer of temporary government shelter. Wrote Akin: "For one week, they were hesitating, not knowing what to do. Then Nate went into the ravaged area and started to erect a shelter for his family, where his house stood before, in defiance of all the notices. Everyone then followed suit, and Trok Tai arose from the ashes" (Akin 1978:26).

A few weeks later, in December, Nate led some of his clients to petition for flats in government housing projects. Since their homes had been destroyed in the fire, they were given priority, and in April they were summoned to draw lots for apartments. When they learned that only some of them would get these, Nate went to the press. He then led the residents to visit the director of the Public Welfare Department, and eventually to the chief of the Housing Section. Ultimately they were all given apartments. Meanwhile, the city continued to press for eviction by fining the slum dwellers for rebuilding their homes and backed up the fines by refusing to grant house numbers. This meant that the residents could not gain connections to public utilities. Nate then convinced the abbot of the temple, who was friendly with Nate's brother, to sell electricity to him, and through him to the rest of the community. Nate was also active in convincing all the slum dwellers to refuse to move in defiance of the eviction. Again, Nate might have been arrested for these actions had it not been for his relationship with the local police chief (Akin 1978:27).

While the middle-ground resistance proved relatively effective, the dependence on patron–client ties constituted a weak point—namely, the difficulty of preserving the status and authority of the leader who could best utilize those ties. With his success at getting electricity restored to the community, Nate had lifted his prestige to perhaps its highest level. However, *nakleng* status is fragile. Nate found himself in trouble when the share fund he had organized collapsed. In the wake of the fire, many of the participants were unable to meet their obligations, and Nate could not make good on his guarantee for all the defaulters. He thus broke the code of the *nakleng*, failing to honor his commitments to his clients in the process. Nate's reputation suffered another blow when the Roman Catholic Association donated rice to those who had lost their homes in the fire. Nate was asked to distribute the rice, which was only sufficient for twenty of the eighty households whose homes had been destroyed. He put the poorest at the top of the list and the richest at the bottom, and was criticized for failing to think first of his own friends and clients. Shortly thereafter, Nate, who had intended to give his sons the apartment he had been alloted after the fire, left the community to live there himself (Akin 1978:30). When Nate proved unable to live up to his *nakleng* obligations of honor and loyalty, his status declined and he left the community.

By the end of 1969, the temple and the Crown Property Bureau were nearing a resolution of the dispute over land ownership. Without the threat and benevolence of the *nakleng* to ensure unity, and without his patron–client ties, individual families were left isolated. Those seeking eviction took advantage of this, and lawyers sent letters to each home, asking to talk. Residents were then offered 2,000 baht (then about U.S. $100) to move. This household-by-household approach invoked both fear and greed, and broke the solidarity of the community. Many accepted the deal and left.

Violence threatened only once at Trok Tai, during the last attempt at eviction in 1973, when residents put up barriers to stop the workers from razing their homes (*Bangkok Post*, 29 August 1973, 3). When the workers arrived, residents prepared to defend the barriers, and police, the army, and reporters rushed to the scene. Nate, who had returned to help in the resistance, went to meet Suwit Yodmani, son-in-law of the prime minister (*Daily News*, 28 August 1973).[11] Subsequently the city governor postponed the eviction order "on humanitarian grounds" (*Bangkok Post*, 29 August 1973, 3), and a compromise was reached allowing forty-nine families to stay on a narrow strip of land between the new shop houses and the canal (Igel 1993).[12]

Under the authoritarian political regime, connections, influence, and patron–client ties were the primary means of resistance. Nate did not spend time cultivating the press, nor did he work through formal bureaucratic channels in his resistance to eviction. On only one occasion did he go to the press, and that was in an attempt to secure apartments at a government housing project for victims of the fire, not to resist eviction. His visit to a reporter was meant to apply pressure to a recalcitrant bureaucrat, as his pursuit of resources through formal channels had stalled. That he never used these tactics to resist eviction indicates his distrust of them and his confidence in patron–client ties.

Nate's gender and educational background played an important role. His status as *nakleng* was based on his "manliness." He was able to hold the community together because of the respect and fear that a *nakleng* induced. All the officials he dealt with were men. His status as a *nakleng* helped him get along well with police. The military authoritarian system, led by soldiers and based on personal ties with male officials, was more easily manipulated by men. As for education, in Nate's case, it was not formal education but rather knowledge of how to deal with nobility and the bureaucracy that determined his choice of tactics. It was also this knowledge, and the success of his tactics, that ensured his position as leader. Yet it should be stressed that Nate was not chosen as leader because of his knowledge, but because of his connections. In the community resided a retired railway official and a teacher, both of whom were better educated and at least equally knowledgeable concerning the political system.

Changes in the Political Opportunity Structure

In October 1973, student-led demonstrations succeeded in overthrowing the military authoritarian regime and sending its leaders into exile. Elections were held in 1975, and since that time Thailand has had an elected parliament for nearly twenty-two of the twenty-five years. Coalition governments have been multiparty and unstable, with little cohesion among the parties. In January 2001, the eleventh election since 1973 was held—an average of one election every two and a half years. The instability and the parliamentary nature of the post-1973 period have led to a very different political opportunity structure and have had considerable impact on tactics. While none of the old tactics have disappeared entirely, new ones have emerged and grown in importance.

The political changes of the 1970s were partly due to the rapid economic development during the late 1950s and the 1960s, closely tied to a policy of anti-communism to ensure the flow of U.S. aid, which set in motion significant changes in the social structure (Anderson 1977). Of these changes, three are particularly important to understanding developments in slum communities. First, as part of attempts to deter communism, the government expanded the bureaucracy. Much of this expansion involved agencies to assist the poor. This created a group of civil servants who began to collect information and expend budgets on poor communities. (A few of these bureaucrats later left the government to form NGOs.) The government had begun to form agencies to deal with slums as early as 1960 when it established a Community Improvement Office under the control of the Bangkok Metropolitan Administration (BMA). Although in the beginning this body was involved mainly in eviction, by 1964 it had become involved in slum improvement. Initially efforts were modest, but one aspect of the program that would have long-term effects was the establishment of community committees in the improved slums. Subsequently, the National Housing Administration (NHA), a state enterprise under the direction of the national government, was established, with one of its objectives being the improvement of slum communities. Like the BMA, it established community committees in the areas it developed (Sopon

1992:98–99). Eventually a number of non-governmental organizations (NGOs) were established to aid slum communities, and they also organized committees. The BMA took responsibility for all these committees in 1988, and most large communities now have a committee with new members elected every two years. Since the communities elect these committees, it is not unusual for a *nakleng* to become the community leader, as we saw for Trok Tai.

Second, growth was led primarily by the urban sector, and especially by Bangkok. Even in the slums, many people were benefiting from the economic growth. Consequently, rural-to-urban migration was high during this period.[13] Land in Bangkok was becoming more valuable and evictions were more frequent, with the evicted often moving to other slum communities.[14] All these factors increased overcrowding, weakened established social relations and the sense of community, and opened the way for new leadership in slum communities.

Third, "the middle class" or, more accurately, middle-class elements (see Chapter 7), expanded dramatically, and with it came educational opportunities, media expansion, and parliament. Some people in the slums managed to become part of the new middle-class elements; all were affected by the new political culture and the rise of middle-class–oriented institutions. The massive expansion of the educational system to accommodate middle-class elements in the sixties and seventies, and the entry of the students onto the political stage provided ample lessons concerning the effectiveness of protests, demonstrations, and other techniques. Meanwhile, the parliament opened a new channel to government, a channel where numbers of votes were important and political parties competed for those votes. Also, the new culture proved somewhat sympathetic to the urban poor. Many of the bureaucrats, and the NGO leaders who aided slum communities, were part of the new middle-class elements. Finally, the expansion of middle-class strata allowed for a huge expansion in the size and importance of the media. The largely uncensored press made possible a new range of tactics and opened a channel to a sympathetic audience. In more recent years, investigative reports on television and, to a lesser degree, radio talk shows, have also proved important. The resistance to eviction at Thep Prathan and Bankhrua sought to take advantage of these new opportunities.

NEW METHODS AND NEW LEADERSHIP: THEP PRATHAN

Like Trok Tai, Thep Prathan is an old community, originally settled more than eighty years ago on land owned by the monarchy. The original settlers planted gardens and orchards, and dug fishponds. When the Crown Property Bureau was established, the residents were asked to sign leases, and the community grew and developed until it included a market, schools and theaters, various small-scale industries, and even a bank. Walkways were built and public utilities extended into the community. With long-term leases on the land, many residents built permanent houses. The community had many beautiful old wooden houses; however, with eviction looming for nearly three decades, most had fallen into a state of disrepair long before a settlement was finally reached, adding to the difficulties of residents.

By the 1960s the land had become quite valuable, partly through the efforts of the residents and partly through the expansion of the city. Their longtime occupancy and their work in improving the land would be the basis of the residents' claims to a share in it.[15] In 1965, rumors spread through the community that a prominent banker had laid plans to evict the residents and build a shopping complex on the site of the slum. At that time, the small fire station was withdrawn from the community—a result, say residents, of collusion between the banker and the municipal government. Within three months, the attempts at arson began.[16] After six tries, on Chinese New Year, January 1966, a fire destroyed a large section of the community.[17] After the fire, the city banned reconstruction of the destroyed homes and began to offer compensation to other community members to induce them to leave. It also began to evict residents a few at a time along the edges of the community to avoid provoking a unified response. In Thep Prathan community, arson proved only partly successful. Although part of the community left, the rest managed to regroup. This was largely the result of the appearance of new kinds of organization, new types of leadership, and new forms of resistance.

At about that time, slum dwellers of Thep Prathan organized a community committee. The establishment of official community leadership generally provides a sense of legitimacy to community leaders. Perhaps more important, the community has an officially sanctioned leader to deal with landlords, officials, politicians, financial institutions, and charitable organizations. Thep Prathan, however, did not at first benefit from the establishment of a community committee. It was openly opposed to the Crown Property Bureau (CPB), and although the community rightly considered the CPB an organization separate from the monarchy, others were wary, and so they were unable to obtain formal recognition. Furthermore, Thep Prathan found itself in opposition to the municipal government and to powerful business interests (*Thep Prathan*, n.d., 7–8).

The first leader of Thep Prathan was a prominent community member who was a construction contractor. He was soon forced to quit when he found he could no longer obtain government construction contracts. Other leaders were also prominent, relatively wealthy, older members of the community. One who was particularly wealthy for a poor community, the owner of a gas station, was asked to donate so much money that he eventually left Thep Prathan.[18] Ultimately the leadership fell upon a medical doctor, a woman whose business came not from the government but from the community.

The developers, or perhaps their agents, reportedly pursued both legal and illegal means of eviction. In addition to pursuing the case in court and the alleged arson attempts, the developers, and the municipality, reportedly threatened the residents with rumors, thugs, and police (*Thep Prathan*, n.d., 10; interview, Thep Prathan community leader, January 1994). Along with the threats came offers of compensation for those who left voluntarily. These threats were made to individual households, not to the community as a whole, and residents claim that the compensation offered was not always paid. The developers sought to take advantage of the illiterate and the naive by sending in people with documents for residents to sign; the documents were designed to relieve the slum dwellers of their claims (*Thep Prathan*, n.d., 10; interview, Thep Prathan community leader, January 1994).

Nor did the developers and the municipality ignore the leadership. When elected leaders began gathering evidence to support their case, the developers hired thieves to steal the evidence. The thieves were unsuccessful, and the committee made it standard practice for all members to keep a copy of the documents. The developers threatened leaders, and at times gunshots were heard as a demonstration of the seriousness of those threats. The leader of the community was informed by a local youth that eight men had been hired to kill her (*Bangkok Post*, 10 August 1989, 2; interview, Thep Prathan community leader, January 1994).

In facing these aggressive attempts at eviction, Thep Prathan leaders could look to a number of other communities and organizations for advice. During this period, the number of people involved in attempts to aid slum residents increased considerably with the appearance of NGOs. By 1992, there were at least thirty-two registered and nineteen unregistered NGOs. In addition, there were nine government organizations, nine educational institutes, nine student groups, and six "special agencies" (Sopon 1992:101). NGOs sought to share the successful tactics of each community with other communities, and to put community leaders in contact with each other.

Facing the Crown Property Bureau, and without recognition from abroad, money, or powerful friends, Thep Prathan community leaders found it impossible to establish a foundation or an NGO, as Pratheep was doing in the nearby Khlong Toei slum (Chapter 3). With a wariness of confrontation and the continual danger of being accused of lèse-majesté—a danger that constrained press coverage of the story—the community was limited in its range of possible tactics. Some sort of institution seemed necessary in order to gain official recognition and legal status.

On the advice of an academic who had long been active in helping slum communities, in 1981 Thep Prathan community leaders decided to establish a credit-union cooperative. Here, too, they met with considerable resistance from the developers. During the one-year probationary period, the developers sent around men dressed to look like government officials to tell members of the community that the cooperative was a scam and they would lose their money. With few members and little money, the Thep Prathan credit-union cooperative turned to an established credit union for assistance. After six months of countering further rumors and threats from the developers, the cooperative finally succeeded in gaining official recognition (interview with the leader of Thep Prathan, February 1994).

Faced with long years of delays, increased attention in the media, a legally recognized entity in opposition, pressure from an elected prime minister,[19] and no end to the confrontation in sight, the developers finally agreed to negotiate a settlement. The company would develop most of the land, setting aside a small plot for the community, and would also build new apartments on it. The slum dwellers would help pay for their new homes through the credit-union cooperative. The contract was finally signed in 1989, as a birthday gift to the queen, and the dispute was declared "solved."

Thep Prathan represents just one example of new styles of leadership and methods of resistance. It grew out of an earlier era, when slum communities were only beginning to overcome their isolation from each other. This isolation was ended for many communities with the rise of a group of people whose occupations involved working for the development of all slum communities. NGOs, community committees, academics, reporters assigned to cover slum evictions, and other interested parties have come to form a fairly close-knit group. At frequent formal gatherings and through discussion and informal contact, tactics are shared and assistance provided. Individuals from one community now often join demonstrations organized by another, which shows the increasing strength of horizontal ties in and between slum communities (interviews, Duang Prateep Foundation, December 1993; Community Development Office, Dusit District, February 1994; *Bangkok Post,* 20 December 1993, 1). In many cases, a well-known NGO leader will be called in to serve as mediator in eviction proceedings. Ties to this group of people are not based on the type of male-oriented *nakleng* ties that proved successful under the military government. Consequently, women leaders, such as the doctor at Thep Prathan, have become more common. Women have also played an important role in Bankhrua, a Muslim community in downtown Bangkok that has been resisting eviction for many years.

BANKHRUA: TACTICS OF RESISTANCE UNDER UNSTABLE PARLIAMENTARY RULE

Like Trok Tai, Bankhrua is located along a canal in the heart of Bangkok.[20] It officially comprises three separate communities in two districts of Bangkok. In Bankhrua, the threatened eviction was due to the construction of a tollway "collection and distribution road (CD Road)"—an extended entrance/exit ramp—and the land was being expropriated by the Expressway and Rapid Transit Authority (ETA) regardless of ownership. Residents vacated the path of the main tollway route, which is now in operation, but resisted eviction related to the planned ramp.

Bankhrua was settled by Cham Muslims captured in battle and brought to Bangkok in the early nineteenth century (Phonthip and Saowapha 1989). At the time, the area was outside the city and consisted of unused fields. As Bangkok expanded, Bankhrua was absorbed into the city and eventually became quite densely populated. Ethnic Chinese and northeastern Thai moved into the community. Solidarity among the Cham remained strong, however, with three mosques as religious centers and two cemeteries as reminders of their heritage. The planned expressway ramp would have passed through one of the cemeteries and over one of the mosques.

Although Bankhrua is classified as a slum community, it has always had both relatively rich and quite poor residents. The current official term "*chumchon ae at,*" or congested community, is particularly appropriate to Bankhrua. Initially the well-to-do were high-ranking naval officers or traders. Bankhrua was known locally for its high-quality silk, and in the 1950s the main source of wealth changed when Jim Thompson and a few residents of Bankhrua made a fortune marketing silk overseas; others benefited to a lesser degree. This created a greater disparity of income within the community. While this has led to some resentment, the eviction attempt united the community against an external enemy.

In the past, leadership in Bankhrua came from the imams and members of the mosque committees. Bankhrua also had its patrons, with, in earlier times, both silk and dye factories being locally owned, and its *nakleng,* similar to Nate. By the mid-1990s, the factories were gone, and if younger community leaders are to be believed, the *nakleng* belonged to the past.[21] In 1978, Bankhrua became the site of the first major development effort of the NHA, with the support of the World Bank. As part of that development effort, the NHA sought a leader and a committee to represent the community, and in 1981 the first elected committee was formed. Community committees exist alongside the mosque committees and are responsible for development and communication with the government. There is some overlap, which facilitates cooperation. With the threat of eviction, a "Special Working Committee" was established. This committee consulted with the imams on all decisions, and about half of the members were also on community committees. The committee planned, organized, and coordinated resistance. This complex structure of leadership stands in sharp contrast to the informal leadership of Trok Tai. Yet, outside of the religious sector, Bankhrua had as little leadership as Trok Tai until the arrival of development agencies and eviction notices.

Bankhrua committees reveal interesting patterns. Of the eight imams and their assistants, seven were over sixty. Members of mosque committees were also older, nearly three-quarters were over fifty and many were not very active in the community. The Haj, which required considerable savings, was an important qualification. Some residents believe that membership was more a matter of respect and prestige than responsibility. Community committee members tended to be younger:

about 75 percent were under fifty. Around 25 percent were women, and one committee comprised nearly 50 percent women at one time. Two of the three communities have had women presidents. A good community leader must obviously spend a great deal of time in the community, so those who work there, such as "housemothers" *(maeban)*[22] or small shop owners, have an advantage (Saowapha, Phonthip, and Duangphon 1989:41). Over one-quarter classified their occupational status as *rap jang,* which translates loosely as "employee," a category that can include anyone from a secretary to a bank clerk to a day laborer. This was followed closely by "trader" (*khakhai,* a small-scale retailer) and "housemother." Committee members also included teachers, students, state enterprise employees, and a soldier (NCO). As for the Special Working Committee, none of the members were over fifty, most were well-educated, and occupations included people used to dealing with government, such as an employee of the city, two state enterprise workers, a teacher, and two who work in the media. Many in this group were of the same age cohort as the students who organized the demonstrations in 1973, and some participated in the demonstrations. Members were from families long resident in the community; and they were in careers where advancement could not be easily threatened by their participation.

While most "newsworthy" resistance is exceptional, much of the long, wearing process is at the everyday level. Leaders of the community say they were harassed and repeatedly threatened, and were offered large bribes to end the struggle. Threats are an effective tactic of oppression, as they force a continuous reaction. Over the last decade, the community has had to adopt almost a siege mentality: residents watch for strangers entering the community, question them regarding their destination, and ask someone to accompany them. One of the first things residents did was to organize a twenty-four-hour patrol, mainly to prevent fires. Residents claim to have caught at least one arsonist pouring benzene and say there have been "tens of" attempts at arson (*Nation,* 18 September 1994).

A second constant challenge for community leaders was maintaining solidarity. ETA tactics aim at breaking down this solidarity by offering compensation to individual households. Residents were also offered land of their own at Ban Rom Klao, on the outskirts of Bangkok. The ETA several times imposed deadlines for claiming compensation, forcing residents to contemplate the possibility of being left with nothing as a result of their ongoing resistance. The shared Islamic identity was an important factor in maintaining solidarity.

Another important everyday tactic is to gain support from outside the community. Again, Islam and the rich cultural diversity of Bankhrua were helpful in this endeavor. Bankhrua won the support of the academic community at least in part because of its unique heritage, and the resultant personal ties with academics. It also won the support of many Muslim politicians and organizations and developed ties with NGOs that promoted both development and democracy. Unlike the relations Nate developed with the police, politicians, and government officials, however, these ties were not just between men, but often between women, or between men and women.

Another everyday activity was the pursuit of information, both of strategies of the opposition and of technical data. The community gave weight to reason and debate, and successful debate requires evidence. Here Bankhrua had an advantage over many other slum communities. The wealth generated by the silk industry in the 1960s gave many the opportunity to pursue secondary, vocational, and in some cases even tertiary education. Bankhrua has residents, former residents, and friends in various ministries who, although they did not play an active role, gathered information. It also has friends who helped out of religious sympathy. This network provided Bankhrua with both information of moves that needed to be countered and hard data. The ETA, on the other hand, has sought secrecy. Early on in the struggle, a meeting took place at the ETA in which officials agreed that the ramp must be built and secrecy was the key to success. The "secret" proceedings of this meeting later were leaked to Bankhrua residents and were used in a parliamentary debate on their behalf (*Nation*, 16 September 1988, 1).

Finally, it is important for the community to remain visible. Whereas Nate very rarely resorted to the media, Bankhrua worked hard to publicize its struggle in order to win sympathizers. This was done through Special Working Committee members and their advocates in the media, through friends in academe who wrote columns, and through creating news by staging protests. Here, too, the ETA countered Bankhrua's efforts with its own, claiming that the community was delaying the construction of the expressway, and that its residents were to blame for steadily worsening traffic in Bangkok (*Phujatkan*, 22 April 1994, 13). In addition, the ETA publicized offers of compensation to convince the public that Bankhrua residents were being looked after, but were simply stubborn and selfish.

On the middle ground were activities that occurred intermittently and were more visible. These efforts included petitions to government officials; attempts to have the issue reconsidered by parliament, the cabinet, or other bodies; calls for public debates and hearings; and, most provocative of the methods used by Bankhrua on the middle ground, the demonstration.

In February 1988, a petition was written to then Prime Minister Prem Tinsulanon, requesting that the ramp be eliminated. This was the first of twenty or so petitions written to various politicians. While some of these have won minor concessions, most were ignored. Nevertheless, petitions were an important means of reminding politicians that the issue had not gone away. The petition was also used at times when the Special Working Committee decided the political situation was too delicate to hold protests (*Bangkok Post*, 27 April 1994, 27). The form of the petition ranged from letters written by the Special Working Committee to formal documents such as the one submitted to the Chatchai government, signed by residents, by all twelve Muslim M.P.s, and by two Muslim senators (*Bangkok Post*, 16 September 1988).

A second type of resistance on the middle ground were efforts to enlist the support of elected politicians to overrule the authority of the ETA. In September 1988, an opposition Thai Citizen party (TCP) member from Bangkok called for a debate on the CD road. Elections in Bangkok in 1988 had been hotly contested between the TCP, the Phalang Tham party (PDP), and the Democrat party. Bankhrua had residents who supported each party and a substantial number of votes. The TCP saw a chance to increase its support in Bankhrua while putting the government, and particularly its Muslim M.P.s, on the spot. After a debate in which no one spoke in favor of the CD road, a vote was called, and when all twelve Muslim M.P.s voted against the government, the opposition proposal to reroute the CD road passed. The government called for a recount, which it won; but when a third count was called, the government instead agreed to reconsider. Less than a week after the debate, Suwit Yodmani, the government spokesperson, announced that the CD road through the community had been canceled (*Sayamrat*, 21 September 1988, 1). The ETA soon renewed its efforts to build the ramp, announcing that Bankhrua residents had misunderstood: the ramp would be built, but it would be rerouted to miss the mosque.

Three later attempts to work through elected politicians demonstrate the scope of such efforts. First, Bankhrua residents convinced M.P.s from parties in Bangkok to pursue the issue at the committee level in the House. For example, the leader of the House Environment Committee, a PDP member from Bangkok, pushed a resolution through the committee calling on the ETA to eliminate the CD road. Second, either through M.P.s or on their own, Bankhrua leaders cited acts of parliament that favored their cause. For example, in 1995, an opposition M.P. claimed that the ramp was illegal, as it was being constructed in a historical preservation area. Bankhrua residents also declared that the ramp violated the 1992 National Environmental Act, which required an impact statement (*Bangkok Post*, 17 April 1995, 3; 27 May 1995, 2). Third, Bankhrua residents used the vote. In the 1995 election, Samak Suntharawet, leader of the TCP, declared that his party opposed the building of the CD road and would work to have it canceled. As the rival Phalang Tham party had announced that it would expedite the building of expressways, perhaps 90 percent of residents voted for the TCP (estimate of a community leader, interview, January 1996). The election was held on 2 July, and both the TCP and the PDP joined the new government coalition. Samak reaffirmed his policy to block the ramp. Three days later the TCP announced that it would leave construction of the ramp to the PDP (*Bangkok Post*, 4 July 1995, 1; 6 July 1995, 3). Although ultimately ineffective, these attempts demonstrate the extensive knowledge of the political system that can be gained in reacting to the opportunities allowed by the democratic political structure.

Bankhrua leaders began to seek a public hearing in 1992. In April 1993, the minister of the interior apparently saw public hearings as a means of pacifying the community, and perhaps the Muslim M.P.s in his own party as well, and agreed to the proposal. The hearings, which took place before a committee of neutral experts, were the first of their kind in Thailand. Both the ministry and the ETA, which is responsible to the ministry, strove to limit the scope of the hearings. A seven-day deadline was imposed and the meetings were held in a small, inaccessible room in the ministry headquarters. Publicity was kept to a minimum, and throughout the hearings the ETA apparently tried to follow its policy of maintaining secrecy as far as possible (*Phujatkan*, 21 May 1994, 13).

Bankhrua, however, was depending on publicity and openness to make its views known. At the first meeting, community leaders presented a number of demands: that the hearings be held according to international practices; that the seven-day deadline be dropped; that the meetings be moved to a more accessible site; that they be televised; that the agenda be set in advance; that their experts be allowed to speak and given access to relevant documents. They walked out of the meeting to protest the secret and rushed nature of the hearings. The meeting continued, but later many of the demands were met, as the committee decided to expand the time frame to two months, set an agenda, grant access to documents, and hear experts. The venue was not changed and the hearings were not televised; Bankhrua had to create its own publicity (*Bangkok Post*, 29 April 1993, 25 July 1993).

On 7 October the committee made its report public. In a close vote, it agreed with Bankhrua residents that the ramp should not be built. The report stated that even according to the data of the ETA the CD road was not warranted, and that it might increase traffic problems. Further, it was not economically viable and would cause tremendous and unjust damage to the Bankhrua community. Bankhrua residents felt that they had won an important victory. However, the ETA claimed that the contract could not be changed and that newer data suggested increased usage of the expressway would justify building the ramp. Subsequently, Bankhrua leaders called for a televised public debate on the issue (*Bangkok Post*, 17 April 1995, 3). They also participated in various televised debates about other issues, taking advantage of opportunities to mention Bankhrua.

Finally, Bankhrua residents participated in demonstrations and protests. By protesting against the ramp rather than the government, and by keeping those protests peaceful, Bankhrua remained on the middle ground. A description of one of these demonstrations will reveal the tactics in more detail and exemplify methods in which "weakness" can be used as a strength.

The largest demonstrations held by Bankhrua began on 18 April 1994, and were to continue until a satisfactory response was received. Extensive preparations were made, with groups assigned to security duties in the community and at the rally site, to food preparation, to "rapid reaction," and to supervise the speakers platform. The leaders of each group formed a coordinating committee. Some 8,000 baht (U.S. $325) was collected from community residents to finance the demonstration.

On the first day of the protest Bankhrua residents met at the mosque. To dramatize their determination, and to strengthen it, they walked to the cemetery and dug three graves, stating that they would give up their lives before they would give up their homes. After praying, they formed a procession, complete with a Muslim burial casket to complete the symbolism, and marched to Government House. The procession was led by community members in wheelchairs, pushed part of the time by children, and included the old and the very young. A platform for public speaking was constructed, and thirteen representatives, led by the Special Working Committee and the imams, went to meet with the ETA governor and the deputy minister of the interior in charge of the ETA. At times negotiations grew heated, with one woman from Bankhrua pounding a table and proclaiming that Muslims worldwide would support the community if they were not given justice. Yet negotiations continued throughout the three-day protest. Other organizations sent representatives to support Bankhrua, including prodemocracy NGOs, Muslim organizations, student groups, slum organizations, and slum dwellers from another community. After three days of protests and negotiations, an agreement was reached. Bankhrua residents insisted on a "Memorandum of Understanding" signed by the deputy minister and community leaders. The memorandum included four points: (1) that the CD road remained a problem and would be solved according to reason and evidence; (2) that any new information would be submitted to the Public Hearings Committee for advice before the government made a decision, and any legal problems would be referred to the attorney general; (3) that the government would use the Public Hearings Committee and its report as the basis of its analysis; and (4) that a final decision would be made by October 1994.

Press coverage of the protests in both Thai and English was extensive and mostly favorable. Pictures of the demonstrators focused on women in Muslim dress at prayer, on children and the old, and on the Muslim coffin carried along to symbolize their determination. Articles were written that chronicled the conflict from its beginnings, and members of the Public Hearings Committee were interviewed. While much attention was paid to the "exotic" nature of the Cham Muslim community, it was all positive and expanded the coverage, a point that the community well realized.

Bankhrua residents have strayed beyond the middle ground into violence only defensively. In November 1991 an ETA survey crew, accompanied by police, arrived to designate homes to be razed. Residents had constructed a barrier of chairs, tables, and other materials to prevent the survey crew and their police escort from entering the community. As riot police together with traffic police, numbering perhaps two hundred in all, advanced, residents defended their barrier with water hoses and threw stones at them. As more violence threatened, a former community leader who, like Nate, had good relations with both the police and community youths, arrived to mediate. The police and survey crew departed without completing the survey (*Bangkok Post*, 13 November 1991, 1; *Nation*, 13 November 1991, 1; *Matichon*, 13 November 1991, 1). Pictures of police in riot gear appeared in later articles about the eviction, juxtaposed with photos of smiling community residents or of women and children protesting. The police were described as outnumbering the surveyors five to one (*Khao phiset*, 11 November 1991, 66) and as "hundreds of commandos" (*Sayam Post*, 18 April 1994, 3). Violence has been limited to defensive reactions and has been rare. Residents have instead chosen the least provocative forms of resistance. When surveyors returned a year later with three hundred riot police, Bankhrua residents made only a brief attempt to block the entrance to the community, contenting themselves with shouting insults and, after the surveyors had departed, tearing down the eviction notices. They also removed all house numbers, thus making it difficult to identify which houses had been marked for demolition (*Bangkok Post*, 22 December 1992, 2).

In the examples of both Bankhrua and Thep Prathan, we can see that slum dwellers quickly learn the opportunities available under new political opportunity structures when it is essential to their survival. Thep Prathan began its struggle under the old regime and fought much of it during the mid-1970s when protests were common. Its tactics reflect that background. Bankhrua, on the other hand, began its struggle under the new parliament of the 1980s, and we see a much greater use of the formal political institutions. It is hardly necessary to point out that the stakes involved and the desperation inherent in the struggle led Bankhrua leaders to learn far more about the way those institutions function than the vast majority of Thais, including those with much more formal education.

With the assistance of NGOs and other slum development agencies and activists, communities can pursue a wide variety of tactics that may lead to higher compensation or even to some form of land sharing. However, NGOs are not active in all parts of Bangkok. In Dusit district, for example, the community development officer reported that only two NGOs were working in slum communities, one assisting children and one promoting AIDS awareness. The *nakleng* of Taopun reported that no NGOs were active near the Bangsu market, although there are at least three large slums in the area. Without NGO assistance, communities often continue to rely on traditional leadership. However, as we saw in Chapter 4, traditional leadership has also undergone significant change in the last two decades. A further look at this change in urban poor communities will provide some perspective.

Changes in Traditional Leadership: Taopun

In Chapter 4, I introduced the traditional-style *nakleng* C.K., who has his head-quarters in a slum in Taopun, and outlined his rise to power. Mr. C.K. has provided informal leadership to slum communities in his neighborhood. For example, one slum dweller relates her personal experience when Mr. C.K. saved her and others from eviction:

> I have lived here for more than forty years. The place where I live these days is a home that Mr. C.K. built for us: one hundred families that were about to be evicted by the owner so the land could be sold. . . . When Mr. C.K. found out about the problem, he went to ask to buy the land from the landowner. . . . After Mr. C.K. bought the land, he built [an apartment building] of 100 rooms to share out among us (*"Luk phuchai"* 1989:12).[23]

Mr. C.K. apparently did not collect rent for these apartments (*Deli Niu,* 13 November 1989, 24). He owned a lot of land in the community then, claiming that he had acquired most of it when people came asking him to buy it, in some cases to prevent seizure (interview with Mr. C.K., February 1994; *Khao krong,* 21 June 1990, 14). After a fire in the slum community at Soi Wat Pradu, about a mile away from Taopun, residents also came to Mr. C.K. to ask for his assistance. He donated 5,000 baht each (U.S. $200) to over a hundred families to help them start over (interview with Mr. C.K., February 1994).

While Mr. C.K.'s wealth and ambition have been a great help to many members of the community, problems have also emerged. He averred that he had withdrawn from the lucrative illegal gambling racket and become a legitimate entrepreneur. One of his most successful businesses was real-estate development, at least prior to the economic crisis of 1997. While Mr. C.K. the *nakleng* and politician may wish to help slum dwellers, Mr. C.K. the landowner and developer may have different interests. In one of his projects Mr. C.K. built condominiums on land formerly occupied by slum dwellers. The land where the condominiums are now located is behind the market, and prior to development was not accessible by road. Mr. C.K. himself did not evict the community; the former landowner had them evicted before Mr. C.K. purchased the property. However, since Mr. C.K. owns much of the land in the area, it would have been difficult to sell the land to any other party. Oddly, or perhaps not, that community did not come to Mr. C.K. for assistance, and even though it is practically in his backyard, he did not offer to help them—although he did help a few individuals (interview with Mr. C.K., February 1994). When asked about the condominiums, Mr. C.K. responded: "We have helped some, have solved a few problems. I don't know what more than this we can do, because we must think of ourselves too. We can't always think of others. If we are to help others, we must have [money] first" (*Khao krong*, 21 June 1990, 12).

Although Mr. C.K. is in a powerful position to help slum dwellers in his community, in the long term his presence may create a number of problems. In addition to the conflict of interest mentioned above, others also come to mind. Patron–client ties, especially in their current distorted form, are seldom as benign as the patrons would have us believe, and clients may be too dependent—or too afraid—to object. Slum dwellers under Mr. C.K.'s protection are helped; they do not help themselves. There are no NGOs in the area to help fight eviction, the community leadership is largely inactive, and the slums in the area are isolated from other slum communities. NGOs and government agencies may be reluctant to become involved in communities under the control of a person as potentially threatening as Mr. C.K., even if the communities would accept their help.

Mr. C.K.'s methods have often proven effective. Yet they prevent the development of other methods. It is likely that Mr. C.K. himself would wish to prevent demonstrations and protests. Any reports in the press that might hint that things are not well in slum communities near him would be interpreted as attacks on his honor and his ability to protect his own. The communities are in a situation of dependence on Mr. C.K.—a dependence he encourages and preserves. He has done much to earn their trust: his aid continues to ensure that communities in the area are better off than most other slum communities. Yet Mr. C.K., like Nate, may fail his community, especially after becoming a landowner and developer.

The potential threat from Mr. C.K.'s business ventures, however, is balanced against his political activities. He had long sought to enter politics, and in 2000, he finally succeeded, winning a seat in the senate.[24] If he wishes to continue his political career, he will need the votes of slum community residents and will have to continue to work for them. In the senate, he may also have access to state resources and may be able to provide even more assistance. The threat is thus likely in abeyance for as long as Mr. C.K. retains his political ambitions. We should also keep in mind that there are other similar individuals who have been less politically successful, whose business activities remain threatening to their communities.

New Leadership, New Weapons, New Society

These cases of slum communities show the same transition in leadership styles that has occurred at other levels of society. However, at the community level, when it comes to national rather than local politics, the transition has been more reactive to changes in the government. This is not surprising when we recall that national politics in the past had little impact on the lives of Thai villagers; only when they began to have a clear and direct impact did villagers find it necessary to react. In examining congested urban communities, we found that they really began to assume their current congested shape during the period of strongly authoritarian rule—that is, during the 1960s. At that time, the *nakleng* was the most appropriate leader to deal with government authorities, particularly the police. Only later, with the change in political structures, did new styles of leadership and new tactics develop.

We can see the transition quite clearly in the cases examined here, if we begin with the earliest and follow the changes in leadership over time. In Trok Tai, Nate, a *nakleng,* relied mainly on personal contacts with the local police chief and others. His masculinity was important in projecting the *nakleng* image and in developing those contacts with the male police chief and male officials in the military authoritarian political structure. In addition, Nate's practical knowledge of the ways to deal with bureaucrats and the upper class were important factors. Later, in Thep Prathan, the leader was well-educated, a doctor whose patrons were from the community; thus the developers could not pressure her economically in the struggle. Finally, in Bankhrua, leaders were generally younger, better-educated, and situated in positions in the media and in low-level bureaucratic jobs with minimal opportunity for advancement. (In both Trok Tai and Bankhrua, there were members of the community with more powerful positions in the bureaucracy who were afraid to get involved.) Younger, better-educated leaders were more skilled in searching out information and had personal connections with activists, academics, and the media. Unlike in the military and the bureaucracy, gender is not particularly important in developing ties to these groups. Dealings with the bureaucracy tended to be less personal and more formal in these later cases, as with the memorandum that Bankhrua leaders insisted the ETA chief sign.

The nature of leadership and power has changed in other ways over the last two decades. In particular, the structure of leadership has become more complex, with the leaders of individual slums looking outside their communities to leaders of NGOs and government agencies, or to rich and powerful *nakleng* like Mr. C.K., for guidance and assistance. As in the countryside, the increasingly complex structure of leadership also signals further erosion of vertical patron–client ties. For example, by extending patron–client ties to other communities, Mr. C.K. and other patrons are required to rely on cash rather than personal relationships to ensure loyalty.

Tactics of the struggle against eviction have expanded with the decline of patron–client ties and the rise of new types of leaders. In Trok Tai, resistance was based primarily on patron–client ties—between the leader and the community, and between the leader and the local police chief. All resistance attempts came about through the leading patron in the community; when he was discredited, the resistance failed. In Thep Prathan and Bankhrua, we saw the growth and the effectiveness of new tactics as they were wielded by slum dwellers, NGOs, and slum community leaders. New tactics included both middle-class–style tactics such as hiring lawyers and establishing foundations, and populist tactics such as protests and demonstrations. It is in Taopun, where the traditional leader has evolved into a rich and powerful *jaopho* and entrepreneur, that we saw no evidence of the use of the new methods. Partly, this is because Mr. C.K. had no need to use such methods and no desire to appear weak; partly, it was because his mere presence prevented the development of these methods. Yet the case of Nate demonstrates how fragile the honor of a *nakleng* can be, and how vulnerable the community is if the *nakleng* fails.

In many ways, Bankhrua is not a typical slum community. It is much older than the average community, has some relatively wealthy and well-educated residents, and is Muslim. All these factors have influenced its tactics, expanding the available repertoire. However, all communities have unique features that enable some tactics and rule out others. The wider range of tactics available to Bankhrua demonstrates more of the repertoire in use, which, as Tilly argued, is fairly standard, for at least three reasons. First, the political structure is the same for all communities, offering similar opportunities for resistance. Second, communities are aware of others facing the same problems and learn from their actions. NGOs organize occasional meetings of community leaders where tactics are discussed; in this way, knowledge and experience are spread to communities that lack formal education. Third, NGOs and academics provide advice to communities resisting eviction, further standardizing the repertoire.

The repertoire of protest was transformed with the changes in the political structure during the 1970s. Although personal ties remain important, for example in procuring information, they are no longer the primary concern of those resisting eviction. Instead, a variety of tactics are pursued, aiming at different targets, from the prime minister to elected politicians to government agencies to the public. Competition among political parties has also created opportunities as politicians have sought to win support in elections by assisting the community.

While many aspects of the political opportunity structure have changed, at least one aspect has not: there is still no means for the public to influence the political input structure. Trok Tai had no part in the decision concerning landownership in the community, and once it was decided, could only resist the looming eviction. Similarly, the expressway was designed by bureaucrats and technocrats, with no input from the community. Other than cabinet approval, even elected politicians had little input, and the ETA signed the contract without taking into account the views of those affected. When public hearings were finally held several years after the contract was signed, the ETA simply claimed that the contract could not be changed. According to a Ministry of the Interior adviser: "They fear this could set a precedent. If people start calling for public hearings on every major development project, what would happen to the administration's ability to get things done?" (*Bangkok Post*, 25 July 1993). What would happen, if Kitschelt (1986) is correct, would be popular participation in the political input structure, and perhaps less resistance after policies are announced. Not only might this prove less conflictual, but in a nation like Thailand, where the state avoids using force, it might also expedite policy if agreement were reached in the policy formation stage. Although the new constitution formalized the public hearing in the political process, it has remained only a forum for the government to explain the decisions it has already made. It has thus become a forum of conflict rather than a forum of resolution.[25]

The Bankhrua case also demonstrates that, in employing many of the weapons of the weak, perceived weakness is actually a strength.[26] The elderly, the disabled, children, and women played significant roles in demonstrations and were prominent in press photos. This provided important contrasts with their foes, almost invariably male bureaucrats, who were seen as oppressors. The elderly, the disabled, children, and women were not simply subjects of photographs, however. As one woman leader put it: "Women have played a major role in this demonstration, for example, in kitchen work, or in basic health services. . . . Some Bankhrua women are still 'housemothers' but have an income from weaving silk. . . . These women can come together and protest fully" (*Thairat*, 22 April 1994, 5; see also *Bangkok Post*, 18 April 1994). Women, the disabled, and the elderly in slum communities in Thailand are often close to home, both physically and emotionally. Any threat to the home draws them into the political sphere in its defense. One key member of the fire patrol is an elderly woman who is at home, near the entrance to the community, all day long (*Nation*, 18 September 1994). At community meetings, the predominance of women was so noticeable that, before I even thought to ask, community leaders told me that men do not attend meetings but participate in demonstrations and other actions. Some of the fieriest speeches at those meetings came from elderly women, and often the leadership had to exercise a calming influence.

The increase in the numbers of community leaders who are women is striking when compared to the small numbers of women engaged in politics at the national level. Data on congested community leadership are collected at the district level, and then not always very carefully, so it is difficult to obtain statistical information. In a sample of eight congested communities in Rajathewi district in 1994 (one of the districts of Bankhrua, in the middle of their struggle), fourteen of sixty-five members, some 22 percent, were women. Furthermore, four of the eight committees were all-male. Where women had broken the participation barrier, they made up fourteen of forty-five members, or 31 percent.[27] In these leadership positions we see the intersection between the private and public spheres. Women leaders of slum communities in the fight against eviction are protecting their homes and families. In doing so, they are engaging in public political activity. By building on their strength in the private sphere, women are developing considerable power in the public sphere—power that can be employed for political purposes.[28]

It is not just in the communities, however, that women leaders play important roles. In the bureaucracy, women are often channeled into positions where they can work with the needy rather than into traditional positions of power. Furthermore, other women in Bangkok, freed from traditional domestic duties by maids and appliances, often involve themselves in community service or charity work. These women, both former bureaucrats and volunteer workers, often occupy important positions in the network of NGOs.[29]

The changes in tactics and in leadership also reflect, and enhance, more basic transformations in Thai culture and society. At one level are the more obvious connections between ideology, political structure, and tactics. For example, in 1968 Thailand was under a military dictatorship. Under a military government, connections to the police force would be expected to play an effective role in resistance to eviction while demonstrations would not. Between 1973 and 1976, the ideological left and right ensnared many slum communities and leaders in ideological battles. Demonstrations during this period were quite common and were considered indicators of ideology. After about 1980, the struggle between the left and the right eased, and demonstrations could again focus on eviction as an issue rather than an ideological challenge. Although the ideological struggle of the seventies may have benefited lower classes as a whole, and certainly did much to raise class-consciousness, populist tactics have proven more effective for the individual community when they were no longer thought of as class struggle.

At a more fundamental level, we see changes brought about by the democratic movement in Thailand affecting the attitudes of slum dwellers. The democratic movement has promoted the idea of the equality of all individuals. Slum dwellers who go to the residence of the prime minister to protest are assuming that they have an equal right to be heard, not just through their patrons, but as citizens. Protest, then, is also an indicator of an attitudinal change. Slum dwellers are beginning to believe that the government belongs to them and that they have a right to make demands of it.

Although slum dwellers have been increasingly willing to make class-based demands of the state, the relationship to their patrons complicates any simple portrayal of a rise of class-based resistance to eviction. Class-based resistance is largely aimed at the state; resistance to eviction from private landowners—patrons of the community—takes different forms. As one experienced analyst put it: "In general, resistance to eviction from private land is considerably more subdued than resistance to eviction from public land. Many slum dwellers facing eviction feel that the landlords' behavior has been acceptable in the past, allowing them to stay on their land for low rents. They are, therefore, willing to leave (Somsook 1983: 277)."[30] In other words, private owners are often treated as patrons and their wishes are respected. On the other hand, eviction by one of the arms of the state is almost invariably resisted. Resistance to eviction may be less a challenge to private property than to a state that is failing in its responsibilities to all its citizens. Thus slum dwellers balance their patron–client ties and their class ties: both may be maintained.[31] Meanwhile, the changes in attitude toward the state will benefit the slum community residents as they become more willing to make demands and more capable of making their needs known. At the same time, the spread of these attitudes into what are generally thought to be the poorest and least-educated of the Bangkok population is a positive sign for the development of a more democratic society.

Although I have focused here on urban communities, the same changes in the political opportunity structure have affected rural areas and have brought the tactics of the middle ground there more into line with tactics in the cities. Easier transportation and communication, and access to resources, have allowed peasant communities to organize demonstrations both in the provinces and in Bangkok itself. Initially, most of these protests were led by local notables (who were also powerful *hua khanaen*), and often the villagers were paid to participate. But what works for notables can work for the villagers as well. The best-known example of farmers organizing and taking their grievances to Bangkok began in March and April of 1996. At that time, a number of associations of farmers, workers, and slum dwellers from different parts of the country came to Bangkok to air their grievances at Government House, the official residence of the prime minister. They formed an umbrella organization known as the Assembly of the Poor to present their demands.[32] Eventually the demonstrators came to number perhaps as many as thirteen thousand as the demonstrations were reported in the press, and as others with grievances organized and joined them. Still others, by threatening to join the demonstrators in Bangkok, were able to achieve dialogues with provincial authorities. Regular demonstrations have been held since that time, particularly during the dry season when the fields lay fallow. In these demonstrations, much the same repertoire of tactics was employed as at Bankhrua. Successful tactics become widely known, as they are spread through press reports and by activists. Organizations form, resources are pooled, often with the help of NGOs, and the opportunities offered by the democratic system are exploited. What makes this particular example interesting is the interaction among the protestors: the direct sharing of past experiences of resistance among farmers, workers, slum dwellers, and activists.

Included in the Assembly of the Poor were a group of farmers from Suphanburi who were resisting eviction from their land by provincial authorities who wanted to build an administrative center. Both tactics of eviction and of resistance are remarkably similar to those of Bankhrua. Over a three-year period, residents sent representatives to present their grievances to parliamentary committees, sent a protest letter to the prime minister, made a complaint to the Ministry of the Interior, sought assistance from the Thammasat University Law faculty, met with the Council of State, and gained the support of students from Ramkhamhaeng University. They also brought their grievances to a meeting of Thai and foreign NGOs, and finally joined the protests of the Assembly of the Poor in Bangkok (*Bangkok Post*, Internet edition, 23 May 1996). The government sought to break down the unity of the protestors, offering compensation and the implicit threat that those who did not accept it would be left with nothing. Contractors were then sent in to begin work on land already procured—a visible symbol of the threat. Clashes between officials and villagers and students took place, and at one point a health station was burned (ibid.). The similarity in tactics on the middle ground is an indication of the importance of the changes in the political opportunity structure on the repertoire, including both the new possibilities democracy affords and the better communications, transportation, and education that have reduced the isolation of most villagers.

Finally, Bankhrua, Thep Prathan, and the Assembly of the Poor demonstrate that, at least among the poor, democratic structures lead to democratic values. Democracy is learned and utilized quickly when the political opportunity structure allows it and the threat of eviction requires it. Authoritarianism requires different methods, teaching different lessons. In addition, democracy opens up greater access to the middle ground, perhaps making resort to violence less likely. This is not to say that democracy necessarily brings better results. Still, residents, and those who witness struggles, learn a great deal about the way democracy works, and the way it should work. Especially among the poor, democracy, rather than development, leads to democratic knowledge and participation. In the process, they may force their concerns onto the political agenda and narrow the gap between national politics and local concerns. Of course, a focus on local concerns might require the parliament to divert more of its attention and the national budget away from the interests of Bangkok and middle-class elements, which may not be easy to achieve.

Let us now turn to the role of the diverse middle-class elements in the democratization process, their struggles to forge an identity, their relationship to both the upper and lower classes, and their attitudes toward leadership and democracy.

CHAPTER 7

Thai Middle-Class Elements
Leading in Democracy?

The newly rich in Thailand have invariably been described as a new middle class. That this newly rich middle class is responsible for the democratic uprising of 1992 is taken for granted by many. Yet there has been surprisingly little debate over just what constitutes the middle class in Thailand. Rather, it has been left undefined, as if somehow everyone knows just what it is and all that remains is to determine how it functions; thus it can be used to explain everything. In Chapter 1, I challenged the argument that the middle class brings about democracy in simple straightforward fashion. Though middle-class elements have certainly played a part in the process, democracy came about as a result of a combination of factors. Economic development had led to large-scale migration to the city. This movement, along with economic development, had created both lower- and middle-class elements in Bangkok migrants who, by self-selection and circumstance, were open to change and exposed to new ideas from other parts of the country, and from other countries. Gradually the political culture evolved, drawing largely on rural traditions of participation, on the notion of *phudi*-style leadership, and on democratic ideals from abroad. This new political culture was less amenable to dictatorial styles. The emergence of parties and parliament in 1968 and 1969 provided organizations and a brief opportunity for people to learn about democracy by practicing it, before it was abruptly ended through a coup in 1971. This evolution of political culture, and the lower- and middle-class strata in Bangkok who not only came to accept it but helped to shape it, were behind the democratic uprising in 1973.

Here, I shall discuss the rise of the newly rich and the nature of Thai middle-class elements in more detail. I begin by looking at the way "middle class" has been conceived in the literature. Then I describe some of the ways the middle class has been both conceived and constructed in Thailand and go on to examine the role of middle-class elements in politics, particularly since the rise of the newly rich. Finally I address the question of democracy and leadership in regard to middle-class elements.

Academic literature on the development of middle classes can, for my purposes, be divided into structural and historical approaches. In the first, the middle class is described according to its position in the social structure, the appropriate structural criteria being a matter of considerable debate. For example, for Marx, the criterion was relationship to the means of production.[1] For Mills (1956), it was necessary to distinguish between the old middle class, which consisted of independent farmers and small entrepreneurs, and the "new" or white-collar middle class, comprised of salaried professionals. For Weber (1946), criteria included lifestyle and status. For Giddens (1980), qualifications were the main criteria. Each of these definitions produces a different "middle class," and while there may be considerable overlap, each may act in different ways. To the Thai case, this is particularly relevant, as many traditionally high-status occupations do not provide the financial means for a middle-class lifestyle, while traditionally low-status occupations do, producing an unusually high amount of fragmentation of the various structurally defined middle classes.

The historical approach to class formation is best exemplified in E. P. Thompson's description of the English working class. Thompson (1968) argued that classes create themselves. This type of approach has been applied to the middle class by Frykman and Lofgren (1987). According to them, the middle class constructs a distinct lifestyle in order to set itself apart from both the aristocracy and the lower classes. It then claims superiority for that lifestyle and attempts to impose it upon other classes. In this way, the middle class constructs itself, in the same way that a wall is constructed, brick-by-brick, attribute-by-attribute, using discourse as mortar until there is a coherent shared view of who is middle-class, and who is not. At that point, those who share those attributes become "the middle class." Only the wall is built according to a plan, while class consciousness, I argue, is not. Several problems are clear in this approach. First, a middle class cannot invent itself out of nothing—before they can construct a lifestyle, middle-class elements must exist. Thus, neglecting the structurally defined classes is as problematic as neglecting the historical process. Second, this approach underestimates the constraints upon the ways in which the middle class can construct a distinct lifestyle (Ellin 1991:821).[2] Classes not only construct, they are constructed by the capitalist system, and by external actors. For example, middle-class media constructions are restricted by the need for profit. On the other hand, there might be fewer, or at least different, limitations on academic constructions. Both media and academe are international in scope.

In describing the making of the English working classes, Thompson stressed the formation of working-class organizations and culture, whereas Frykman and Lofgren emphasized the development of middle-class culture. Yet, the middle class is ideally suited to construct itself and its culture in ways not readily available to the working class—namely, *discursively*. Segments within it are responsible for writing and editing newspapers and magazines, advertising copy, and textbooks; for radio and television programming; and for teaching students. In these ways, it is able to construct itself academically, ideologically, and culturally. To understand how the middle class is being created, then, I will discuss how it has developed structurally, within the context of the way it has been constructed discursively. By examining both academic discourse and media constructions, contrasts inherent in the different mix of educational and monetary aspects are clear.

Discovering the Middle Class in Thai History

In her 1992 dissertation, Jiraporn Witayasakpan wrote that by the end of the nineteenth century commercial theater became viable as a result of the rise of "the middle class" in Thailand. This she attributed to "expansion of trade, western education, and the bureaucracy (Jiraporn 1992:3)."[3] "The middle class which emerged ... encompassed merchants, bureaucrats, and intellectuals with western-style education and distinct tastes towards western elements" (Jiraporn 1992:43). The late nineteenth century seems to be the earliest date offered for the appearance of "the middle class," although Jiraporn is not unique in pointing to this time period.[4]

Although not new, this group did grow rapidly at the turn of the century. While the number of merchants had been increasing since the Bowring Treaty of 1855, the semihereditary bureaucracy was transformed into a salaried civil service and expanded dramatically during the 1890s. Siffin estimated that "the salaried bureaucracy more than doubled in size between 1892 and 1899." By 1900, he estimated, there was a bureaucracy of some twenty-five thousand, which grew to about eighty thousand officials by the year 1918 (Siffin 1966:94). The structural middle class of the period was composed largely of traders, independent farmers, and civil servants, including academics. There was also a sprinkling of journalists.

Descriptions of the Thai middle class of this period focus on the salaried intellectuals and bureaucrats. It was this salaried middle class, according to several influential analyses, that was responsible for the 1932 overthrow of the absolute monarchy. Thawatt Mokarapong argued that "with the spread of education . . . a new class—the intelligentsia—began to emerge. . . . Dissatisfied intelligentsia . . . became the principal supporters of the revolution" (Thawatt 1972:86–87, 77–78). Although here Thawatt defined the group according to education, in his description of the leaders, Thawatt observes that Pridi Phanomyong was born "of a typical lower middle-class family," Phibun Songkhram "was a son of a simple farmer of considerable means," Tua Laphanukrom was born to "a middle-class family," and so on (Thawatt 1972:5ff.). Benjamin Batson argued that the coup resulted from the introduction of a salary tax. According to him, "The tax affected mainly middle class government officials and employees of Western-style firms" (Batson 1974:75). Virginia Thompson argued that "groups of European-trained junior officials, largely drawn from the middle class, were the theorists behind the revolt" (Thompson 1941:61). On the left, Udom Sisuwan argued in 1950 that, after the 1932 overthrow of the absolute monarchy, power "fell into the hands of the petty capitalist class, midlevel capitalists, and the Land-Lord class" (cited in Reynolds and Hong 1983:81–82).

Recent analyses by Thai scholars have assigned a greater role to the extrabureaucratic middle class. Chanwit Kasetsiri wrote that the period since the reforms at the turn of the century "saw the development of a new class . . . the middle class with one part in military and civilian government service . . . and the other part outside government service, perhaps as writers or journalists, including entrepreneurs and traders. New leaders of the middle class spearheaded the change of government" (Chanwit 1992:37). Nakharin Mektrairat defined a middle class of those with "independent occupations" (Nakharin 1992:85–90). This middle class, he argued, developed during the period from 1857 to 1927, though it had existed even earlier (Nakharin 1992:85). Nakharin then reclaimed the "revolution" from mid-level soldiers and bureaucrats for the wider middle class:

> The middle class outside government service did not play a role in seizing power. . . . That task fell to the mid-level civil servants and soldiers. However, the act of seizing power took place in circumstances where the middle class outside government service had already helped to destroy the legitimacy of the upper class to govern . . . almost completely. (Nakharin 1992:105)[5]

When the military and the bureaucracy acted on the side of democracy, they were considered middle-class. When the military later opposed democratic rule in 1992, they were defined as outside of the middle class. The middle class, apparently, must always act on the side of democracy, at least in the 1990s construction.

Discarding the Middle Class

The discursive middle class, conceptualized as a combination of independent entrepreneurs and white-collar bureaucrats, was disaggregated and then dropped from academic literature describing the 1950s and 1960s. This occurred in a two-part process. In the fifties, G. William Skinner (1957, 1958) analyzed Chinese communities in Thailand in this way:

> There are what appear to be two middle classes, or at least two major middle-class groupings—the Chinese and the Thai. They overlap for the most part in stratification, but the mean status of the Chinese middle class is appreciably higher. The latter consists of most ethnic Chinese in occupations of highest and mid-high status, i.e., occupations of relatively high income which involve no

manual labor. . . . The Thai middle class, consisting mainly of those in mid-high status occupations (government employees, small entrepreneurs, teachers, newspapermen, clerks, secretaries, and so on), is strongly white collar in flavor. (Skinner 1957:307–308)

Skinner here made the primary division ethnicity rather than class, and then linked that ethnic division to "old" and "white-collar" middle classes: thus we have an old middle class of independent entrepreneurs, the Chinese, and a white-collar middle class, the Thais. That the Chinese described by Skinner might more accurately be called Sino-Thai was obscured in his constant references to "the Chinese." That there were Thai entrepreneurs and Sino-Thai bureaucrats is ignored, and the shared middle-class culture described in Jiraporn's analysis of theater has disappeared from the analysis.

While Skinner had transformed "the old middle class" into "the Chinese," it remained for Fred Riggs and William Siffin (1966) to turn the (Thai) white-collar middle class into the bureaucracy. Wrote Siffin: "the emerging middle class was a bureaucratic class" (Siffin 1966:134). Riggs and Siffin thus made the conceptual shift from white-collar middle class to "the [Thai] bureaucracy." There remained but one minor problem with this view: the large number of Sino-Thais in the bureaucracy. This long ignored fact was addressed by Chai-anan Samudavanija, who argued that, due to the socialization process of the bureaucracy, "a son of a Chinese immigrant will remain Chinese if he chooses to be a businessman, but once he enters the bureaucracy his ethnic identity disappears and he becomes a *kharatchakan* or civil servant" (Chai-anan 1991:65).

The elimination of the middle class from the discourse is central to the analysis of David Wilson. He explained the apparent stability of Thai society by pointing to the absence of a middle class, arguing that "the society of the Thai is characterized by a gross two-class structure ("consisting of an extremely large agrarian segment and a small ruling segment"), in which the classes are physically as well as economically separated and differential status is satisfactorily justified (Wilson 1962:274–275)."[6] As for the roles generally played by middle classes, according to Wilson, "The more intimate economic relationship concerned in transfer of goods and services between town and country takes place through Chinese traders. These people as aliens are easily contained politically..." (Wilson 1962:275). Meanwhile, in 1958, the new military government suppressed debate on the left and Udom's work was censored. Thus by the late 1960s, scholarly discourse held, there was no middle class, and as a result the Thai political system was extremely stable.[7] Writing the middle class out of the discourse ensured that it could not create itself or develop into a coherent social class. It also meant that when "the middle class" returned to the discourse in the 1970s, it was considered new.

"New" Middle Classes: The Rise of the Newly Rich

During this period when academics were busy defining the middle class out of existence, middle-class strata actually began to undergo another rapid expansion. Much of the growth was in services and sales, with education and media sectors also expanding dramatically. The occupational distribution of Thai workers for 1960, 1970, 1980, and 1990 is summarized in Table 8.1. The white-collar middle class will be found in categories A, B, C, D, and I; these categories have grown more rapidly than the total workforce in every period since 1960, increasing from 9.85 percent of the total workforce in 1960 to 20.2 percent by 1990. These newly rich middle-class elements, concentrated in the sales, technical, and services sectors of the economy, have flooded a structural middle class formerly composed largely of small traders, intellectuals, and bureaucrats.

As the newly rich middle-class elements multiplied, the higher education system was expanded to meet their needs. Enrollment in universities climbed from less than 25 thousand in 1950 to well over 600 thousand by 1990. There was a concomitant growth in the number and size of universities and in the number of academics. More Thais were being socialized in the higher educational system, taught by the same group of academics who were creating the discursive middle class.

While these academics, as teachers of the newly rich, enjoyed high social status (see Table 8.2), their income was not congruent with that status. In terms of status, soldiers and police at some ranks are also part of the middle class. Writers and journalists, who play a key role in constructing the middle class, rank quite low in terms of status. The lowest status occupation is a euphemism for prostitution; yet many who practice it are paid more than journalists, nurses, teachers, and even professors. Thus, status and income may widely diverge, with teachers, bureaucrats, and academics, for example, often unable to afford the lifestyle their status might seem to indicate is appropriate.

As we have seen, "the middle class" is not truly new; rather, it was defined out of existence during the fifties and sixties. The emergence of the newly rich was so striking that later writers could no longer ignore what they now saw as "the middle class." Because the growth occurred during a period of political change, it was rather simple to attribute all of the changes to this "new" group. Analytically, it is rather dubious to conflate these various elements, old and new, into a single middle class. The prostitute, the university professor, the bank manager, the independent farmer, the owner of a Chinese traditional medicine shop, the police officer, and the soldier are all "middle-class" under various definitions, yet they have little in common. Nevertheless, descriptions of "the middle class" and the identification of times when it has "acted" have become the basis for the discursive construction of a middle class.

Table 7.1. Occupational Groups in Thailand Ages 11 and Up: 1960, 1970, 1980, 1990

Occupation	1960 Total	1970 Total (% increase)	1980 Total (% increase)	1990[a] Total (% increase)
A. Professional, technical, and related workers	173,960	284,104 (63.3%)	665,255 (134.2%)	1,397,100 (110.0%)
B. Administrative, executive managerial workers, and government officials	26,191	246,591 (841.5%)	434,682 (76.3%)	864,000 (98.8%)
C. Clerical and related workers	154,303	190,238 (23.3%)	389,226 104.6%)	763,000 (96.0%)
D. Sales workers	735,457	833,607 (13.3%)	1,591,268 (90.9%)	2,472,400 (55.4%)
E. Agricultural, fishers, forestry workers, and hunters	11,332,489	13,217,416 (16.6%)	16,838,477 (27.4%)	21,096,500 (25.3%)
F. Miners, quarrymen, and related workers	26,255	42,605 (62.3%)	59,405 (39.4%)	24,600 (-58.6%)
G. Transport equipment operators and related workers	146,610	225,204 (55.7%)	369,207 (63.9%)	606,600 (64.3%)
H. Craftsmen, production workers, and laborers	806,205	1,109,943 (37.7%)	2,232,356 (101.1%)	3,514,000 (57.4%)
I. Service workers	273,375	471,999 (72.7%)	663,386 (40.4%)	924,200 (39.3%)
J. Workers not classifiable by occupation or unknown	99,259	30,560 (-69.2%)	38,180 (24.9%)	61,300 (60.6%)
K. New entrants	64,880	197,869 (205.0%)	---[b] (---[b])	---[b] (---[b])
L. All workers	13,836,984	16,850,136 (21.8%)	23,281,442 (38.2%)	31,724,300 (36.3%)

[a] Census data for 1990 is for workers ages 13 or older.

[b] This category was eliminated in the 1980 census.

The "New" Discursive Middle Class

The first of these supposed "actions" of the middle class, attributed to it only in retrospect, was the 1973 uprising that brought down the military dictatorship and installed democratic rule. The uprising was student-led but soon came to include people of all classes. The events of 1973 demonstrated that concerted action could overthrow an unpopular government. New leaders emerged, leaders willing to work to effect change. This group of former student leaders has become the conscience of the constructed middle class and has contributed greatly to its creation.

That the 1973 uprising has been identified in academic discourse as the beginning of middle-class political activity does not mean that it actually was a middle-class uprising. Only in retrospect did this interpretation of events gradually evolve. Originally, the demonstrations were credited to the public in general and the students in particular. "Through the leadership of the country's youth, a mighty force had congealed and made itself evident—people power" (Theh Chongkhadikij, *Bangkok Post,* cited in Zimmerman, 1974:515). Scholars followed this characterization, attributing the uprising to students and "the people," "people from all walks of life," and "members of the public" (Withayakan 1993:77; Heinze 1974: 498; Race 1974:198).

Among the first to see the 1973 uprising in middle-class terms was Benedict Anderson. He began by describing the changes in class structure that had resulted from the expansion of the economy in the sixties. In his view, this created a "new petty bourgeoisie," the newly rich, responsible for the success of the uprising:

> There is no doubt the new bourgeois strata contributed decisively to the huge new crowds that came out in support of students' and intellectuals' demands.
> . . . Indeed, it can be argued that these strata ensured the *success* of the demonstrations—had the crowds been composed of slum-dwellers rather than generally well-dressed urbanites, the dictators might have won fuller support for their repression. (Anderson 1977:18)

Likhit Dhiravegin (1985) of Thammasat University wrote a similar article, describing the development of "the middle class" during the sixties and attributing the events of the seventies to its new participation in politics. This argument has dominated in the Thai intellectual discourse (see, e.g., Ockey 1992:chap. 8).

Other scholarship, while attributing the primary role to students, has reemphasized the part played by older intellectuals and academics in the uprising (Withayakon 1993:chap. 5; Khamhaeng 1994; Flood 1975:61). It might thus be argued that the educated "middle class" instigated the 1973 uprising. In the Thai case, scholars seem to have made the connection in reverse, noting the advent of

Table 7.2. Occupations Ranked by Status

Rank	Occupation	Status Points
1	Doctor, veterinarian, pharmacist	82.9
2	Cabinet minister	81.8
3	Ambassador	79.7
4	Military officer: general	76.4
5	Provincial governor or equivalent	75.0
6	Architect, engineer	74.1
7	University professor	72.6
8	Nurse	71.5
9	Senator, M.P.	70.0
10	Physical sciences	68.7
11	Lawyer, judge, prosecutor	68.5
12	Military officer: lieutenant, colonel	67.2
13	Airport/Port officials, e.g., pilot, navigator	66.7
14	Manager, entrepreneur	66.4
15	Police officer: general (rank)	65.8
16	Natural sciences	65.4
17	Teacher	64.4
18	Shop owner	63.8
19	District officer and similar	63.3
19	Economist/accountant	63.3
21	Statistician and similar	61.6
22	Restaurant/Hotel manager	61.0
23	Police: lieutenant, colonel	59.5
24	Social sciences	57.9
25	Social worker	57.5
26	Foreman	56.8
27	Priest or minister	56.8
28	Farm manager	56.3
29	Manager-Marketing	55.6
30	Mid-level civil servant	55.3
31	Large-scale farmer	54.3
35	Soldier: NCO	51.2
38	Heir	50.1
39	Medium-scale farmer	49.6
40	Writer	49.4
41	Journalist	48.4
43	Village and *tambon* leaders	47.5
47	Police officers: NCOs	42.7
60	Sales representative	39.6
89	Service woman, e.g., masseuse, "partner"	17.6

Source: Adapted from Suphawong 1991, tables 4 and 5, ranked by urban response.

democracy, then searching out a middle class that must have created it. This also led to a reexamination of the 1932 overthrow of the absolute monarchy to discover if a middle class was present at that time, or, alternatively if perhaps it had not been a democratic revolution after all.[8]

In 1976, this idea of a connection between the middle class and democracy was undermined when student demonstrations again erupted in violence. Support for the students failed to materialize, and the military returned to power in a coup. Although the events of 6 October were initially characterized as "left" against "right," analysis soon turned to consider the role of "the middle class." The 6 October massacre demonstrated that there was no single unified middle class with a clear awareness of its interests: there were middle-class elements on both sides. Many of the educated members of the middle class strata were again calling for a more just society. But, as Anderson pointed out, many of the newly rich middle-class elements turned against them:

> We are to visualize then a very insecure, suddenly created bourgeois strata . . .
> faced by straitened economic circumstances and the menace of worse troubles
> still to come . . . haunted by the fear that . . . their ascent from backstreet dust
> would end where it had begun. . . . Such, I think, is the explanation of why
> many of the same people who sincerely supported the mass demonstrations
> of October 1973 welcomed the return to dictatorship three years later.
> (Anderson 1977:19)

Anderson is perceptive in emphasizing the very newness of their riches as the source of insecurity in the newly rich middle-class elements and of their support for a return to authoritarian government. Yet, there is a reluctance to recognize that "the middle class" was divided by the event. The students who were massacred are not described as "middle-class." Similarly, Wyatt writes of the same event: "Judging only by its members' behavior, one might conclude that the growth of a middle class has strengthened a traditionalistic sort of Thai political conservatism. . . . While they would support the overthrow of the Thanom-Praphas regime in 1973, they also would join the right-wing reaction against the political chaos of 1976" (Wyatt 1982:296). Again the middle class is depicted as singular and opposed to the uprising.

The 6 October massacre was construed by the martial-law regime as a victory over communism. Not until the mid-1980s, after the Communist party of Thailand had been destroyed and the economy had taken off under parliamentary rule, could a reconstruction take place. In that reconstruction, the events were described as a massacre of the same students who had fought for democracy and won in 1973. The extent of the reconstruction became evident during an election campaign in 1988, when Bangkok governor Chamlong Simuang, who would lead the 1992 uprising, was accused of supporting the "right wing" in the 1976 events. Chamlong vehemently denied any role in what was described in the press at the time as "the incident in which scores of students were killed by frenzied right-wing mobs" (*Bangkok Post,* 7 October 1988, 3). The middle class was still being portrayed as singular, although in the reconstruction it switched sides.

The extent of the reconstruction of the events of 1973 and 1976 can be seen most clearly in the retrospective work of a leader of the 1973 uprising, Thirayut Bunmi (1994). Thirayut never mentioned the middle class; he wrote instead of the 14 October 1973 "generation" *(run).* On closer examination, this "generation" is not an age cohort but a constructed group. But by describing the group as a "generation," Thirayut constructs a "new" middle class, based on the initial rise of the newly rich and distinct from those who might share a similar class position, yet which did not share in the experiences of 1973, 1976, and eventually 1992. Thirayut expanded the generation to include anyone from the ages of thirty to fifty, then ascribed to it three essential characteristics. Most important, they had experienced the events of October 1973, October 1976, and May 1992, which served to define the "generation," constituting a sort of (ideological) touchstone to determine membership. Membership did not depend on having been physically present, but on belief in the goals espoused. Thirayut then made it clear that he meant something very like a middle class, defining it in terms of lifestyle, which he described as one that accepted Western culture—Elvis, the Beatles, long hair, and jeans. It included those who wore Bally shoes, ate at McDonald's, used the newest computers, lived in luxurious townhouses, and stayed in mountain and seaside resorts (Thirayut 1994:14–15). Finally, he outlined the occupations of his "generation," again in middle-class terms: "People of this generation are usually technocrats, experts, "professional" [this word is in English] . . . but there are a few who are owners of enterprises, usually new businesses . . . such as the hotel industry, newspapers, computers, and electronics, but these are still a minority" (Thirayut 1994: 23).[9] He also pointed out that his "generation" was active in parliamentary politics and NGOs, and supported environmentalism and culture.

Thirayut's article exemplifies a second aspect of the role played by the 1973 and 1976 leadership in the construction of the middle class. Thirayut mentioned that his "generation" was voluble in the newspapers, and indeed his article first appeared in *Sayam Post,* then in English in the *Bangkok Post.* As columnists and reporters, those of Thirayut's "generation" were in key positions to construct the middle class. He failed to mention several other occupations where leaders of the uprisings of 1973 and 1976 are in such a position. Thirayut was also a professor at Thammasat University. Seksan Prasertkul, another 1973 student leader, was a columnist for *Phujatkan* newspaper, a prolific author, and dean of political science at Thammasat. The most notable success in the media has been Somkiat Onwimon, a university lecturer who signed the petition calling for a new constitution in the leadup to the 1973 uprising. Somkiat went on to become a prime-time news anchor, and is credited with popularizing the news through bringing in techniques such as investigative reporting and advocacy.[10] From these positions, leaders of the 1973 uprising, consciously and unconsciously, were constructing the middle class while providing a visible reminder of the uprisings that have become the touchstone of middle-class consciousness.

Capitalism and the Construction of the Middle Class

Whereas attempts were made to construct a middle-class ideologically according to the ideals of the uprisings, its daily lifestyle has been shaped by consumer capitalism. We can get an idea of the scope of this influence through an examination of the growth of the media, advertising, and market research.

The size and the pervasiveness of the media have increased tremendously over the last forty years. The clearest example is television. In 1955, there was only one black-and-white channel, available only in Bangkok and the surrounding area. By late 1994, there were four regular channels, two cable television packages, an educational channel, and plans under way for at least two UHF channels (Vivat 1994). By the 1990s, there were over 8.5 million television sets in use (*Thailand in Figures,* 1994), and by the end of the decade 89 percent of homes had a television set (2000 Population and Housing Census), so that nearly everyone had access to television in the home or somewhere in the community. Television helped to construct a middle-class lifestyle with virtually all programming—from soap operas with "middle-class" settings to game shows with "middle-class" contestants and prizes, to commercials aimed at middle-class consumers—depicting ideal "middle-class" people, products, and ways of life.[11] Other media have expanded rapidly as well. This is evident in the rise in advertising expenditures, from 1.5 billion baht in 1979 to 49 billion baht in 2000. This is particularly striking in television advertising, from 667 million in 1979 to 32 billion in 2000 (*Thailand in Figures,* various dates; *Bangkok Post,* 13 January 2001, B8).

Advertising expenditures also demonstrate the growth of some of the most influential constructors under capitalism, the advertising agencies: of the eighteen listed in *Thailand Company Information 1990–91,* two were established in the 1960s, six in the 1970s, and ten in the 1980s. Advertising expenditures by category indicate that the images being constructed were largely middle-class (see *Bangkok Post,* 3 January 1995, 19). Most housing estates, which ranked at the top, are aimed at the consumer middle class. Office machines and equipment, ranking second, are aimed at the manager, the purchasing agent, or the private entrepreneur. Ranking third, department stores and shopping malls are the replacement for traditional markets, the epitome of middle-class consumerism, all under one roof. These shopping malls provide a showcase of middle-class culture, where those who aspire to this status can see the types of furniture they should own, the clothes they should wear, and the places where they should dine. Furthermore, the workers of these modern capitalist markets often belong to middle-class strata. Passenger cars (ranked sixth) and petroleum products (ranked eighth) are also middle-class goods, and cosmetics (ranked ninth) have only recently spread beyond the consumer middle class. Only shampoos/conditioners (ranked fourth), cosmetics (ninth), and dairy products (tenth) aim at a wider audience. Finally, the media (ranked fifth) was marketing itself quite heavily, indicating the need of new outlets to rely on the established ones to get under way.

The companies that spent the most on advertising in 1992 (through November) included Lever Brothers, Nestlé, Proctor and Gamble, Colgate-Palmolive, National, and Toyota. Only four Thai companies were in the top ten; two developers of housing projects, one pharmaceutical company, and the franchisee for Coca-Cola in Thailand (*Khukhaeng Thurakit,* 7–13 December 1992, 22). Of the top ten advertising agencies by 1994 billings, only one, Spa, was wholly Thai-owned; it ranked tenth and had the lowest rate of growth (*Bangkok Post,* 3 January 1995, 22); the others all had a significant foreign ownership component. Thus advertising agencies were dominated by Western companies and the leading advertisers were Western. It is not surprising, then, that the middle-class lifestyle constructed through advertising is not too dissimilar from that familiar to those in the West. Nor is it surprising that Thirayut and his readers thought of the middle class in terms of Bally shoes, jeans, and McDonald's.[12]

While it is not possible to outline in detail the middle-class lifestyle constructed through advertising, it is important to point out the differences in the middle class constructed by consumer capitalism and that constructed around the events of 1973, 1976, and 1992. One example should suffice. The middle class constructed by the uprisings deemphasized differences of ethnicity and gender by focusing on large crowds of people with the primary similarity that of class.[13] The implication was that women and men act similarly and equally, and while this is not always true in practice, many NGOs, where some of the most idealistic of the participants of 1973 and 1976 gravitated, were indeed led by women—the same group, primarily, that leads the Thai women's movement. The construction of gender roles by consumer capitalism through advertising is quite different. In advertisements, women worry about clean houses and clothes, and about looking more beautiful; men impress beautiful women by buying expensive imported whisky and fancy cars.

Newly rich consumerism also created an entirely new industry, market research, which rushed in to survey and measure. Market researchers assumed the existence of "the middle class," then set about trying to determine its lifestyle. From such firms, we learn that 72 percent of "middle-class" Thai women like to shop in department stores, 60 percent like to eat out on weekends, 68 percent like to watch television, and 89 percent of "middle-class" families own their own homes (Laifsatai 1987; Chiwit khwampenyu . . . 1986). These surveys often appear in newspapers and magazines, telling "the middle class" how it should act, then measuring again how it does act, in a self-perpetuating process.

The constructions of the advertisers have mingled freely with academic constructions in the press, where many academics write columns, as well as on television, where talk shows mediated by academics became quite popular. This blending of constructions is also apparent in the writings of Thirayut and in the way the 1992 uprising was conceptualized.

THE MOBILE TELEPHONE MOB AND THE 1992 UPRISING

That the media, academics, and others were busily constructing a middle class, and connecting it with democracy, had a profound effect on the way the 1992 uprising was interpreted. The media soon designated the protestors "the mobile telephone mob" and "the automobile mob." The press made explicit comparisons to the 1973 uprising, seeking to tie together the newly rich, the protests, and the earlier touchstones of middle-classness. The Social Science Association of Thailand even went so far as to produce a survey "proving" that the protestors were predominantly middle-class.[14] Thus, from the beginning, the uprising of 1992 was constructed as a middle-class event.

Initially most academics followed along this path with relatively little questioning. Thirayut wrote in June that "it has never happened that a mob anywhere has been so full of automobiles, mobile phones, hand-held radios, and workers of the 'white collar' type . . ." (*Sayamrat sapda wichan,* 14 June 1992, 12.) It was, said Thirayut, a "yuppie" revolution (ibid.). Likhit Dhiravegin argued that the event was of the same order as the 1973 and 1976 uprisings, connecting the newly rich to democracy and even to the 1976 demonstrations that many of them had opposed (Likhit 1992). Anek Laothamathat wrote several articles for various journals, published them in popular form in the weekly *Matichon sutsapda,* and then as a book entitled *Mob mu thu* (Mobile telephone mob). Anek, a student leader in 1976, attributed the uprising to the middle class and to "entrepreneurs."[15] He reconstructed the earlier uprisings as well, calling the students "proxy" for the middle class in those earlier events (Anek 1993:61).

Not long after the uprising, the Political Economy Center of Chulalongkorn University organized a conference in "an attempt to come to grips with the phenomenon of the 'middle class' in the protests of May 1992" (Sungsidh and Pasuk 1993:27). Aimed at an academic audience, the analysis is more sophisticated, and several of the authors sought to determine the nature of "the middle class" in structural terms. There was no agreement on definitions, yet there was an assumption that there was a middle class, and only one middle class. The introduction set the tone for much of the book:

Many protestors arrived at the demonstration site in their large cars, carrying their hand phones. . . . Local newspaper [sic] reported that the majority of the demonstrators were "middle class." They included business executives, stockbrokers, civil servants, owners of small and medium businesses, civil servants, academics, other white-collar workers, and educated persons. Students and political activists were present, but formed a small minority of the crowd. . . . The typical member of the "mob" was a well-off, well-educated, white-collar worker. (Sungsidh and Pasuk 1993:27–28) [16]

Some of the papers in the collection did tentatively question the role of the middle class in the uprising. Yet the focus remained on "the middle class." Sungsidh Piriyarangsan, for example, wrote of the reasons organized labor did not join the uprising before writing briefly of the role of slum dwellers. Voravidh Charoenlert pointed out that many of the dead and injured were not middle-class, but concluded: "The victory of democratic forces is not possible if it lacks the support and the combat that comes from the middle class" (Sungsidh and Pasuk 1993:139). Nitthi Aewsriwong reminded us that the middle class does not necessarily believe in either democracy or equality, as Anderson and others had pointed out after the 1976 massacre, a point recent constructions of the middle class have largely ignored. Perhaps most intriguing is an article by Teeranat Karnjana-uksorn, who correctly pointed out that by most definitions, including family background and income, the soldiers who fired on the demonstrators were also "middle-class." On the whole, however, even the more sophisticated analyses in this book credit "the middle class" with the uprising of 1992.

In the construction of the events of 1992, we see coming together all the strands of the analysis presented here. It was the first popular uprising where an awareness of the middle class had already developed, and thus the first time an uprising was attributed to it from the outset. This uprising was associated constantly with the earlier ones, the ideological touchstone for determining membership in the middle class. The military, despite its arguably middle-class nature as pointed out by Teeranat, was not considered part of the middle class because it took the wrong side in the conflict. Yet retired Lieutenant General Chamlong Simuang, who led the protestors, was considered middle-class. The middle class was also identified in terms of consumer goods, particularly the automobile and the mobile phone, in an attempt to connect the newly rich middle-class elements with the ideological preferences of those in academe and in the media who were busily creating the middle class discursively. And finally, the constructed middle class attempted to take over the event, minimizing the role of others and denying them any credit.

The middle class did play an important role in the 1992 uprising by providing leadership; [17] yet when fighting erupted, they were not in the forefront. The occupational backgrounds of those killed and injured have been documented in *100 Wan Wirachon Prachathipatai*. Of the thirty-eight dead (where information was available), only one was a businessperson, one a government employee, one a teacher, and one an engineer. At least twenty belonged to lower classes, and ten more were students. (The other four were street vendors.) Even more telling, of the thirty-four where information is available, not one had graduated from a university (*100 Wan Wirachon Prachathipatai* 1992:3–5). Of the 176 injured where information is available, only twenty-three clearly belonged to the middle or upper classes, though some of the others may, by some definitions, have belonged to a lower-middle class (*100 Wan Wirachon Prachathipatai* 1992:8). Yet, initially, constructions of the uprising (with the notable exception of Nitthi) almost invariably cited the earlier survey that had claimed 52 percent of demonstrators had a degree rather than admitting that not one of the dead had such a qualification. Only slowly—and after the image of a middle-class uprising was firmly entrenched in the public discourse—did questioning begin in earnest.[18]

Despite the many books and articles that describe the uprising as a middle-class victory, the discursively constructed middle class is not unaware that, with many courageous individual exceptions, it went home when the shooting started while others fought on. Various accounts, encouraged by those who supported the military government, claim that Chamlong led the people to their deaths. The implications of this argument are twofold. First, it shifts some of the blame for the killing from the military to Chamlong, who might otherwise be seen as the hero of the uprising. Second, it implies that the demonstrations would have succeeded without violence if only Chamlong had not provoked the troops, in the process absolving "the middle class" for leaving when the shooting began. While this construction of the events may be outside the mainstream, it is widely known, and may account for the fact that Chamlong's party actually lost seats in Bangkok in the ensuing election.[19]

Middle-Class Elements and Political Reform

In the wake of the 1992 uprising, some middle-class elements apparently decided they would have to protect their democracy from corruption and vote buying themselves, rather than allow the military the excuse to do it for them. In the short term, constitutional amendments were passed to make the military-promulgated constitution more acceptable. At the same time, some reformers began to call for a new constitution that would be more democratic, focusing on provisions to eliminate vote buying and corruption.[20] Reformers decided that politicians should not be allowed to subvert this new constitution, and so they called for a constitutional assembly to be created to prepare a draft. After some give-and-take over the procedures to be followed, in 1996 such a body was established.

The new assembly was chosen through a combination of indirect election and parliamentary selection. In the first stage, candidates over the age of thirty-five who held at least a B.A. degree registered in their home provinces for election to the assembly. In provinces where more than ten people registered, an election was held among the candidates, who then chose the top ten prospective members. The resulting 760 names from the 76 provinces were submitted to the parliament, which then selected one candidate from each province. To these 76 indirectly elected candidates were added 23 experts. Up to 450 experts could be nominated by the universities, drawn from the fields of political science and law, and from those with experience in public administration or politics; again the parliament chose from this pool. The result was an assembly made up largely of middle-class elements, with a heavy concentration of academic "experts." This assembly then spent the next year drafting a new constitution.

Once the Constitutional Drafting Assembly was chosen, it met and distributed responsibilities among several committees, including one responsible for producing a draft of a constitution. Various public hearings were held along the way, and public submissions encouraged, ostensibly allowing the public to present its ideas. Although it is not clear whether public opinion had any impact on the actual draft, this did allow the Constitutional Drafting Assembly to declare the draft a "people's constitution" and gave broader middle-class elements an opportunity to feel as if they had participated. The draft constitution produced by the assembly was passed by the parliament in 1997, after a strong media campaign supported by academics and aimed largely at other middle-class elements (McCargo 1998:22–23). A clear attempt was made by the writers to control the political process that would follow the enactment of the constitution. The constitution is extremely detailed and complex in spelling out not only the institutions and how they will function, but also the duties and responsibilities of citizens and the state. Even the basic policies of the state, which all governments must pursue, are delineated (Thai Constitution, Section 5).

We can get a sense of the attitudes toward democracy of the powerful middle-class elements who wrote the constitution, of the media and academics who promoted it, and of those middle-class elements who supported it by looking at some of its provisions. Three sets of attitudes are worth particular consideration: attitudes toward the lower classes; attitudes toward politicians, especially provincial politicians; and attitudes toward technocrats.

At the heart of the reforms lies the same possessiveness toward democracy that we have seen in the 1992 uprising. The twin problems of vote buying and corruption became the main targets of reform. This formulation made corrupt politicians and the lower classes who sold their votes the saboteurs of Thai democracy. Middle-class elements apparently believed that the lower classes were not capable of effective participation in democratic politics. The evidence of this incapacity was the practice of vote buying, which they assumed was confined to the lower classes—a practice that made it impossible for "good people" (that is, those acceptable to middle-class elements) to win elections. The corrupt politicians who won elections were then obliged to recoup the investments they had made in buying votes through more corruption.

The solutions to these problems, in regard to lower classes, were twofold. First, the constitution required the government to set a national education policy appropriate to the economy, and the society, that would teach democratic principles (Thai Constitution, Section 5, Clause 81). Apparently it was thought that the poor sold their votes because they lacked the education of the middle-class elements, and therefore were unable to understand democracy. Education was thus seen as the best long-term solution to vote buying. Perhaps in the same spirit, decentralization of decision making was given priority. Villagers in particular and the lower classes in general would be able to practice democracy by deciding local issues at the local level (Thai Constitution, Section 5, Clause 78). In addition, the drafters of the constitution decided to distance the electorate from the cabinet, where important decision making takes place (see Chapter 3). Consequently, they installed a provision requiring all cabinet ministers to resign from the parliament on appointment (Thai Constitution, Section 7, Clause 204). Thus, under the new constitution, no serving constituency M.P. directly responsible to the predominantly lower-class electorate can be a member of the cabinet.

The new constitution also sought to undermine the power of provincial politicians. The most important provision here is the one just discussed: preventing constituency-based M.P.s from joining the cabinet. A second interesting provision will likely have little effect on corrupt politicians, but effectively bars the lower classes from running for parliament: all candidates must have at least completed a university undergraduate degree (Thai Constitution, Section 6, Clause 107).[21] Here the fascinating—and revealing—assumption is that if politicians had a (middle-class) university education, they would not be corrupt. In addition, a number of new institutions with sweeping powers were created to investigate corruption and prevent vote buying.

Finally, the middle-class elements who supported the new constitution put in place provisions designed to encourage "good" people to both regulate and dominate politics. Here we find a willingness to trust technocrats, almost all of them men at present (Connors 1999). An Election Commission was created whose five members were given sweeping powers to disqualify candidates on the charge of vote buying (Thai Constitution, Section 6, Part 4). By thus disqualifying a candidate, the five members of the commission can overrule the choice of tens of thousands of voters.[22] The powers of the National Counter Corruption Commission were also increased (Thai Constitution, Section 10, Part 2). In particular, it was given the authority, with the approval of the Constitutional Court, to ban corrupt politicians from holding office for a period of five years (Thai Constitution, Section 10, Clause 307). An elected senate was created and members or supporters of political parties were barred from participation there. Strict limitations were imposed on campaigns for candidates as well. In that way, middle-class elements who supported the constitution sought to keep the senate free of what they saw as the unsavory nature of political parties and the electoral process,[23] allowing more "good" people to win. Finally, in the same spirit, a party-list system was created for the House of Representatives. While party-list systems are a common means of strengthening political parties, the Thai system includes a provision that is meant to ensure that all cabinet members come from the party list. If a constituency M.P. resigns to join the cabinet, a by-election is held, and the M.P. who resigned must pay for the election. If a party-list M.P. resigns to join the cabinet, the next person on the party list takes the seat in parliament (Thai Constitution, Section 6, Clause 119 [1]). Therefore, if a party-list M.P. becomes a minister, the party retains the seat; whereas, if a constituency M.P. becomes a minister, the seat must be contested. In this way, it was hoped, the cabinet would be composed of people unsullied by electoral politics, without attachments to provincial constituencies.[24] Finally, the party-list system opens the way for more Bangkokians to enter parliament, and of course the cabinet, at the expense of provincial politicians.[25]

The same possessiveness with regard to democracy that we saw in the claims of responsibility for the democratic uprising of 1992 is evident in the constitution, which contains provisions that seem designed to increase the control of middle-class elements over the political process, over "their" democracy. At the same time, there is a host of provisions that can be employed to make demands of the state itself. These provisions are most accessible to middle-class elements but open to all. The constitution, for example, includes a freedom of information provision allowing citizens increased access to government-held information (Thai Constitution, Section 3, Clause 58). It requires the government to provide for public hearings in some circumstances (Thai Constitution, Section 3, Clause 59–61); and it gives individuals the right to sue state institutions in court if their rights have been violated (Thai Constitution, Section 3, Clause 62).[26] Such provisions are most effective for people with access to financial and legal resources.

We should not ignore the hopeful attitudes underlying the new constitution. Despite the lack of trust in the ("uneducated") lower classes, the constitution does demonstrate a belief that, through carefully engineered laws and institutions closely regulated by technocrats, democracy can be successful. Not all middle-class elements have accepted this principle, but the writing and promulgation of the constitution certainly propagated this belief that Thai democracy can be repaired. In this sense, the constitution has helped to further promote democracy as an ideological touchstone for the middle class that is being constructed. Unfortunately, as McCargo (2002:114, 117) pointed out, the new constitution "overengineered" the political structure, leading to challenges to election results in over three-quarters of the constituencies and repeat elections in about one-quarter. Such challenges, McCargo observed, undermine the legitimacy of the electoral process itself. Furthermore, with supposedly independent regulatory bodies also increasingly subject to political manipulation, the constitutional foundation of the state may rapidly lose much of its legitimacy among middle-class elements.

Conclusions

By now it should be clear that it is, at best, analytically dubious to speak of a single middle class in Thailand. Rather, there are diverse elements that have not yet converged into a single social class. As Giddens (1980) pointed out, in order for a middle class to become consolidated, a closure of mobility is necessary. In Thailand, not only has there been no closure, but middle-class elements continue to expand, adding more newly rich to the mixture.

The differences in the middle-class fragments are clearest between the consumer middle class, many of them newly rich, and the status middle class, many of whom are in the media and academe. Despite considerable overlap, these two groups are fairly distinct in terms of income and education. Many in the consumer middle class are relatively well off but not necessarily highly educated. The owners of medium- and small-size enterprises often fit into this category. In contrast, academics, teachers, and social workers are well educated and enjoy high social status but have incomes at the low end of the middle-class strata. Not surprisingly, this difference manifests itself in the two strands of construction of the middle class. The status middle class, with its high levels of education and its positions in universities, the media, and NGOs, has stressed a class based on an ideology associated with the uprisings of 1973, 1976, and 1992—an ideology of democracy; thus, high-status groups compensate for their lower income through influence over culture. The consumer middle-class construction is based instead on owning cars and mobile phones, and on making money. The 1992 uprising demonstrated the discursive attempts to draw together these two strands.

That middle-class culture is still fragmentary and under heavy construction has not prevented middle-class cultural imperialism. It is not malicious in intent, often going unnoticed. Where it is intended, it has usually been an attempt by reformists to promote democracy by associating it with fragmented and diverse middle-class elements that have shown only limited and sporadic support for democratic government. The unfortunate side effect, however, has been a conviction on the part of the constructed middle class that democracy belongs to it, and that the lower classes are not capable of participating effectively in a democratic system (Ockey 2001). The frustration with vote buying is the most dramatic testimony to this attitude: frequently the poor are blamed for it rather than those doing the buying. Denying the role of lower classes in the uprisings that brought about democracy is a necessary corollary of this conclusion that the poor are neither worthy nor capable of participation in the democratic system.

The frenzied construction under way reflects both the fragmentation and the struggle for middle-class culture. Reformist academics seek to associate the middle class, particularly the newly rich, with democracy, while advertisers aim at consumption and an associated need for a high-growth economy. When economic downturn was associated with democracy in the 1970s, the newly rich turned on the students and academics and supported a coup. This legacy is one reason academics were so pleased when the newly rich middle-class elements supported democracy in 1992. Academics sought to consolidate that qualified support, with only limited success, after high economic growth was associated with democracy during the 1980s. The high levels of support for the Thai Rak Thai government even as it attempted to silence its critics and impose limitations on the media are a reminder of the fragility of the support for democracy among middle-class elements.

Ultimately, however, despite the differences in the various fragments, it may be the overlap that is most important. Out of this overlap, and out of the power of the discourse, may eventually emerge a coherent social middle class with democracy as an ideological touchstone and economic prosperity as the binding force. As middle-class culture becomes more intricate and solid, and moves toward greater consensus, the fragmented middle classes will tend to conflate, perhaps even without closure of mobility.[27] In the meantime, it seems safe to conclude that there is no "middle class" in Thailand. Rather there are many different fragments in the process of becoming.

Conclusion

Much of the literature on democratization contends that it is the process of modernization which is responsible for the emergence of democracy.[1] I have argued here that, while modernization may play a part, indigenous traditions of participation are also influential in the development of democracy. As the standard modernizationist position has long been established, some may find it perverse for me to insist that the ethic of participation existed long before the westernization and economic development of the 1960s. Yet it seems even more perverse to insist that Southeast Asians in large numbers were willing to fight and die for purely Western or modern or global foreign values, without any local cultural underpinnings. The kind of commitment demonstrated in the democratic uprisings in the Philippines, Indonesia, Burma, and Thailand can only be explained by examining cultural continuities as well as changes.

In describing indigenous forms of participation in politics, I have taken issue with the assertion of Asian values proponents that Asian cultures are inherently authoritarian, either now or in the past. Rather, I have argued, like many other scholars, that throughout Southeast Asia, centralized authoritarian traditions have existed alongside participatory local ones. In fact, prior to the arrival of the colonial powers, those local traditions were far more relevant to the lives of most villagers. However, as the technology and administrative expertise of the colonialists were applied in Southeast Asia, including in Thailand by central Thai leaders, the centralized authoritarian tradition began a long struggle to extend its control into the villages, and to undermine the local participatory traditions in the process. Economic development, a modernized military, and the beginnings of industrialization (perhaps most evident in the construction of railroads), contributed to this process by increasing central resources, power, and control, a process that peaked in Thailand during the Sarit era. The legitimacy of the authoritarian patterns of leadership were then slowly eroded by urbanization, which brought the village participatory tradition into the cities, and by forces of globalization as democratic values reinforced and reshaped participatory traditions.

The debate over the origins of democracy has important implications for how democratization is conceived, adapted, and implemented. If democracy comes about as the result of modernization and the impact of foreign ideas, then, as Huntington (1968) contended long ago, authoritarian rule can be justified if it brings about stability and economic development. In other words, by encouraging economic development, authoritarian rule initiates democracy. My counter argument is that an authoritarian regime simply intensifies authoritarian patterns of leadership, making it all the more difficult for democratic attitudes to realize themselves. Those attitudes then must come from the outside—through the processes of "globalization"—or from below—from long-standing participatory traditions at the village level, or both, developing in opposition to the authoritarian regime. The results are often antagonism between emerging democratic ideas and authoritarian attitudes, a delay for democracy, and in some cases open conflict and killing—as in Burma, Indonesia, and Thailand. I argued that the best way to promote democratic ideas is to introduce a system of democracy and encourage meaningful participation in it: democratic attitudes and patterns are only institutionalized under democratic rule.[2]

A second important implication of the debate on the origins of democratization concerns the roles enacted by middle and lower classes in emerging democracies. If it is modernization and the impact of foreign ideas on the middle strata that bring about democracy, then their participation in democracies should be maximized, while that of the lower classes should be minimized. As Dahl (1971) pointed out, this is the path taken by Western nations, which began with property requirements for voting. On the other hand, if we accept the premise that there are indigenous patterns of participation already present, then the primary task is to discover a way to integrate those traditions: broad-based participation is to be encouraged and effectively channeled into democratic institutions.

Another important aspect of the origins of democratization merits brief mention. If modernization and foreign ideas are indeed its basis, then democracy is at worst a foreign imposition and at best an aspect of globalization, and democracies should be similar, perhaps ultimately identical, in all parts of the globe. If, on the other hand, democracy has its origins in indigenous traditions of political participation, then it is firmly rooted in local culture, and diversity is more likely to be preserved in democratic forms of government.

Thai Patterns of Leadership, Participation, and Democracy

Turning specifically to Thailand, there have been significant transitions in styles of leadership, participation, and legitimacy with the reform of the administrative system in the 1890s, then again at the time of the 1932 overthrow of the absolute monarchy, the rise of the Sarit regime, and in the mid-1970s. The 1890s saw not only the reformation of the bureaucracy along Western colonial lines, but also the arrival of much of the same technology being employed elsewhere in Southeast Asia to expand central power. In 1932 the toppling of the absolute monarchy dealt a blow to traditional forms of legitimacy, especially those associated with the king. Attempts were made to replace that legitimacy by employing the rhetoric of democracy, strengthening the state, and relying on provincial notables and their networks, rather than by building up political parties or other political institutions. A few years later, authoritarian leadership and the power of the state were strengthened during the war years, as army commander Phibun became prime minister and sought to militarize society. In the process, he tried to build up mass-based organizations, but they were organized from the top down, and participation was tightly controlled by Phibun and his inner circle. This reinforced authoritarian patterns of leadership, despite increased participation.

The end of World War II saw a brief opening up of opportunities for participatory leadership; however, again it was the provincial notables and their networks of clients who were left to provide organization to the emerging political parties. Military intervention in the political system prevented the development of democratic political organizations such as political parties, which in any event would have been difficult. Meanwhile, the expansion of the armed forces, with American support, created a large enough military to impose authoritarian rule after 1958 on a scale never known before: authoritarian patterns of rule spread throughout the society, from the center to the villages, as elections and popular participation were largely eradicated.

Although Sarit was able to eliminate the institutions of participation, he could not so easily destroy the ethic of participation. Instead, he sought to channel it into development efforts and into anticommunism, with some success. However, larger social processes were under way that were to strengthen the tradition of participation even as authoritarian patterns were weakening under Sarit's successor, Thanom. The first transition back to more participatory forms took place in Thailand, partly because, when strongman Sarit passed from the scene in 1963, his successor lacked personal charisma and was not able to consolidate his rule as thoroughly as had Sarit. More important, Sarit had divided actual and symbolic leadership when he consolidated his power: while he held actual power, the monarch had symbolic power. When Sarit died, the monarch remained, and it was he, rather than the not very charismatic Thanom, who became the focus of legitimacy. When the monarchy exhibited some support for greater democratization in the late 1960s, the strength of the Thanom regime was further undermined.

By the mid-1970s, the transition to new styles of leadership in Thailand had proceeded to the point where *phudi* leaders were more acceptable than *nakleng* leaders, particularly in urban areas. The transition to new styles of leadership in the seventies took several years. The prime ministers during the 1973–1976 period, while clearly from the *phudi* tradition, were from essentially the same social backgrounds as their predecessors, except that they were civilians rather than soldiers. Only in the late 1970s was there a shift to a new generation of leadership, followed by a more gradual transition to parliamentary rule. This later transition eventually brought new types of leaders to the fore, both *phudi* and new *nakleng,* more often with provincial backgrounds, with business experience, and with Thai educations from a different set of schools from those of their predecessors (Ockey 1996).

The transition in style of leadership was also related to a change in constituency. Under military rule, the leadership was only very indirectly dependent on ordinary citizens. The main constituency was the military itself and, to a lesser degree, the bureaucracy. In both those constituencies, patron–client ties were reinforced by structure. The transition in style of leadership in the 1970s included a widening of constituency to include all voters. Unable to continue to rely on structure, potential leaders then shored up weakening patron–client ties through vote buying and violence. I have pointed out that one particularly important segment of the widened constituency are women, who make up approximately half of all voters. Nevertheless, women candidates for parliament did not benefit from the transition to new styles of leadership in large numbers. Women who are leaders in Thai society outlined a number of obstacles that remain, including the difficulty in overcoming stereotypes, which apparently are different at the national than at the local level. Breaking down those stereotypes has proven difficult and has proceeded slowly, although we identified the emergence of the *jaomae* as one figure with considerable potential to break down the stereotypes and the barriers they impose.

There is a further dilemma for women in seeking to gain leadership positions. As we noted in Chapter 3, women in village Thailand have participated in politics only informally. Thus there is at best a very limited indigenous tradition of such participation for women, and change has indeed had to come largely through the process of modernization and the impact of Western ideas. And yet, important differences between the lower and upper classes remain. Upper-class women, including even the *jaomae* Chamoi Tipso, find that they must adhere to certain feminine stereotypes if they are to succeed. Yet some of those very stereotypes constrain their opportunities to participate in politics. On the other hand, lower-class and rural women like Kim Haw or Arunee Sito, in rural politics or labor politics respectively, have been able to ignore the feminine stereotypes and act as would any male leader. Rural and lower-class women are less restricted in the ways they can behave, but also less likely to enter politics. As Prateep Ungsongtham pointed out, there is a difference in the images that women must project at "higher" levels of society, where urban traditions of gender relations prevail. Perhaps as women are drawn increasingly into informal types of politics, as at Bankhrua and Thep Prathan communities, they will become more willing to assume leadership positions in the political sphere. Then, as with Prateep, they will be in a position to try to alter the stereotypes imposed by urban traditions of gender relations. In the end, change from below, from those lower in the societal hierarchy may be as important as the change through modernization.

The general trend in the transition of styles of leadership was complicated by variations in the pace of change among particular social groups and in different places. One of the differences explored was that between middle and lower classes; equally important were those between urban and rural voters. This study of patterns of leadership in the democratization process provides some evidence for the important role played by middle-class elements in initiating democracy. In particular, they are at the forefront of the change in attitudes—the change in political culture. Young, mostly middle-class–oriented students provided the leadership for the 1973 uprising. However, I have pointed out that the urban poor and workers were also strongly exposed to the wrenching changes wrought by location, lifestyle, status, and globalization, and have comprised a large part of all the crowds that have demonstrated for democracy. Thus it may be more accurate to say that urbanites in general, rather than middle-class elements, played the key role. Of course, new middle-class strata, the urban poor, and workers were often recent migrants, with the legacy of village-level participation still strong among them, so that the change must also be seen as combined with continuity. The lower classes were bolder in their demands for democracy in Thailand than the middle-class elements, at least in 1992 where evidence is available. Furthermore, while middle-class fragments may have been prodemocratic in seeking to initiate democracy, it is also important to consider their later attempts to consolidate their own position in the social structure. This has hindered the further progress of democracy, as middle-class elements seek to prevent expansion of economic and political benefits to the lower classes that might diminish their own share and affect their attempts to consolidate their identity. This has been most evident in the media and the new constitution, but also in the distaste of these strata for provincial politicians who cater to their rural constituencies. Such figures are inevitably depicted as corrupt, while their constituents are blamed for selling their votes.

Sarit played on the traditional *nakleng* style of leadership to reshape participation in the villages. The key figure in this new pattern has been the provincial notable, who is all too often a new-style *nakleng,* or a *jaopho,* and may also be a powerful political party faction leader. By linking the national to the local, particularly in their distribution of resources and their role in the factionalized political parties, new *nakleng* have shaped contemporary Thai democracy. Their use of vote buying and patronage to strengthen patron–client ties has reinforced their position and undermined the development of other forms of participation in national politics. For the most part, participation in national politics has come through these *nakleng.* However, the efforts of the Assembly of the Poor and other NGOs and, in a different way, Thaksin's populism, are beginning to change that.

The 1997 Thai constitution and related policies attempt to deal with corruption and vote buying by increasing education and decentralizing politics. However, breaking this pattern will require more. It will require that the countryside be brought into national politics in a meaningful way. As we saw in Chapter 7, democratic participation is the best means of learning and institutionalizing democracy. This means that the attitudes of middle-class elements toward democracy have to change further, so that there is a greater willingness to involve the lower classes. However, even this may not be enough. The neoliberal policies promoted by international economic policymakers allow little scope for the promotion of redistributive policies. And of course the powerful provincial notables have a strong stake in maintaining a system that gives them personal credit for any benefits that come out of Bangkok.

Ironically, then, it is the economic interests of the Bangkok middle-class fragments, combined with the desire of the (detested) provincial notables to retain their power, that have undermined Thai democracy. It is in the interests of big business and these middle-class elements, both concentrated in Bangkok, to promote policies that benefit Bangkok at the expense of the provinces. Meanwhile, in the provinces, a new style of patronage-oriented *nakleng* has emerged, one who relies on generosity, and often corruption, to strengthen the increasingly tenuous patron–client ties. Some of these new-style *nakleng* have further transformed into *jaopho,* increasingly preying on their constituents rather than just providing patronage; yet it is the new-style *nakleng,* the *jaopho,* and the corrupt politician who most effectively bring growth, so they often win election. This, rather than an inability to understand democracy, seems to be the primary difference between urban and rural attitudes. It is worth noting that, in 1975, the Social Action party implemented a policy that sought to reverse the long-standing flow of money from the provinces to Bangkok (Girling 1981:203). The party went from 18 seats to 45 seats with the implementation of this policy. And when Thaksin Shinawatra's Thai Rak Thai party promoted policies designed to help villages in the 2001 election, it won a resounding victory, defeating longtime patronage-oriented politicians in a number of constituencies. So it seems clear that there is support in the provinces for a policy platform that would benefit them.

While the ethic of participation in the villages may have been eroded by Sarit's authoritarianism, we see that the urban and rural lower classes can participate democratically, as they did in the Assembly of the Poor, in Bangkok slum communities, and in past democratic uprisings. The democratic deficit rests in the link between national and local participation. To put it another way, a gap exists between local and national for most in the rural and urban lower classes. Rarely does it appear as though they can participate in national politics in any effective way, except through the provincial (and community) notables. Rarely do they see the benefits of government policies, except through the provincial notables. Those same provincial notables are the faction leaders who are the key links in the political parties as well. This gap between national and local—in the areas of participation, politics, and policy—seems to be the most significant problem not only for leadership but also for the development of democracy in Thailand. It is this gap that the Thai Rak Thai party has sought to exploit.

The Democratic Deficiency:
The Gulf between National and Local Politics

The gap that exists between local and national politics, particularly in the countryside but affecting many urban poor as well, can also be traced back as far as the absolute monarchy and has endured through all the transitions in styles of leadership. Under the monarchy, decisions made in villages were of little concern to central monarchs, as long as their tax and conscription needs were met. Conversely, decisions taken at the center often had an impact on the villages, but they were in a reactive position: they had no thought of participating in the decision-making process of the center, only of resistance to the policies that emerged. The chasm between leadership styles was also quite wide. Only the village leader was in a position to bridge the gap, and then to a limited extent, through a series of other leaders at the district and provincial levels. In other words, central policies were made according to the needs of the center, not the villages. This gap between villages and the center has never been closed, and only partly bridged.

The bureaucratic reforms of the late nineteenth century reshaped the nature of this gulf but did not significantly narrow it. As part of the reform process, *phuyaiban* were elected. But as the position increasingly required the *phuyaiban* to represent the government, few were willing to take it on. Consequently, a gap opened between the leaders chosen by elections organized by the government and the informal leaders who continued to wield influence in local matters. Formal and informal democracy were separate from each other.

With the overthrow of the absolute monarchy, traditional leadership at the center was disrupted. In the provinces, however, rather than building up new political institutions of participation such as political parties, which would have required the development of new styles of legitimacy in the provinces, the new leaders at the center simply turned to already established provincial notables for support and political organization.[3] Initially, parties were not allowed to develop because central leaders feared competition in the parliament. During the nationalist period prior to and during World War II, Phibun organized groups to support government leaders and policies, but entirely without input from the villagers. These organizations were directive rather than participatory. After World War II, political parties finally emerged. However, on every occasion up until the 1980s, they were given little time to prepare for the first election and survived only for short periods, after which they were banned and had their assets confiscated. Under these circumstances, parties had little choice but to turn to local notables for organization. Furthermore, there is no indication that any of the major parties were ever inclined to build the kind of organizations that might have bridged the gap between villages and the center, even if it had been practical. Government parties turned to the Ministry of the Interior to win votes, which, of course, was not participatory. With the swing to strong authoritarian rule in 1957, even the selection of local leadership in the villages became directive.

The Sarit government again shifted the divergency between village and national politics. Under Sarit, the central government took a greater interest in development as a means of counterinsurgency. Development money available from the central government gave villages a financial incentive to interact with the state. It was the *nakleng*, with his connections to the bureaucracy, who was in a position to procure those resources. This meant that participation in national politics took place mostly through the *nakleng*, so that the divide between village and local politics was preserved in a way that served the interests of these powerful figures and the bureaucrats who worked with them.

The restoration of parliamentary rule and the early phase of the transition to democratic patterns of leadership in 1969 and 1973 saw one unsuccessful attempt to bridge the gap between center and villages. After the 1973 uprising, the Democracy Propagation Program was established to promote understanding of democracy, particularly in rural areas. From the beginning, it was directed primarily by academics, with students doing much of the teaching and organizing of workers and peasants (Morell and Chai-anan 1981:151ff.). It is important to note that much of the participation of such groups was extraparliamentary and extrainstitutional. Students, in particular, were not old enough to run for office, or even to vote at the time. Nevertheless, left-wing parties did develop; and even some centrist parties, such as the Social Action party, advocated policies designed to help poor villagers. As others have noted (e.g., Morell and Chai-anan 1981:167–169), and I have pointed out in Chapter 7, the attempt to activate workers and peasants was a major contributing factor in the 1976 massacre at Thammasat University by right-wing forces. Attempts to bridge the gulf between national and local by organizing and mobilizing the poor, farmers, and workers were also quashed.

The destruction of the organized left by the Thanin government (1976–1977), followed by the provisions of the constitution of 1978 that were designed to prevent its reemergence, combined to limit participation in politics, especially by the left (Ockey 1992:57ff.). Unwillingness to espouse left-oriented policies, and the desire of provincial notables (many of them *jaopho*) to keep their constituents dependent on themselves rather than the political parties or the government, further contributed to a decade and a half where there were few attempts to appeal to rural constituents through concrete policy proposals. Although nongovernmental organizations slowly developed, then proliferated during the period, they chose to work at the grassroots level and were issue-oriented rather than policy-oriented. In other words, they also failed to bridge the gap between local and national politics by neglecting national politics—again, in many cases, due to an unwillingness to openly espouse leftist policies. Meanwhile, the economic disparity between rich and poor, urban and rural areas continued to widen. With growing resources and no competition, provincial notables continued to buy off participation, shoring up increasingly fragile patron–client ties with money and violence.

The extent of the divide between national and local was evident in the writing of the 1997 constitution and influenced the outcome. While conservative reformers strengthened both new and existing institutions to fight corruption and vote buying in ways that would rely on technocrats and undermine participation in national politics, grassroots political activists introduced measures designed to increase participation in local politics (McCargo 1999; Connors 1999). The result is a constitution that, for example, prevents nearly all rural Thais from running for parliament because they lack university qualifications, while allowing them to participate in newly developed public hearings on important local issues. This neatly preserved the divide between national and local. At the same time, however, it entailed attempts to get rid of the provincial notables without providing a replacement, a virtual impossibility.

While the new constitution did little to bridge the gap between local and national, three related trends proffered some hope. First, although local politics may have seemed divorced from national politics to many poor, especially in rural areas, the two are, of course, intricately related. Building a dam or an oil pipeline, to take two prominent examples, is a policy decided at the national level with a direct impact locally. In the past, going to the provincial notable was the only effective way to protest such decisions. Now, with the development of formal institutions for participation at the local level, including the public hearing, there are alternative channels for dissent. Thus far, however, they have been largely ineffective.

Second, organizations such as the Assembly of the Poor and various NGOs have been assisting the poor in utilizing these channels and in trying to increase their effectiveness. The Assembly of the Poor in particular has also been active in promoting participation through protests in Bangkok, a technique previously possible only with the assistance of provincial notables, due to the cost involved in traveling to Bangkok and the need for some familiarity with the capital and its ways. The Assembly of the Poor has developed links to many other NGOs and to many rural areas, so that an informal network now exists. However, the focus of the assembly has mainly been issue- rather than policy-oriented, and many seem content to retain that focus.

Third, the economic crisis has undermined the independence of provincial notables within the party system. During the economic boom, they could fund the election campaigns of large factions. The crisis left many of them in debt, and they were forced to turn elsewhere for funds. Those in government were able to rely on patronage. Others turned to wealthy Bangkok-based tycoons, and particularly to Thaksin Shinawatra and his Thai Rak Thai party. The economic crisis, then, has given Thai Rak Thai the opportunity to impose some control over its provincial notables. The party has also sought to forge direct relationships with the poor, especially the rural poor, through clear policies designed to help them, such as that which provides a revolving fund of one million baht for every village, and the policy for subsidized national health care, which limits the cost of medical care to 30 baht per visit. The party has also recruited an extensive membership. However, the many provincial notables recruited by Thai Rak Thai will wish to retain their personal influence. Ironically, the return of prosperity may make it more difficult for Thai Rak Thai to develop and maintain a direct relationship with the poor, when the provincial notables seek to reassert themselves. The changes brought about by Thaksin and Thai Rak Thai remain fragile, and are linked to Thaksin himself in the public mind. Many may be reversed when he leaves the scene.

Nevertheless, if Thaksin does succeed in changing the political system as he hopes, he may also reshape patterns of participation in ways comparable to Sarit. I have pointed out that there has long been a gulf between local concerns and national politics, a gulf that, while seldom bridged, has paid big dividends in the parliament when exploited, first by SAP and now by Thai Rak Thai. The populist policies of Thai Rak Thai were deliberately formulated to appeal to voters in the countryside. They are clearly stated and provide concrete benefits. Thus rural voters can choose a party with a policy platform that meets their needs. This has the potential to bring rural voters into the national political system in ways never sustained in the past. At the same time, Thai Rak Thai has accomplished this without encouraging participation. Instead, Thaksin, and to a lesser degree the Thai Rak Thai party, have established themselves as the new patrons of rural voters, at the expense of the provincial notables and in a similar relationship of dependency. Constitutional provisions aimed at increasing education and participation in the countryside have proceeded slowly, or been derailed. Power has been increasingly centralized in the hands of Thaksin and his close allies, and criticism and competition have been actively discouraged. This, of course, is exactly the tack that was taken by Sarit.

Two years into the Thai Rak Thai term, Prawet Wasi, who played a major role in developing the 1997 constitution, spoke up regarding the populist policies of Thai Rak Thai. According to the *Bangkok Post* (24 May 2003), Prawet argued that: "It's not good giving rural communities too much money because that only makes them weak. Generosity should end now and attention should be shifted to training people in management and helping them make their communities prosper without having to rely on money and 'external' power." Prawet nicely highlighted the dependency encouraged by Thai Rak Thai. Yet his interest in participation of those in the countryside remains purely local—just as the constitution encourages those in the rural areas to participate in local but not national politics, at least until they have university degrees. Thus the choices, for now, are limited. On the one hand is a political party led by a new *nakleng*-style politician who seeks to benefit them while discouraging participation and encouraging dependency; on the other are well-meaning *phudi* who want them to participate, but only locally, and to seek self-sufficiency without the access to resources that Thai Rak Thai's populist policies provide. (The neoliberal policies of the Democrat party seek the same outcome as the *phudi*.) Neither the new *nakleng* nor the *phudi* wish to allow extensive meaningful participation in determining the future of Thai politics.

Leadership and Thai Politics

One of the advantages of democracy is that it opens the way for charismatic leadership to function within a legal-rational system. In turn, democracy seems to function best when at least occasionally an inspirational leader emerges to capture the popular imagination. One of the biggest problems of Thai democracy has been the failure to produce such popular charismatic national leaders. Since the 1970s, it has had a series of sometimes good, sometimes not so good, but never inspiring democratic leaders. That has made any effort to promote dramatic change difficult. As Diamond (1999) observed, weak, ineffective leadership in democracies can result in nostalgia for authoritarianism. The original muted reaction to the coup of 1991 may indicate just such nostalgia. The high levels of support for Thaksin, even —perhaps especially—when he has acted somewhat autocratically in his "CEO" style, reflect the same nostalgia. Nor can we be certain that it will not grow stronger, so that more authoritarian styles of leadership return.

The reasons for the failure to produce popular inspirational leaders are, in part, results of the nature of the contemporary monarchy. In consolidating his rule, Sarit divided symbolic leadership from actual leadership, using the monarchy to prop up his authoritarian regime. Perhaps in reaction to this manipulation, the king under Thanom supported democratic change, and has even been depicted as a democratic king. In some senses, this is true. On many occasions over the years, the king has supported democracy, albeit a conservative kind of democracy (Niti 1999; Hewison 1997). Furthermore, he is popular, and there is no doubt that he would easily win any election. Yet there too lies the problem. A king cannot contest an election; while he can support democracy, he cannot be democratic. He cannot submit legislation or face a vote of no confidence. To be king, he must act as a king and not democratically. For a symbolic leader, that does not pose a problem. However, when the monarch becomes the model of an ideal leader, and elected leaders are measured against him, democracy suffers, particularly when the monarchy is above criticism while political leaders are not. An elected leader cannot act like a king, emulating a monarchical style of leadership, just as a king cannot act like an elected leader.

There is a more direct explanation for the failure to elect inspirational leaders since Sarit divided symbolic and actual leadership. Conservative royalists fear that allowing a political leader to develop a truly national constituency would mean competition with the monarchy, which they see as dangerous. And so a nationally elected leader has not been seriously considered, despite calls for such a system. Thailand has, nevertheless, moved incrementally and informally toward it. In recent years, the media have depicted elections as a contest between two rival candidates for prime minister rather than a contest between parties. And the new party-list system provides for M.P.s who are not linked to a single constituency. Since the revival of the monarchy under Sarit, political leadership has been overshadowed by symbolic leadership. Not until Thaksin has any leader managed consistently to gain such a share of the limelight. Thaksin, as a party-list candidate whose party won nearly half the seats, is perhaps as close as possible to being a prime minister with a national constituency. He has been the strongest elected leader of the modern era. However, he is still one of a hundred party-list candidates, all with the same type of constituency based on the party, not the nation.

Under the 1997 constitution, perhaps fewer, larger, and stronger parties will eventuate, leading to at least occasional charismatic leaders with broad-based support; however, many obstacles will have to be overcome. The procession of non-charismatic leaders, some with no concern for a national constituency, has eroded support for democracy. At the same time, the lack of a truly national political leader has encouraged the monarchy to play a more active role in politics than was envisioned in the constitution (Niti 1999:102). While this may be necessary to preserve democracy in the short term, it may also weaken it over the long term. Thus, for now, the strength of the monarchy, a continuation of a traditional form of leadership, may inadvertently be slowing down the transition to more democratic patterns of leadership.[4] Weber, and many political scientists since his time have struggled with the paradox inherent in charismatic leadership and its potential for change. Charisma can create a Mahatma Gandhi, Sukarno, or John F. Kennedy; or it can create an Adolph Hitler or a Benito Mussolini. In a democracy, a democratically elected inspirational leader can express the highest hopes and dreams of the people—or can destroy the democratic system. This is a dilemma faced by many new democracies. In Thailand it has been structurally avoided for elected leaders. However, shifting the problem from the political system to the symbol of traditional leadership has not solved the dilemma of charismatic inspirational leadership; it has only introduced new complications in its stead.

NOTES

Chapter 1. Changing Patterns of Leadership, Culture, Power, and Democracy

1. Scholars such as Wm. Theodore DeBary (1998), Andrew Nathan (1986, especially pp. 24ff. on remonstrance), and Tu Wei-Ming (1998, on human rights), and politicians such as Kim Dae Jung (1994, responding to Lee's comments in Zakaria 1994) and Anwar Ibrahim (1996) have pointed out some of the participatory elements of Asian cultures. But their refutation has been based on court culture and in some cases the ability to adapt foreign ideas. A useful summary of the "Asian Values" debate is Subramaniam 2000.

2. Those who attribute democratization to the middle classes include, among many others, Anderson 1977, Likhit 1985, Sungsidh and Pasuk 1993, and Anek 1993. I have covered the literature on the middle class and democratization in detail in chapter 7.

3. I do not mean to imply that traditional culture was unchanging, although the pace of change was generally much slower. I have simply chosen the mid-1800s as a convenient starting point. On changes in the nature of leadership and participation prior to the mid-1800s, see Akin 1996; Thak 1974:226–235; and Pasuk and Baker 1995:chap. 7.

4. Administratively, the kingdom was divided into inner provinces, outer provinces, and tributary states. Inner provinces were subdivided into four classes, only one of which was ruled directly. On the geographical aspects of administration, see Tambiah 1976: chaps. 7, 8, and 10; Bunnag 1977:17–39. There were also regional variations. Administratively, the regions of Thailand were governed by different ministers: the north by *mahatthai* (civil affairs), the South by *kalahom* (military affairs), and the coastal provinces by *phrakhlang* (finance). See Pasuk and Baker 1995:216; Vickery 1970.

5. It was not simply distance, but remoteness. A distant village easily accessible by ship was easier to control than a nearer village accessible only through a difficult overland journey.

6. I use "headman" here to emphasize that during this period village leaders were male. That is no longer necessarily the case.

7. See also Pasuk and Baker 1995:218.

8. Hong 1999 discusses some fascinating exceptions to this general pattern and the struggle to police the margins.

9. Yot's 1990 work is based on his 1986 English-language dissertation.

10. I shall return to this point in chapter 4, when I describe the lives of some women leaders.

11. As indicated by this odd comment in the conclusion: "In particular, individual styles of leadership could make a great difference. With General Arthit rather than General Prem in control of the government, the results might have been totally different." No further explanation is given. See Sombat and Montri 1991:173.

12. Neher (1992) took a different approach. He did not write about the nature of leadership per se but outlined the pattern of coups and elections, and the high degree of continuity in terms of policy between regimes despite origin.

13. See Siffin (1966:94). This process has been well documented for the various ministries. The two most important for our purposes are the Defense Ministry (see Battye 1974) and the Interior Ministry (see Bunnag 1977). Anderson (1978) argues that this amounted to internal colonialism.

14. See Scott 1976a and Scott 1976b, especially chap. 3.

15. Bunnag's characterization is somewhat different from mine, as he has viewed things from the perspective of the Ministry of the Interior. While he has made the point I have stressed here regarding the shift in the status of headmen to "quasi-officials" and its implications, he also cited records describing *nakleng* leaders as bandits and emphasized the obstacles to government policies presented by the apathy of the villagers and their (well-founded) suspicions of the central government.

16. The gap between local concerns and national politics always existed, of course. What was new was the way this gap became tied to the formal institutions of leadership in the village, which in turn led to a deeper division between formal and informal leadership.

17. Pasuk and Baker 1995:186–189 provide a variety of figures on migration from the 1950s to 1990s. The growth in Bangkok was due to a combination of high birth rates, temporary migration, and permanent migration. Temporary and permanent migration to provincial and regional centers and migration from one rural area to another were also high.

18. During this period, many migrants worked as hawkers and *samlo* (pedicab) drivers, two of the occupations that were organized into unions during this period.

19. It should be pointed out that the changes in political participation have been directly affected by international factors, and not just through the process of modernization. Colonialism influenced the administrative reforms of the late nineteenth century. The depression was one cause of the 1932 uprising. The Cold War and the war in Vietnam contributed to the ability of Sarit and his successor Thanom to impose authoritarian rule. President Jimmy Carter's human rights policies had an impact on the decision to democratize in the late 1970s. IMF and World Bank influence have supported policies that widen the economic gap between the rich and poor. I have chosen to focus primarily on domestic politics for the sake of clarity.

20. This biography of Thaksin is drawn from Plai-oh, 1987: 53–54, 80, 86, 148; *Bangkok Post,* 3 June 1991, 32; *Khao phiset,* 3 May 1989, 12; Ukrist, 1998; *Bangkok Post,* 7 February 1995, 3; and Sarakun, 1993.

21. For further details on the listings and on Thaksin's government contracts and concessions, see Ukrist 1998.

22. According to one report, of the 106 million baht in donations reported by Thai Rak Thai for December 2000, the month prior to the election, 105 million came from Thaksin's wife, Pojaman. See *Nation,* 4 January 2001, A2.

23. It should be noted that Banhan succeeded mostly through contracts won through competitive bidding, while Thaksin was more successful at securing large-scale monopoly concessions.

24. Mulder (1992b) associates "the mother" with *khunna* and "the father" with the interpenetration of *khunna* and *decha*.

25. Interestingly, rumors have circulated concerning the sexual orientation of some of the *phudi* prime ministers since 1976. Whatever the source or truth of these rumors, they do indicate that these prime ministers are perceived much differently than the "manly" Sarit, who was the subject of many rumors of large numbers of mistresses and minor wives.

26. Although often characterized as urban and rural differences, the division is really class-based, with the urban-poor voters grouped with the rural voters. In part, the distinction is blurred because middle- and upper-class voters are concentrated in urban areas. I have provided justification for grouping urban-poor voters with rural voters in chapter 6.

27. Thai Rak Thai, with its populist policies, has aimed to take advantage of this gap.

Chapter 2. Leadership, Political Parties, Factions, and Patronage

1. McCargo 1997b. He designated them as "real" and "authentic" respectively.

2. McCargo (1997b:131) concluded that Western political parties are increasingly moving away from the ideal model, so Thai political parties are not very different from Western ones. In the sense that Western political parties do not rise to the ideal either, this is no doubt correct. But the fact that both differ from the ideal does not necessarily make them similar.

3. With some variations in emphasis, this is the consensus in nearly all the literature on political parties. One of the most detailed analyses of how factions function in Thai parties is Buntham 1988; one of the best analyses of the ways that parties function is Kramon 1982.

4. His discussion of his preferred method of analysis consists of two sentences: "Actual Thai parties do not conform to the ideal types of the 'real' or 'authentic' party. Rather, they represent uneasy composites of both the 'real' and 'authentic'" (McCargo 1997b:121–122).

5. Parties were allowed from 1945 to 1951, 1955 to 1958, 1968 to 1971, and 1974 to 1976. Civilian governments were ostensibly in power from 1945 to 1951; however, after the coup of 1947, the government served at the pleasure of the military, not the parliament.

6. Given the decentralized nature of political leadership in village Thailand, strongly centralized parties with effective local branches would have been difficult, if not impossible, to develop. Furthermore, nearly all strongly centralized political parties in Southeast Asia have grown out of independence movements, something Thailand lacked. Linking provincial notables and their electoral networks more effectively to parties might have been possible.

7. He also eliminated local elections and appointed *kamnan* and *phuyaiban,* further weakening the link between participation and politics.

8. In 1988, under Thailand's first elected prime minister since 1976, the government chose to hold only one parliamentary session a year with only twelve days of meetings, in spite of a large backlog of legislation. Although the session was eventually expanded, this was clearly an attempt to contain conflict and prevent the parliament from overturning the

government (see *Bangkok Post,* 19 August 1988, 1). This pattern has continued in various forms. A recent visit to the parliament demonstrated how small a role it plays in government since the new constitution came into effect. As cabinet members are no longer members of the parliament, only those called to answer interpellations came to the meeting. Only two of the 36 ministers were sitting in their seats in the chamber. Even though the parliament now has 500 members, there were approximately 150 present in the meeting. Furthermore, since voting now works electronically, one member can vote for any number of colleagues by using their identification cards.

9. See, for one example, *Bangkok Post,* 15 June 1988, 5. The election process in this village is described as follows: "Usually Kamnan Boonchan would call a meeting of the villagers and inform them whom to vote for, simply telling them the candidate he has chosen is a 'good person.'"

10. Historically, the exception has been the Democrat party, which has branches organized in a number of rural areas. However, these branches are usually tied to individuals more closely than to the party, and their main purpose has been to influence intraparty elections (see Chai-anan 1981:174–189). The 1997 constitution and related political party laws provide financial incentives to parties based on membership. However, as of 2 June 2003, the Election Commission reported party branches for major parties as follows: Democrat 193; Rasadon 42; Chat Phattana 35; Chat Thai 18; Thai Rak Thai 8. Thus incentives for membership have not led to the development of local branch networks. I thank Sunh Arunrugstichai for providing this information.

11. The most powerful *hua khanaen* usually belong to more than one of these types. These categories are based on those in Phoemphong and Sisomphop 1988:28–30; Setphon 1988:39–44; Kramon, Sombun, and Pricha 1988:57–61; and on interviews with members of parliament, *hua khanaen,* and citizens.

12. Setphon 1988:77–79, 98–100. Setphon claims that in some cases voters will be moved out of one district and into several others. They vote in each new district. In other cases, names will disappear from the voting lists.

13. Often the most powerful *hua khanaen* are actually *kamnan.* In these cases, however, the power may stem from their authority as influential figures and not from their political position.

14. Arghiros 2001, esp. 100–101; 223ff. In a particularly interesting analysis, *Nation,* 28 June 1988, 8 outlined the reliance of the now defunct Ruam Thai party on the tobacco industry. According to the article, some 100,000 workers in eight northern provinces were then employed by tobacco factories. In the 1988 election, Ruam Thai won 26 of its 35 seats in the north (8 in the northeast and 1 in the south).

15. Phichai, Somchaet, and Worawit n.d.:58. One of the candidates from Pattani—the eventual victor—organized his campaign around the provincial Islamic Council members, even going so far as to set up his campaign headquarters in the Islamic Council building. *Bangkok Post,* 9 December 2000, 3 described how candidates attempt to convince people they have the support of one monk, Luang Pho Khun Parisuttho.

16. A good recent example is the defense of Thaksin Shinawatra by Luangta Maha Bua when the National Counter Corruption Commission was considering whether to ban Thaksin from politics in 2000; see *Bangkok Post,* 12 December 2000, 3.

17. Perhaps the best analysis of the role of monks in the election process is Arghiros 2001, especially 201ff.

18. One good example of this type of activity was the group of M.P.s identified only as "young and idealistic" founded by some of the leaders of the October 14 uprising. The group was reported to have a membership of about forty, from both government and opposition parties. "In forming and joining the group, these young MPs hope to keep their political idealism alive and cooperate with one another in sponsoring and legislating bills that they believe will serve the public interest"; see *Nation,* 5 September 1988, 8. Many of these same M.P.s have remained in parliament since the 1980s, and most joined the Thai Rak Thai party for the 2001 election. Within a single party, they may become a more coherent faction.

19. Some of these relationships are described in *Nachun sutsapda,* 15 January 2001, 28–30.

20. I have described the process in detail for Kitsangkhom in Ockey 1994.

21. Charges of buying votes in parliament have been almost as rife as charges of buying votes in elections, and equally convincing. Among the most credible is the admission of former Prime Minister Khukrit Pramot, who said he bribed M.P.s while he was prime minister and claimed that ministers pay M.P.s for votes of confidence on a regular basis. See *Bangkok Post,* 1 April 1990, 3.

22. The opportunities for patronage are based on the budget of the ministry, the number of employees, control over state enterprises, and the role of the ministry in granting licenses, concessions, and permits to business and individuals. (The Ministry of Commerce, for example, has the smallest budget but controls export quotas and is thus sought after.) Bidhya 2001 provides rankings of the desirability of various ministries before the recent bureaucratic reform.

23. After the 1988 election, for example, 121 were appointed. See *Bangkok Post,* 21 October 1990, 7. Of the 121, 100 were M.P.s.

24. See *Bangkok Post,* 2 November 1988, 2. This article described the appointment of the latest group of 27 advisers, calling them a "growing army" and pointing out that one of them was on trial for attempting to smuggle some 10 million baht (400,000 U.S. dollars) worth of ivory out of the country. The next day the order to appoint this particular group of advisers was canceled without explanation. See *Bangkok Post,* 3 November 1988, 1.

25. There have also been frequent reports that high-level civil servants must buy important or lucrative positions. In a censure debate in parliament, one M.P. claimed that, for a policeman to be appointed inspector, he had to pay 3 million baht (120,000 U.S. dollars); for superintendent, 5 million baht; for commander, 7 million baht; and for police director-general, 50 million baht (2 million U.S. dollars); see *Bangkok Post,* 19 July 1990, 1. On the following day, Wasit Dechakhunthon, a retired high-level police officer admitted that positions had been bought "as recently as two years ago"; see *Bangkok Post,* 20 July 1990, 6. For a recent case, see *Krungthep Thurakit,* 3 April 2003; *Bangkok Post,* 29 March 2003, 4 April 2003; *Nachun Sutsapda,* 7 April 2003.

26. The Election Commission (EC) called new elections in sixty-two constituencies, so these numbers changed before the results were certified. Even after the results were certified, the EC continued to investigate charges of vote buying, declaring that it would disqualify sitting members of the House for a period of up to three and a half years after the election.

I have used the list of M.P.s initially certified, together with the additional party list M.P.s who took the places of those who joined the cabinet.

27. In the 1990s, the proportion of reelected M.P.s ranged from 67 to 84% of seats, with the 84% in 1996 marking the highest proportion ever. Turnover was higher in the 1980s.

28. By my count, which is likely incomplete, at least thirty-four new M.P.s are relatives of current or former M.P.s, and at least a dozen are close aides.

29. The initial election was followed by several more to replace those disqualified for violating election laws.

30. The number of parties with more than 20 seats in each election since the restoration of democracy in 1979 is as follows: 1979:5; 1983:4; 1986:5; 1988:6; 1992a:6; 1992b:6; 1995:6; 1996:6; 2001:5. The increasing size of the parliament makes this number a somewhat arbitrary figure. However, 20 seats have generally been enough to make a party attractive as a coalition partner. The large expansion of the parliament in 2001 also fits well with this division, as all parties with 20 or more seats managed to secure party list seats, widening the gap between the two categories. The smallest of the parties with more than 20 seats in 2001 had 29; the largest party with fewer than 20 seats had 14. The number of parties with fewer than 20 members has declined throughout the last decade. In 2001, only 8 parties won seats, and 2 of those won only 1 seat each.

31. *Bangkok Post*, 30 January 2001, internet edition.

32. Reports of vote buying, including detailed descriptions, appeared on an almost daily basis in the Thai and English-language press during the election campaign. A good summary is *Bangkok Post* (Perspective), 14 January 2001, 1, 3.

33. Interview, December 2000.

34. *Bangkok Post* (Perspective), 14 January 2001, 1.

35. The Thai Farmers Bank research report is vol. 6, no. 68, 28 December 2000, and the Thai Farmers Bank web site is http://www.tfb.co.th. The research report is summarized in the "Insider" column of *Bangkok Post*, 4 January 2001, B10. The calculation comes from "Insider" as well.

36. Riker (1962). Ben Anderson originally pointed this out to me over a decade ago. Note that in theory the minimum winning coalition is half the total number of seats in parliament plus one. In practice, however, the minimum winning coalition has been somewhat larger, since the continuing loyalty of factions and faction members cannot be assured.

37. The struggle over cabinet seats is discussed in some detail in the Thai and English-language press. See, for example, the internet editions of *Nation*, 16 February 2001; 23 January 2001; 18 February 2001; and *Bangkok Post*, 17 February 2001; 18 February 2001. See also Nelson 2002.

38. In addition to Thaksin himself, whose family corporation controls AIS, party list M.P. and Minister of Commerce Adisai Bodharamik's family corporation controls TT&T, and party list MP Veerachai Veeramethikul is the son-in-law of the founder of Charoen Pokphand group, which controls Wireless Communication Service, CP Orange, Telecom-Asia, and Bitco, and formerly supported the New Aspiration party (see *Bangkok Post*, 9 January 2001; 19 February 2001; 20 February 2001). When TRT won the election, telecommunication stocks immediately jumped in value.

39. Nuannoi and Nophanan 2002:80. The proposal to reform the telecommunications

sector was initiated by the previous government, to bring policy into line with WTO-mandated changes. However, earlier proposals would have been revenue neutral for the government.

40. Another example of this kind of legalized state patronage is the Thai Asset Management Corporation. Senator Karoon Sai-ngam claimed that the government would be taking on 300 billion baht in bad loans, including debt from Shinawatra Thai (with 1.7 billion baht in debts), run by the family of Thaksin, Thai Telephone & Telecommunications (with 44 billion baht in debts), run by the family of Commerce Minister Adisai Bodharamik, and various other politically connected firms; see *Bangkok Post*, 15 September 2001. After that time, the mandate of the TAMC was expanded.

41. These events were widely reported in the Thai press at the time. For example, see *Bangkok Post*, 31 August 2001, 8 September 2001; *Perspective*, 16 September 2001. The new constitution contributed to this crisis by excluding sitting constituency M.P.s from cabinet positions.

42. Attempts to increase patronage have also been evident in the bureaucratic reform, which created six new ministries (an increase from 14 to 20), and in the decision to appoint "assistant ministers."

43. For the impact of the crisis on Thailand, see Pasuk and Baker 2000. For a good summary of the contemporary economy see Jarvis 2002. While reports of donations to political parties in the middle of a term are not a good indicator, and must be treated very skeptically, they are nevertheless interesting. According to Election Commission statistics, in the year 2000, the year prior to the election, Thai Rak Thai reported donations of 304,409,954 baht as compared to 148,942,702 for the Democrat party. In the first five months of 2003, the Democrat party raised 10,234,034 to 15,492,400 for Thai Rak Thai. So the gap in funding reported has narrowed somewhat, at least temporarily. See www.ect.go.th.

44. Reports thus far have been mixed. Opposition party M.P. Nipit Intarasombat claimed that, "household debt, especially farmers', had increased by an average 8,184 baht last year, while Shin Corp's revenue had risen from 5.5 billion baht in 2001 to 15.2 billion baht last year [2002]" (*Bangkok Post*, 13 March 2003, 3). The government prefers to point to the economic growth rate, forecast to reach 6% in 2003. The National Economic and Social Development Board reported that the unemployment rate in rural areas had dropped below the rate in urban areas by 2003, and that household income had risen by 9.8% (*Bangkok Post*, 28 June 2003).

45. In the 1970s, Kitsangkhom (Social Action party) promoted similar village-based funds, also with considerable success. Advocating policies that directly benefited rural people was possible for the Social Action party because it had no provincial notables holding seats at the time it developed the policies.

46. I thank Sunh Arunrugstichai for providing this information.

47. According to the 1990 Population and Housing Census, in rural areas, just 38.6% owned a color television. Some 26.2% owned a black-and-white television, with some households no doubt owning both, so that the total must be less than the sum of the two categories combined. By the time of the 2000 Population and Housing Census, 88.7% of rural households owned a television (black-and-white and color television sets were combined into a single category in the 2000 census).

48. One particularly interesting campaign, just under way at the time this manuscript went to press, is that to suppress "dark influences." Since many provincial notables could be so classified, this campaign may be an attempt to erode the power of the factions. If past experience and preliminary reports prove accurate in forecasting the results, the attack will fall largely on Thai Rak Thai's competitors. In the initial list of provinces with the highest reported number of influential figures, three of the top four were provinces where Democrat party members held the most seats, including Nakhon Sithammarat, where the Democrats swept all 10 seats, and Trang, home province of former Prime Minister Chuan Leekphai. For the 15 provinces with 21 or more influential figures reported, 21.5% (28/130) of all Democrat party M.P.s were affected; just 15% (45/294) of Thai Rak Thai M.P.s were affected. While this was only the preliminary list, it did raise suspicions. See *Bangkok Post,* 21 May 2003.

49. In order to become a cabinet minister, Thaksin had to divest, so the ownership is now with the family conglomerate.

50. The best work on the electronic media is Ubonrat 2001. On the press, see McCargo 2000. Some specific examples of attempts to exert influence are described in "Muting the Messenger" (*Nation,* 20 August 2001). The impact on contemporary television is nicely described by "Chang Noi" in *Nation,* 18 March 2002. "The TV space once filled by information, criticism, and debate now hosts more game shows, entertainment magazines, and football. The decline of serious social dramas makes way for tales about family-inheritance disputes featuring huge fortunes, gory bullet-ridden deaths, and male villains who abuse women. Flicking across TV channels one night at drama time, Chang Noi found two scenes of women being beaten and one rape. While this dark age lasts, the citizens will switch off their brains, sit back, and enjoy sex, violence, and farce."

51. Organic laws established along with the constitution also mandate increased levels of basic free education, an important structural change that may eventually bring about change. However, an assumption was made that more educated M.P.s and voters would be less susceptible to patronage politics, which may not be correct. Furthermore, thus far educational reforms have been stymied by powerful interests.

Chapter 3. Women and Leadership

1. Nantanee 1977:25, table 10, reported that in two villages surveyed, 71 percent of respondents reported that women controlled family finances, with another 12 percent of houses where responsibility was shared. In only 8 percent did the husband control finances. (Note, however, as Nantanee did, that in the case of families who are on the edge of starvation, this entails responsibility and anguish rather than power.)

2. *Bangkok Post,* 8 March 2003, outlook section, page 1, provides some additional figures.

3. Richter and Bencha 1992:1–2 pointed to rural-to-urban migration as an important factor in changing the roles and status of women. Also important, according to Richter and Bencha, are lower fertility rates, delayed marriage, and increased employment outside the homes and fields.

4. Juree 1994:518 addressed this same paradox of clinging to family and tradition in

the midst of change in similar terms: "Living in an alien setting among unfamiliar faces with people whose norms and life situations differ from their own motivates migrants to look to their family members and kinfolk for comfort and support." She also noted that migrants often form fictive kinship relations with other migrants.

5. According to Reynolds 1999:565–566, "Nearly half (9 out of 22) of the women [who became leaders of their countries in the 1980s and 1990s] were either the wives or daughters of former national leaders and, of these, only [two] were not assassinated."

6. This approach will omit some relationships, since it does not account for women M.P.s who have taken the surnames of their spouses. Data are through February 2001, based on parliamentary and Ministry of Interior records.

7. To take a few more examples, the father of Poonsuk Lohachot of Nan province was an M.P. Sisakun Techaphaibun of Nakhon Sithamarat is married to an M.P; her older brother is also an M.P. Siripan Jurimat of Roi-et is the niece of an M.P. and has a brother who is also an M.P. Karuna Chitchop, Mukda Phongsombat, Mayura Uraken, and Charinrat Wongchai are all married to politicians. See *Bangkok Post,* 29 August 1988:31; *Nation,* 19 November 1996.

8. Since small families are now the norm in Thailand, this criterion does not distinguish women M.P.s from other women.

9. There are women who are possible candidates, including Sudarat Keyuraphan, a leader of the Bangkok M.P.s in the Thai Rak Thai party, Paweena Hongsakun, secretary-general of Chat Phatthana, and perhaps Suphatra Masadit of the Democrat party, whose time may have passed.

10. Juree 1994 briefly discussed the same phenomenon in the Thai context, arguing that because women do not have direct access to power, they learn techniques of exercising power indirectly through their husbands.

11. Siti Hartinah Suharto reportedly played a similar role in kinship politics in Indonesia. According to the *New York Times,* 16 January 1998, D5, Suharto's "closest confidante through most of his presidency was his wife, Siti Hartinah Suharto, and many Indonesians believe that her death two years ago at age 76 explains many of the recent excesses of the family's business empire. While she controlled businesses of her own, Mrs. Suharto was seen as the family's umpire and peacekeeper, and she was known to veto risky business ventures by her children that might tarnish her husband's reputation."

12. Reynolds 1999 provided some statistical support for this approach to understanding women and leadership, which, of course, is not new. He concluded (1999:572): "Democracy in itself is not necessarily a precursor to the presence of substantial numbers of women in political life. Rather, the determining factors are a nation's familiarity with women in positions of power and the sociopolitical acceptance of women as leaders, governors, and national administrators. Religious practices and ideological movements help determine the baseline for women. . . ."

13. The interview with Chodchoy Soponphanich was conducted in English at her request. All the other interviews were conducted in Thai.

14. Interviewed, 29 January 1997, at Sangsan Thai Foundation, Bangkok Bank headquarters.

15. Chodchoy mentioned some specific problems, including the use of "Mrs." for all

married women, the need for married women to secure their husband's consent for legal transactions, and various other difficulties surrounding divorce, names, and the title Mrs.

16. *Bangkok Post,* 22 November 1999, reveals her intention to run for the senate as part of an effort by NGOs to play a greater role in Thai parliamentary politics.

17. Chodchoy avoided two major obstacles: access to capital and promotion to the top. She founded her own company, and so never had to worry about a glass ceiling. As the daughter of the richest man in Thailand at the time, she could found the company and never had to worry about financing or access to elite circles.

18. It is not surprising that networking was easy for the daughter of the richest woman in Thailand. Networking with Chodchoy would be potentially advantageous for anyone.

19. Interviewed on 15 January 1997, at parliament. I have supplemented the interview notes in a few places with Suphatra's comments in published interviews, especially *Ekonniw* 5 (17 February 1995): 42–43, and *Phraeo* 10 (25 January 1989): 124–134, as noted below.

20. Suphatra had discussed this with many M.P.s from all regions and from many parties, and had come to this conclusion. She added that women usually work at the lowest levels, below the village leaders. Teachers comprise one of the main groups. Female *hua khanaen,* she said, are more common in the Democrat party and in the south.

21. Interviewed at the Duang Prateep Foundation, 20 January 1997. Some additional background information comes from two Duang Prateep Foundation publications, "A Window on the Slums," and "Munnithi Duang Prateep chak wan nan . . . thung wanni . . . phua kansuksa khong dek yak con lae khon yakrai . . . nai sangkhom" (Duang Prateep Foundation from that day . . . until this day . . . for the education of poor children and the poor . . . in society).

22. Chodchoy and Suphatra have often made speeches on women and leadership, and their ideas were quite coherent and polished. Pratheep had spoken mostly on behalf of the poor, and Arunee on behalf of labor, and their opinions on women and leadership were less polished. I found their answers more interesting but more difficult to put in coherent order. It is thus important to see these ideas as separate comments and not give undue weight to their prioritization. Kim Haw had probably thought less about this topic than the others, and her opinions were less developed.

23. Pratheep's phrasing was ambiguous here. It was not clear whether a male lack of understanding of social issues was a consequence of lack of attention to detail. Also in the interview, she pointed out that, while many women are good at details, she (a successful leader) is not.

24. Interviewed in the labor union office at Thai Krieng textile factory on 21 January 1997.

25. According to my interview notes, Arunee said she finished only *po.* 4, or four years of education. According to *Thamniap satri phunam kanplianplaeng* (Register of women leaders of change; Bangkok: Gender and Development Institute, 1996), 122, Arunee finished *mo.* 3, which would be seven years of education. It may be that the last three years came as an adult.

26. That treasurer is on this list of low-level positions indicates how little money was involved. It also may indicate, as mentioned above, that women were trusted in business, sometimes even above men.

27. Interviewed at her pier in Ban Phe on 23 January 1997.

28. For some critical analysis of Suphatra and her spouse, see *Bangkok Post,* 30 August 1999 and 28 December 1998. Suphatra's husband is Lieutenant General Pathompong Kesornsuk, an army general. While it is impossible to know whether he has benefited, his rise has not been that rapid or high, especially when compared to that of Chaisith Shinawatra, the cousin of Prime Minister Thaksin. At one point Pathompong held the post of assistant army chief of staff for civil affairs, not a particularly important position, but one with considerable potential for advancement. On his future prospects, see *Bangkok Post,* 4 March 2003, 3.

29. This criticism is particularly odd in the case of Prateep. In effect, she is being accused of using slum dwellers to further her career. This ignores the fact that her increased status benefits the slum dwellers by attracting attention to their problems—even if we ignore all the concrete things she has done for them. In other words, advancing Prateep's career *is* in their interest.

30. At the same time, this is the kind of claim any good politician makes, so perhaps it only reveals political astuteness rather than an attempt to appear to conform to stereotypes.

Chapter 4. From *Nakleng* to *Jaopho*

1. A limited social security act was promulgated in 1990. However, initially it covered only about 10 percent of workers, nearly all in urban areas. Expansion was slow in the 1990s, especially with the arrival of the financial crisis. See Reinecke 1993 for details of the act.

2. The movie *The Godfather* came out in 1972. I will discuss the economic and political changes of the period and the rise of this social group later. Originally, the noun *jaopho* referred to a type of guardian spirit who was responsible for a limited geographical area. Phasuk Phongpaichit has pointed out that the word *"jaopho"* might have origins in this term. Although this is partly true, the term was used but rarely to describe criminals before the 1970s, and *jaopho* in the modern usage does not have the connotations we might expect if its origins lay in the realm of often benevolent guardian spirits. There are some resonances with the old meaning, yet the modern one is "godfather" and is applied equally to the Italian mafia and to Thai criminal figures. The word "godfather" is sometimes transliterated into Thai as well, having the same meaning as *jaopho.* (The positive meaning of the English "godfather" is translated differently [*pho thun hua*].) In the past, *jaopho* were usually referred to as *nakleng,* and later as *phu mi itthiphon* (influential persons, a term still common), *itthiphon mued* (dark influences), or *itthiphon thuen* (illegal influences). News articles of the past would refer to the leader of a criminal group by his nickname. The word *kaeng* ("gang" transliterated) was also used quite frequently. In the north, the term *"pholiang"* (stepfather) is used to refer to *jaopho* in a somewhat more positive way. More recently there has been a broadening of the meaning of the term *"jaopho"* to include any powerful individual, such as a cabinet minister, whose style resembles that of a godfather.

3. The two quotes used by Johnston are from *Bangkok Times,* 26 May 1898, 21–22.

4. For a good indication of how this attitude has persisted, especially in the south, see "Policeman Challenges Bandit to Gun Duel," *Bangkok Post,* 6 July 1991, 1: "The police chief inspector of Muang District [Yala Province] has challenged a separatist movement leader

to a gun duel. Pol Lt-Col Niyom Anpruang issued the challenge after the bandit leader sent letters to businessmen demanding protection money. Pol Lt-Col Niyom responded to the threats by posting two public billboards written in the Yawi language. The police inspector challenged Samaae Thanam . . . to a duel with pistols." In this case, the police officer sought to protect his own by issuing a personal challenge.

5. Johnston 1980:94 quotes from *Bangkok Times,* 25 April 1913, 3, "it is said that Ai Pia [a *nakleng*] was a kind of Robin Hood, robbing only the rich and often helping the poor."

6. Many emphasize the importance of these threats. A police colonel in Bangkok explained to me that since the central government could not police the villages, the people were forced to rely on the village headmen—who were themselves the crooks. Threats included theft, arson, and violence. Though he was unclear about the specific historical era, he believed that this lay behind the rise of *jaopho* and their participation in politics today. This change in their nature toward greater violence is discussed below.

7. These societies were "secret" only in the content of the bylaws and oaths. The leaders and members were, for the most part, publicly known. See Supharat 1981:28.

8. The first official reference to the secret societies comes in 1824 with the report of a conflict between two societies in Chantaburi; see Supharat 1981:33–34. Supharat believes that the secret societies probably existed at least by the time of Rama II (1809–1824).

9. Supharat (1981) argued that the secret societies were not involved in fixing the rates of the tax farms because she was unable to identify known secret society leaders as tax farmers. That known secret society leaders cannot be identified as openly involved does not preclude their actual involvement, and Hong's argument is convincing.

10. Skinner 1957:141 referred to at least six by 1889.

11. There were also riots in 1895 and 1910. At least one of these riots, that in 1889, resulted directly from a conflict between two secret societies over the supply of labor to three large rice mills, wrote Skinner. Supharat described the event that sparked the riot as a conflict between members of two secret societies but agreed that the underlying cause was the control of labor (Skinner 1957:207–212).

12. This is the apt though not quite literal translation given by Thak 1979. (He gives the literal translation as "horsemen.")

13. See Chit n.d. [1960?]:305–334 for the record of the trial of a policeman who was convicted of killing one of Phao's enemies. The trial was completed after Phao had fled the country.

14. On economic growth, see, e.g., Anderson 1977:13–30, which discusses the development and its effect on class structure; Plai-oh 1987 for details on a somewhat longer period in the north; Pasuk and Baker 1995 and Ockey 1992:chap. 3. The connections between economic growth, democracy, and the rise of the *jaopho* are outlined in Anderson 1990:33–48.

15. For a fascinating look at this process, see Anonymous 1991. While the accuracy of this source cannot be assessed, the story that is told fits remarkably well with the argument outlined by Arlacchi. The protagonist, son of a poor peasant, is introduced by his uncle to the don of a small Mafia family in the early 1950s, where he works for wages during a time of widespread unemployment. The don provides a job on his estate to the nephew of a friend, as a good patron should. We then follow the protagonist as he becomes a hitman, as his Mafia family is wiped out by a newly prominent mafioso who has no respect for the old

ways, then through other Mafia families as a semi-independent gunman, while each family falls to the new, ruthless, entrepreneurial Mafia. We also see as key to the new Mafia the importance of access to government contracts, especially construction contracts, and the growth of the drug trade. Arlacchi is cited in some of the explanatory notes.

16. In fact, the distinction between *nakleng* and *jaopho* today includes both the concept of "honor" and the amount of the stakes being contested.

17. The political activities of Kamnan W. are covered in greater detail in Ockey 1992: chap. 5. Unless otherwise noted, this information comes from interview data.

18. Interview with a government official who requested anonymity. Note that even his enemies do not accuse him of running gambling dens or smuggling narcotics. He *has* been accused of fixing construction bids. *Thairat,* 11 May 1989, 23, and *Matichon,* 12 May 1989, 21, both discuss corruption in bidding practices for development funds in Phichit at the time the governor was moved, although neither identifies a particular culprit.

19. He was a member of parliament in 1975 and 1976 for the Phatthana Changwat party.

20. Although I do not wish to read too much into a business card, the implications of the card are in line with the importance he attaches to this position of *kamnan.* Below his name it reads "Kamnan, Tambon Hua Dong, Muang District, Phichit Province," and only below that does it list his business title at the finance company. Equally interesting, his Bangkok address is listed first, which explains the need for the district and the province of Hua Dong. But surely if Kamnan W. is handing out business cards in Bangkok, it is because of his finance company and not his position of *kamnan?*

21. One even went so far as to say that M.P.s paid bribes to Kamnan W. in order to ensure his support, and that those who wished to be reelected had to vote as he asked.

22. See the front-page article in the local newspaper *Banrao,* 16 June 1989. Kamnan W. provided me with a copy of the petition, which was submitted by a former provincial councilor and several members of the Hua Dong Tambon Council. It outlined the reasons why the recipient was not worthy to receive the award and described in detail the decision-making process, attributing what should have been privileged information to a "reliable source." What is interesting here is the importance Kamnan W. attached to winning this award. His motive was not power or money but prestige.

23. This word, usually rendered as "lineage," means family in its broadest sense, including all relatives, ancestors, and descendants who share the family name. Honor for the family name takes on a deeper meaning, of course, where ancestral worship is an important element of culture.

24. Equally interesting is the expansion to Bangkok in finance and retail trade.

25. Mr. C.K. denies being a *jaopho.* In his own words, "'If you call me a *jaopho,* I'm not.'" The interviewer then summarizes: "[Mr. C.K.] said that a *real jaopho* is a person who has died yet many people remember him and come to pay their respects, adding that he prefers to be considered a *jaopho* in that sense." This is a reference to the old meaning of *jaopho* as a guardian spirit, and the need to invoke this image demonstrates just how much the definition has changed. He then acknowledged the new definition, adding, "'You must understand that I am not a person who keeps hired gunmen to kill people or make money from drug trafficking or employ people to undertake criminal activity'"; see *Bangkok Post,*

14 April 1991, 9. C.K. refers to himself as a *naksu,* a "fighter"; see *Khao krong,* 21 June 1990, 16. More recently, he reinforced this same point of view, "I am not a mafia. I am only a gentleman who is never afraid of anything"; *Bangkok Post* (Perspective), 17 December 2000, 6.

26. In this interview, Mr. C.K. says that from the age of eight he knew Khukrit. Elsewhere, he has said he came to know Khukrit in 1975 when he helped campaign for him. He would have been thirty-one in 1975. See *Matichon sutsapda,* 21 August 1988, 5. I have followed the more recent (which is also the more detailed) explanation here.

27. Mr. C.K. has consistently denied involvement in narcotics, robberies, and killings, and has even denied employing gunmen (e.g., see *Matuphum raisapda,* 24 June 1991, 45). However, as Paul Handly put it, "[Mr. C.K.] made headlines in April 1990 when four of his men shot and nearly killed Charoen Pattanadamrongkit, known as Sia Leng, the top godfather of the northeast"; *Far Eastern Economic Review,* 18 April 1991, 28. He says of his rivals, "Those who are influential [i.e., *jaopho*] know that I do not like drugs and therefore I will not help them" (*Bangkok Post,* 14 April 1991, 9). The implications of his statement are that other Bangkok *jaopho* do smuggle narcotics but that he does not. All *jaopho* strenuously deny any role in drug trafficking—perhaps due in part to U.S. pressure on the Thai government to arrest traffickers.

28. As the *Bangkok Post,* 14 April 1991, 9, put it, "[C.K.] said he is a person who does not say much, adding that 'if you can't understand what I, one of few words, say then force would have to be used.'"

29. One prime example: "I am a *lukphuchai,* certainly. There are many people who love me, I am a person with many friends. I have never been arrogant with anyone. And I have never backed down to anyone." *Matuphum raisapda,* 24 June 1991, 45.

30. C.K. has denied any role in the narcotics trade in almost every interview he has given, which would suggest that rumors, at least, persisted.

31. One of the products sold was a rust protectant from the United States. See *Khao krong,* 21 June 1990, 13.

32. Like C.K., Mayor S. said the *jaopho* is dead; however, he was not referring to the old meaning of *jaopho* but rather to his predecessor in Chonburi, Sia Jiew, who was killed in 1981; see *Prachachat Thurakit,* 20 April 1988, 31, *Matichon sutsapda,* 25 May 1986, 12. In a more recent interview, he stated: "I want to ask, what exactly does *jaopho* mean? Because I don't understand the true meaning. But for me, the villagers have called me that for a long time, so that I feel this word is quite ordinary. But actually, it began because I have a large group of friends. Wherever I go, I know everyone. When my friends come and ask for something, if I can help, I do. Usually, I will help every time. And the important thing is that when I speak with my friends I almost always use the words '*ku' 'mung'* [vulgar terms for 'I' and 'you']. The villagers hear me and think I am a *nakleng* or *phu mi itthiphon* [influential person], and call me *jaopho* of the eastern region." *Matuphum raisapda,* 18 August 1991, 6.

33. On the gambling, see the interview in *Matichon sutsapda,* 25 May 1986, 13, where he admitted to "playing" at Sia Jiew's gambling den for a six-month period.

34. Mayor S. has admitted to running the underground lottery, although he claimed to have given it up. As for smuggling, he denied any role in narcotics but conceded that sometimes he allowed friends to receive smuggled goods from abroad in his territory; see *Prachachat Thurakit,* 20 April 1988, 30. He also expanded into some of the same legitimate businesses as Sia Jiew, particularly real-estate development and the hotel industry.

35. He denies these allegations in *Prachachat thurakit,* 20 April 1988, 30.

36. Ibid.: "I am a prominent *hua khanaen,* wherever I go, I must help with everything." See also the interview with Charun Ngamphichet, one of the M.P.s supported by Mayor S., in *Lak thai,* 28 May 1990, 20: "People come and ask for help and [Mayor S.] helps them, for example, finds them work. . . . To his followers who are close to him, he gives them sales work, by giving them some of the whisky he distributes to sell. He doesn't take a profit. Whoever can make a profit, he gives them all of it. . . . From this point, when there is an election, [he] will ask help and everyone will help—and without asking for money from him."

37. Seri Temeyawet in *Sayamrat sapda wichan,* 27 May 1990, 9. He said that when the mayor wanted a license to distribute whisky in one area, he simply called and asked for it. He was given it immediately, even though the former distributor had held it for twenty years.

38. Mulder also discussed a second form of power that is immoral. This may help explain the distinction often made between "good" and "bad" *jaopho.* The "bad" *jaopho* is more prone to violence and inspires fear rather than respect. "The strongest emotions that [an immoral] power can expect to excite are reverent awe and fear *(kreengklua).* Yet to have the feeling of being protected may stimulate genuine feelings of loyalty and gratefulness..." (Mulder 1992a:18). Thus even a *jaopho* thought of in terms of immoral power could inspire loyalty among his core constituents. I emphasize the second type, those who can be thought to represent amoral power, since they more clearly exemplify the relationship between power and virtue.

39. It should be clear that *jaopho* react to circumstances and events, not to the underlying tensions, which they may not have even considered. The result, however, is the same.

40. This, of course, pushes the *jaopho* in the same direction taken by the *sia* and *nakleng* of the past, of protecting his own community and building up respect and the honor of his family *(trakun),* although not without some differences that will be outlined below.

41. The debate on the importance of patron–client ties and the erosion of those ties under the influence of the market is the theme of Scott 1976 and Popkin 1979. Although they have different views of many aspects of the patron–client relationship, both agree that the market breaks it down.

42. This transition has been portrayed in the movie *Salawin* (Salaween), which came out in 1993. Subtitled *Mu puen phak song* (The Gunman Part Two), the movie is about a father and son who are involved in smuggling timber into Thailand from Burma. The son is far more violent than his father, more concerned with accumulating wealth rapidly, and willing to take great risks to gain power. The son is cruel, vicious, ruthless, and ambitious. The father is polite, dignified, respected, concerned about the welfare of others—and deeply involved in illegal activities.

43. The necessity for good public relations is enhanced by the need for legitimacy in the national arena, as the economic concessions and contracts come from the national government and must be justified before a national audience. *Jaopho* do not need to grant interviews to local newspapers. They do, however, often control local papers and thus discourage potentially damaging investigations.

44. Of course, *jaopho* do engage in economic activities in their own village, but the real money is likely to be elsewhere. Ironically, the *nakleng* protected the community, whereas now the community protects the *jaopho,* who provides social security to individuals.

45. Naturally this has blurred the line between *jaopho* and legitimate business leader. *Jaopho* are business leaders, and business leaders who are not engaged in illegal activities may nevertheless be deeply involved in corruption in order to compete for contracts and concessions. The rather loose popular definition of *jaopho* often includes these corrupt business leaders who are not otherwise participating in illegal activities.

46. Mr. C.K. points out that his own area has an extremely low crime rate. He claims that, according to police statistics for the one thousand houses in his area, there were no thefts. See *Khao phiset*, 13 July 1988, 21.

Chapter 5. God Mothers, Good Mothers, Good Lovers, Godmothers

1. There is, however, a very good article on the role of women in political campaigns, a role that is also often filled by *jaopho*. See Fishel 1996.

2. The rapid expansion of capitalism may lead us to doubt whether this hierarchy is still operative, or if, indeed, it ever was true for the Sino-Thai who comprise many of the entrepreneurs, including criminal ones. This expansion and the consequent greater weight given to economic interests may have exerted greater influence and may explain some of the grumbling often heard about how much women have changed in recent years. Most of it, of course, is simply the ever-present desire for "the good old days."

3. When prostitutes are treated as subjects in literature, they are generally depicted as good-hearted and forced into such activities by evil people or by straitened circumstances. Perhaps the earliest and most noteworthy such novel is K Surankhanang (Kanha Wanthanaphat), *Ying khon chua* [The prostitute or, perhaps Unvirtuous woman], originally published in 1937. Keyes 1984:237, pointed out that prostitutes usually describe themselves in the same ways (see also Kirsch 1985:313). Rachael Harrison 1996, in her discussion of prostitutes in literature, observed that they cannot be seen to give birth, cannot become mothers and part of a family. This reticence surrounding family is also clear in the portrayals of *jaomae* I discuss.

4. De La Loubere (1986:75), who visited Siam in 1687–1688, wrote, "It must not be doubted after this, of what is reported of the Siamese who live in the Woods, to withdraw themselves from the Government, that they frequently rob the Passengers, yet without killing any."

5. See, for example, the case of Khlaeo Thanikun, a reputed Bangkok *jaopho* whose several minor wives made claims to his estate after he was assassinated (Thim ngan Khaosot 1991). I am aware of only one *jaopho* whose wife is visible—she has even been interviewed by the press—and who is portrayed as loyal to her.

6. In interviews conducted in January 1997 and presented in Chapter 3, both a leading woman member of parliament and a leading social activist described themselves to me as "*jai nakleng.*"

7. Earlier, *sua* were occasionally referred to as *jao pho* (godfathers) under the old meaning of the term, as powerful guardian spirits of a particular area. This usage was quite limited.

8. I have chosen for the sake of clarity to use "god father" for the guardian deity and "godfather" for the criminal leader. The two are identical in Thai. The same is true for "god mother" and "godmother."

9. For example, *Jaomae Lim Ko Niew* of Pattani (see *Phayakrut,* 15 April 1988, 32; *Warasan praisani* 43 [November 1986]: 44–49) and *Jaomae Soi Dokmak* (see *Chao krung* 27 [November 1977]: 132–135).

10. The Kuan Yin sect experienced a dramatic resurgence during the 1980s, especially among women in Bangkok. A large temple was built off Lat Phrao Road and later expanded. Kuan Yin amulets became commonplace. Interest spread well beyond the community of adherents, as Kuan Yin became the subject of books and articles in women's magazines and academic journals. For example, the story of Kuan Yin appeared in *Dichan* 13 (30 April 1989): 252–256, and a long serialized "historical novel" began with a factual account of Kuan Yin in the first issue of *Khunying* 1 (June 1995): 151–154. The best academic work on the Kuan Yin sect is Nitthi 1994.

11. While *je* literally means older sister, like other words meaning older, it may also be used to convey respect to someone who is not older.

12. There are references in criminal court records to women *nakleng.* I thank Tamora Loos for confirming this information and sharing some of the cases with me.

13. Police sources confirmed that they were aware of at least one woman gunhand in discussions in January 1997. Interestingly, in the original version of the 1970s-era movie *Mu puen* (The gun hand), in one scene a police officer shoots several masked members of a motorcycle gang. When the masks are removed, the gangsters prove to be women. The police department insisted that scene be cut from the movie. See Anderson 1990.

14. Interview with police in Bangkok, January 1997; interview with the crime editor of a Thai newspaper, January 1997. I do not refer to the sex workers, but to those who control them. Many of these women may be former prostitutes who have risen to power. A condition of that rise seems to be giving up prostitution, for a woman cannot sleep with men for money—that is, act as an object (of desire)—and be powerful, especially given the masculine connotations of the term "power."

15. The original interview appeared in *Khao sot,* 19 August 1997, 1, and 20 August 1997, 1. See also the Internet edition of *Nation,* 20 August 1997 and 22 August 1997.

16. There is a resemblance between the attitudes Oi. B. M. cultivated in her female employees and the ideals for proper behavior held by aristocratic men. See Khin Thitsa 1980:19.

17. In these three cases, as far as I can tell, the men led the women to power. There is much that is important about the character of women who are able to manage gambling dens under the protection of powerful men. In particular, it is interesting that these women can enter into chains of patron–client relations that are so male-dominated. Similarly, there is something compelling about those women who inherit a criminal role from a *jaopho* father or spouse, and are capable of holding it, even expanding it by imposing their will on male subordinates unused to obeying a woman. Those topics, however, must be left to future research, since here I focus on women who have built up their own power.

18. Share schemes, also called chit funds, are a common means of community-based finance in Thailand. Generally, each member of the scheme contributes the same amount to the fund each month. Then all members who have not yet used the fund bid for the right to use it that month. The bid serves as interest on the fund and is divided only among those who have not yet used the fund, so that those who wait the longest profit the most. The organizer is responsible for handling the money and the bidding, for recruiting members,

and for ensuring that all contributors meet their obligations. There are many variants to this basic pattern. In Chamoi's fund, individuals bought into the scheme at fixed amounts. They were paid interest each month that they left their money in the hands of Chamoi, who was responsible for investing it. They could withdraw at any time and retrieve their initial investment. Thus Chamoi's scheme functioned in a manner similar to an informal share market, paying much higher interest (6.5 percent per month, or 75 percent per year) than a bank or most stocks. The scheme was organized, not coincidentally, at a time when the Stock Exchange of Thailand was still fairly new and many trust companies were unreliable, and it catered initially to middle-class elements and the wealthy.

19. The information in this paragraph is drawn primarily from "Chamoi Thipso wira-satri ru satan kan nae" [Chamoi Thipso, a heroine or a Satan?] *Phujatkan rai duan* 5 (August 1985): 33–37.

20. *Jaopho* who wish to become public figures also have to portray themselves in various specific ways, in particular as benefactors (the generous side of the *nakleng* character); but not, generally speaking, as "gentlemen."

21. The assertion was made in the columns of his newspaper, *Sayamrat,* 15 November 1983, 1, 12. See also *Krung Thep '30* 3 (December 1988): 52.

22. *Matichon,* 8, 9, 12, 14, 15, 16 September 1984. Some worried that the Thai Military Bank itself was vulnerable to a collapse of the pyramid scheme, since many officers had gone into debt to the bank to get money to invest in it. A director of the Thai Military Bank (an army general) announced that provisions had been made to prevent such an occurrence. Rumors persisted right up through her arrest that senior military leaders were protecting her to ensure that military officers got their investments back at the expense of other investors. (*Nation,* 23 June 1985, reports a "senior army officer" as saying that "armed forces personnel would get back a large part of their investment and doubted that her promise to pay other clients would be realized." For denials of the rumors, see *Deli Niu,* 28 June 1985, 1, 16; *Nation,* 28 June 1985, 1.)

23. Trial Number 7423/2528. The trial results are summarized and discussed in *Matichon,* 28 July 1985, 3, 21.

24. Unless otherwise noted, the information on Kim Haw comes from a long interview with her in her office at her pier in Ban Phe on 23 January 1997, and from conversations with her "executive secretary," a newspaperman who arranged the appointment and spent most of the day showing me around Ban Phe.

25. "Outstanding Entrepreneur," *GWG Newsletter,* Special Issue, March 1994, 6. This is the newsletter of the Gender Watch Group, Gender and Development Research Institute, Bangkok. The special issue profiles the winners of the institute's Outstanding Women awards for 1994.

26. *GWG Newsletter,* Special Issue, March 1994, 6, put the number of boats at sixty, and total employees at six hundred. In January 1997, Kim Haw told me that she did not know the exact number, but that it had to be over one hundred. The son of her executive secretary estimated that Kim Haw was involved in 80 percent of all the businesses in Ban Phe.

27. *Prachathai,* 1–15 November 1996, 2, has a full-page article on the campaign, where the focus is on Kim Haw and her promotion of her brother's candidacy.

28. Ibid., 1. This is apparently a second printing of this issue (same date and issue number) that varies from the first, which was also given to me. The story may well employ journalistic license.

29. Information on Ubon Bunyachalothon is summarized from several months of press clippings from both Thai and English-language newspapers. For biographical material, I have relied most on her own account, "Pa mai phit . . . Pa mai dai tham" [I am not guilty . . . I didn't do it] *Phujatkan rai sapda*, 26 August 1996, 33, 34, 36. Other important biographical articles include: "Poet chiwit sut phitsadan jaomae withayu" [The most detailed exposé of the life of the Radio Station Godmother], *Thansetthakit*, 22 May 1996, 1, 16, 17; and Siri Nuson, "Ubon Bunyachalothon," *Matichon*, 28 April 1996, 9.

30. *Phujatkan rai sapda*, 26 August 1996, 33. *Thansetthakit*, 22 May 1996, 16, claims she arrived in Bangkok about 1976, with a "chunk" of money gained through some unknown "crooked shortcut." *Thairat*, 14 May 1996, 23 states that by her own account she finished her schooling in Samsuk, then moved to Bangkok. Since her years in Phrakhanong slum are described in detail in the interview, and since *Phujatkan* seems to have checked on her story, I have followed her/their version.

31. *Phujatkan rai sapda*, 26 August 1996, 33, which depicts her as a "red-faced moneylender." Moneylenders are generally not popular in slum communities, and the job is usually shunned due to the resulting unpopularity and the difficulty of collecting loans; see Akin 1975:127–128. It is not the kind of thing a *nakleng* would do, and certainly not in the contractual manner that Ubon employed.

32. At the time, according to the interview, she had recently pawned her television set to survive. It seems unlikely that a moneylender would give 80,000 baht to someone who rented a house in a slum, had no gold or silver, and had just pawned her television set. This is reminiscent of the unexplained money mentioned in *Thansetthakit*, 22 May 1996, 16. The source of Ubon's original capital has been the subject of many rumors and remains a mystery.

33. *Phujatkan rai sapda*, 26 August 1996, 34. This assertion is surprising, as Phalang Mai was a left-wing party, and in the 1980s Ubon was a strong supporter of promilitary parties and of Prime Minister General Suchinda Kraprayun, who was responsible for the massacre of prodemocracy protestors in May of 1992.

34. *Phujatkan rai sapda*, 26 August 1996, mistakenly dates Ubon's support of General Rawi to the 1988 election. In 1986, General Rawi received 30,919 votes. He would have needed 41,398 to have placed third and won election in the three-member election district; see Krasuang mahatthai, Krom kanpokkhrong, Kong kanluaktang, *Raingan wichai kanluaktang samachik sapha phuthaen ratsadon pho. so. 2529* [Research report on the election of members of the House of Representatives, 1986] (Bangkok: n.d. [1986]):387. General Rawi did not run in Yasothon in 1988. *Matichon*, 28 April 1996, 9, also confused these two elections, asserting that Ubon ran for Puang Chon Chao Thai in 1988, and that General Rawi was then head of the party. In 1988, General Athit Kamlang-ek was the leader of Puang Chon Chao Thai, and Ubon ran for the Ruam Thai party.

35. Narong Wongwan was a longtime politician and alleged *jaopho* from Phrae in the north. In 1992, he became the leader of the promilitary Sammakkhitham party, which Ubon joined as well. When Sammakkhitham won the most seats in the election, Narong expected

to be named the new prime minister. At that point the U.S. State Department issued a statement claiming it had evidence that Narong was involved in smuggling narcotics, and that the United States would be forced to reevaluate its relationship with Thailand if he were named prime minister. His candidacy was withdrawn, General Suchinda was named prime minister, and prodemocracy uprisings began shortly thereafter.

36. *Thansetthakit,* 22 May 1996, 17. See also *Thairat,* 12 May 1996, 15, which also mentions the incident and adds that "this *jaomae* has a history of violence" with those who have gotten in the way of her or her family, often meeting with suspicious accidents.

37. *Phujatkan rai sapda,* 26 August 1996, 34. The word I have translated as "firm" *(detkat)* can also be translated as "absolute."

38. Thawi has run for parliament in many elections in district two of Chiang Rai but has only been elected once, in 1992, when he was with Sammakkhitham. He was married to Ubon's daughter Konkanok.

39. *Phujatkan rai sapda,* 26 August 1996, 34. The significance of reference to this powerful image and its relationship to gender is discussed in relation to amulets below.

40. This is Ubon's version of the story. According to *Sayam post,* 15 May 1996, 2, this was the third time she had tried to present him with a gift.

41. See *Phujatkan rai sapda,* 26 August 1996, 33, which states that she sometimes called herself *mae.* All the quotes here and elsewhere use *pa,* however—perhaps an unconscious attempt by journalists to avoid calling Ubon *mae.*

42. She did mention that, when she learned she was being called a *jaomae,* she wanted to both laugh and cry; see *Matichon,* 17 May 1996, 2. She did not entirely neglect the possibility of appealing to femininity, but seems in most cases to raise it yet also to negate it, as with the comment that she wanted to cry but also to laugh, or when she said to *Bangkok Post,* 15 August 1996, "I'm not an influential figure [another (nongendered) term for *jaopho*] but an ordinary old woman who has been divorced for ten years." Why the need to add that she has been divorced for ten years to that statement other than to separate herself from her sex?

43. The discussion took place on 28 January 1997.

44. Various discussions in December 1996 and January 1997.

45. Montesano wrote of a market society that is Sino-Thai and generational, consisting of those who came to Thailand after World War I. He pointed out that it was the first generation where women migrated in substantial numbers, with their families.

46. Or even a monarch. In an interview, the late Khukrit Pramot, aristocrat and former premier, remarked: "Well, if a princess ascends the throne, she'll become a male. . . . She will not be a goddess, she will be a god. . . . If you are the *Phra Chao Yu Hua* [monarch], you can do anything. You see, sex will be gone." See Vilas and Van Beek 1983:200.

47. I cannot resist a brief note on the opposite phenomenon, a female-in-male form, for which I quote from "Transvestite Slugger Snatches Manly Points Win at Lumpini," *Bangkok Post,* 28 February 1998: "A transvestite boxer created a stir at Lumpini Stadium last night when he refused to strip for a weigh-in as required by regulations. Parinya Kiatbusaba, tears rolling down his cheeks, complained: 'The rule is unacceptable. How can I strip in public?' Mr Parinya . . . wears make-up, lipstick and a hair-band to keep flowing hair in place . . . Pongsak (Oven) Sor Bunma, his opponent, who has seen 28 fights in his career, said the bewitching smile would not distract him. 'I will not be shaken by his smile. I will

give him a big lesson so that he will learn that Thai boxing is the game of a real man,' Mr Pongsak said."

48. When prominent Bangkok godfather Khlaeo Thanikun was killed, news articles on his many mistresses proved so popular that *Khaosot* newspaper republished its articles in a booklet. See also n. 5 above.

Chapter 6. Eviction and Changing Roles of Leadership in Bangkok Slum Communities

1. The Assembly of the Poor has also been known as the Forum of the Poor, particularly in its early days.

2. Yap's data indicate that 65% of those living in congested communities were born in Bangkok.

3. Yap gives a total for the Bangkok Metropolitan Region of 1,098,500.

4. Somsook 1983:271: "Communities from which people are being evicted have been in existence for thirty to forty years on average." My own research indicates that this estimate is still accurate, perhaps even a bit low, if temporary communities such as those under overpasses are excluded.

5. Yap 1992:31 gives detailed figures. Kankheha 1997:31, currently the most recent full survey, gives these figures for communities in Bangkok: of 843 total congested communities, 251 have rental agreements, 152 are squatters, and the rest are on their own land. Since many communities have a mixture of arrangements, it is not clear how these numbers are calculated. Unofficial NHA figures, which are reported by districts and subject to inaccuracies, indicate that there were 1,226 congested communities comprising 249,822 households as of 14 December 2000 (no population figure is given); data provided by the NHA, Division of Slum Community Development.

6. And, apparently, only once. In Europe, old forms gave way to new forms over an eighty-year period by about 1850, according to Tilly (1983:465).

7. West and Blumberg, 1990:27, make this point regarding women. Much of their argument applies to the old and the young as well.

8. This case study is drawn primarily from Akin (1978, 1975).

9. There were three major patrons in the community, according to Akin (1978). One died around the time of these events; a second lacked the "heart" of the *nakleng;* and the third, Nate, became the leader in the struggle against eviction.

10. Akin (1978:21) wrote: "Sai was to [*sic*] much of an entrepreneur. He cared much about his profits and losses. . . . Probably, it was because of his lack of the heart of a *nakleng* that he could have managed to become the richest man in Trok Tai."

11. Akin (1978:31) wrote that they met with Narong Kittikachon, son of the prime minister.

12. Interestingly, in a visit to Trok Tai community in December 2000, residents told me that they still do not have a formal leader, as that would just lead to fighting among members of the community. There is at least one patron left in the community, however, who is able to find jobs for a few residents (four at the time) as golf caddies at the nearby Pathum Horse Racing Stadium golf course.

13. See Yap (1992:37, fig. 2.1), which shows that new slums grew most rapidly during the period 1955–1975.

14. Somsook (1983:280n6) cites a National Housing Authority survey (ca. 1981) which found that 37% of those surveyed had moved to the present community following eviction or fire.

15. The arguments are set forth in detail in *Thep Prathan* (n.d.)

16. Since the residents had long-term contracts with the Crown Property Bureau, they could not be legally evicted. The law actually encourages arson as an effective means of eviction. The standard rental contract includes a clause that voids the contract in case of fire. Also, according to municipal regulations, there can be no reconstruction on the site for forty-five days, leaving the victims with no place to go (Yap 1992:39).

17. *Thep Prathan* (n.d.:4–5). *Bangkok Post,* 10 August 1989, 2, says there were seven attempts.

18. Interview, leader of Thep Prathan, February 1994. Most of the donations apparently went to Krathing Daeng.

19. Chatchai Chunhawan of the Chat Thai party pushed for an early agreement. See *Bangkok Post,* 10 August 1989, 2.

20. This case is based on primary research. I have cited relevant articles from the press where possible.

21. Bankhrua is actually divided into three communities, although they cooperate closely in resisting eviction. One of the three communities, Bankhrua Tai, has a small-scale *jaopho* who has some rental housing that is let out to new migrants. According to community leaders, Bankhrua Tai has the greatest problem with gambling and drugs of all three communities, in large part due to the inability to suppress the small-time *jaopho* and his external suppliers, who are connected to those in authority.

22. The emotional significance of this term in explaining women's role in resisting the destruction of their homes should not be overlooked.

23. Apparently he reblocked the land and developed part of it. Interview with Mr. C.K., February 1994.

24. "*Bik* M" 1990:64–65; *Khao phiset,* 16 November 1988, 39. Mr. C.K. apparently wished to run for parliament in the 1995 elections, but his request for support was rejected by the party he had long assisted. Angered, he shifted his support to a new party, though he did not run for parliament himself. The candidate he supported lost in the election. In 2000, a new constitution led to nonparty elections to the senate. Mr. C.K. decided to run in Bangkok and won. His victory was annulled by the Election Commission, whose members suspected that he had bought votes. A new election was held, and he won by an even greater margin.

25. Changes are being formuated, see *Bangkok Post,* 21 January 2001. The proposal from the Prime Minister's Office (Chuan Leekphai government) requires that the hearing be held before decisions are made but does not require the government to heed the results, and the state agency involved will continue to dominate the process.

26. Neuhouser (1989:695–696) made this point in regard to women, pointing out that they are seen as less likely to engage in violence and are thus less threatening to authorities. See also Lawson and Barton 1990:48.

27. Data supplied by the Rajathewi district office. To put this data into perspective, at the time, just 4.4% of M.P.s, 2.6% of senators, 4.9% of provincial council members, and 1.2% of village heads were women (Thomson and Maytinee 1995:66). For recent figures, see Chapter 4.

28. This point draws on the arguments of Neuhouser 1989, Lawson and Barton 1990, and Blumberg 1990.

29. The role of women from middle-class elements in social movements is discussed in detail in Blumberg 1990.

30. Somsook 1983:264 wrote that, in most cases, eviction from private land takes place when land ownership changes hands and there is no patron–client tie between the new owner and the residents.

31. Put more simply, though resistance is increasingly class-based, it is not necessarily class-oriented. Askew 2002:151 fails to make this key distinction.

32. The Assembly of the Poor is covered in detail in Prakan Pintomtaeng, *Kanmuang bon thong thanon: 99 wan samaccha khon jon* [Street politics: 99 days of the Assembly of the Poor] (Bangkok: Kroek University, 1998).

Chapter 7. Thai Middle-Class Elements

1. For a good summary of Marx's views, see Burris 1986.

2. See Anderson 1980, chap. 2, for a further critique of Thompson.

3. I have not distinguished clearly between contemporary and retrospective work as, oddly enough, they seem to follow the same general pattern outlined here. See also n. 6 below.

4. Akin (1969:162) pushed this date back a few years: "By 1850 the Chinese had gained almost complete control of the interregional trade of Thailand. . . . It seems therefore, that besides the two classes of *phrai* [commoners] and *nai* [nobility], there was perhaps another class, an entrepreneurial class of Chinese traders in the middle."

5. These recent attempts to reclaim the 1932 overthrow of the absolute monarchy for "the middle class" should be seen in historical context. Both works were published in 1992 for the sixtieth anniversary of the revolution, just one year after a military coup had ended the latest attempt at parliamentary rule. By 1992, the perceived enemies of democracy were the military and the bureaucracy, which had been getting the credit for 1932 events.

6. Wilson's work appeared before that of Riggs and Siffin, indicating that the pieces were already in place for this elimination of the middle class by the early sixties. Wilson was perhaps thinking of Thai society as a whole and meant that the rural area so dominated the urban area that the urban middle class was insignificant. Riggs and Siffin argued that the relevant polity was the bureaucracy, so the rural areas could be safely ignored.

7. This elimination of the middle class from the discourse during the 1950s and 1960s occurs in both the writings of the time and in retrospective writings. Thompson (1941) wrote of the middle class and Udom (1950) of the petty capitalist class, and Blanchard (1957:411–414) claimed that some 70% of the population of Bangkok was "middle-class," before quoting Skinner almost verbatim. Ten years later there were only "the Chinese" and "the bureaucracy," and references to the middle class disappeared. Retrospective writings

are remarkably similar, with, for example, Jiraporn discovering a middle class at the turn of the century, while other writers claim the development of the middle class took place in the 1960s. This leads to the odd situation in Keyes 1989, where the "new middle class" is credited with the 1932 event (63), yet just fourteen pages later (77) Keyes discusses "the rise of a middle class" during the Sarit era (1957–1963). For Thai authors, this may reflect a tendency to see the middle class, not as a class, but as a generation *(run)*, as does Thirayut 1994.

8. See Reynolds and Lysa 1983 and the special issue of *Pajarayasan* 8 (June–July 1981).

9. Contrast this to what is surely a more accurate description of the nonstudent participants in the 1973 uprising: "government servants, shopkeepers, samlor drivers, workers, and the dispossessed of the city" (Flood 1975:61).

10. Somkiat gained considerable popularity in the 1980s. In 1992, he sided with the military government against the uprising and lost his popularity among the demonstrators.

11. More recently, there has been a return of soap operas depicting the life of the upper classes, particularly turn-of-the-century Chinese tycoons and emerging tycoons, and regional nobility. This fascinating combination may indicate a new focus on the goal and the road to it in the wake of the economic crisis of 1997.

12. The success of advertising in shaping opinion was aptly described by Boonrak Boonyaketmala, dean of the Faculty of Journalism and Mass Communications at Thammasat University: "After TV our society has turned into an oral society, whereby a common culture is born. Consumerism is the common denominator; everyone feels he has to consume. Look, farmers now are wearing jeans and University of Chicago T-shirts. They see that in television [*sic*]. People now have similar frames of reference, the same views, the same tastes" (*Bangkok Post*, 4 August 1989, 7).

13. Given especially the ethnicizing of the middle class prior to 1973, it may have been necessary to deemphasize these differences in order to construct a common class-consciousness. Once the middle class is constructed, it then becomes possible to break it down by gender and ethnicity. One fascinating example of the ways in which ethnicity, gender, and the middle class come together is the rise of the cult of the goddess Kuan Yin; see Nitthi 1994. For an example of breaking the middle class back down ethnically, see Kasian 1994.

14. This survey is reproduced in *Saithan Prachachon*, 33. According to the survey, some 52% of demonstrators claimed an income of over 10,000 baht (US $400). This statistic has been cited regularly. Only rarely has it been noted that some 48% of the demonstrators made less than 10,000 baht. Nor does there seem to be any logical reason to select a cutoff point of 10,000 baht for the middle class.

15. Anek 1992 had earlier made the argument for the contribution of entrepreneurs to democratization in detail.

16. Note the elements of the newly rich that were excluded here: sales workers, taxi drivers, prostitutes, those without an education.

17. Leadership was provided by political parties and NGO leaders. Kanjana Spindler, "May 1992: When the Tide Finally Turned," *Bangkok Post*, 19 May 1993, conflates the NGOs and the middle class: "A handful of Non-Governmental Organizations (NGOs) . . . were leading and organizing the fight for democracy. The May NGOs—university lecturers, doc-

tors, lawyers and company workers. Those were the people who represented the so-called 'middle-class' of the Thai society."

18. McCargo (1997a), Ockey (1999, 2001), and Ji (1997) emphasized the role of the lower classes in the uprising, while Callahan (1998) added an explication of the role of activists and the NGO community. These contributions reveal the more nuanced understandings of many academics, but have not had much impact on public beliefs regarding the middle-class nature of the uprising. The strongly middle-class orientation of the 1997 constitution also seems to have led some academics to rethink the role of the middle class.

19. For some other reasons, see McCargo 1997a: 263–274.

20. The best accounts of the drafting of the new constitution are McCargo 1998 and Connors 1999. Connors provides an account of the events leading from 1992 to the formation of the constitutional assembly.

21. Pasuk and Baker 2000:118 claimed that this excluded 90% of adults from running for parliament, and over 95% in rural areas. Of course, corrupt politicians can easily subvert this requirement.

22. The first Election Commission was made up of five men, all Bangkok residents. Four of the five were former bureaucrats—one in the interior ministry, three in the justice ministry; the fifth was an engineer who had become a political activist. The Election Commission is selected by the Senate from a list of nominees chosen through a complicated process that gives the bureaucracy, particularly the judiciary, a strong role. See Thai Constitution, Section 6, Clause 138, for the details of the process.

23. Frequently expressed in the phrase *nakkanmuang nam nao* or "stagnant water politicians." I do not mean to imply that middle-class supporters of the constitution thought all politicians were unsavory, but they did believe the system favored such politicians.

24. Thaksin, a supporter of the constitution, pointed out, "We will have two societies in one, those from the constituencies to form the government and those hundred, who have a good image, to run it" (*Asiaweek,* 10 October 1997, 24).

25. As Pasuk and Baker 2000:118 put it: "The addition of the party list was expected to increase the number of MPs who stood for 'national' (i.e. Bangkok) interests." There is a provision (Thai Constitution, Section 6, Clause 99 [1]) that requires the party list to represent the different regions "in a just manner." As far as I can tell, no attempt has been made to enforce this extremely vague provision, nor has the regional distribution of party lists ever been publicly discussed. The background of party-list candidates provided by the Election Commission on its webpage includes detailed information on education, a contact address, identification numbers, parents, and other information, but does not include either place of birth or place of residence. See http://202.183.203.226/.

26. Pasuk and Baker 2000:111–112 have argued that there were two clear "groups" involved in the drafting of the constitution: one conservative, made up of bureaucrats and entrepreneurs; the other liberal, made up of activists. The liberal group, they maintain, is primarily responsible for decentralization and the rights clauses of the constitution.

27. One of the most interesting analyses of the middle classes in Bangkok is Askew's (2002:chap. 6) examination of a middle-class housing estate and the characteristics and attitudes of the people who live there. While he argued (2002:192–193) that there was no "community" in the sense we saw in Bankhrua and other congested communities, he did

identify similarities in problems and aspirations, and a "sense of place." His focus, however, was on the neighborhood rather than national politics or democratic attitudes.

Conclusion

1. See Huntington 1991 for a good summary of this literature.

2. This was particularly evident in the analysis of congested communities of Bangkok, and in the activities of the Assembly of the Poor. More generally, Stodgill (1974:365) described the results of an experiment conducted by Lewin and Lippit in 1938:

> Members of authoritarian groups made more submissive reactions to the leader, however, and treated him less as an equal than was the case in the democratic group. In the authoritarian group, members became progressively more submissive to the leader, demanding attention and approval. Although members of the authoritarian group tended to respond to the leader rather than to initiate interaction with each other, they hesitated to approach him because to do so might further reduce their personal power and freedom of movement. The democratic form of leadership, on the other hand, tended to increase the freedom of action of group members.

Although this is a description of an experiment conducted on a small group of young people, the results are in line with the conclusions I draw in Chapter 6.

3. Of course, which leaders in the provinces proved capable of adapting to the new situation varied considerably from place to place. The main point here, however, is that organization, and with it considerable power and legitimacy, was devolved to provincial notables.

4. Hewison (1997:58–74) discusses the role of the monarchy and democratization in detail.

SELECTED BIBLIOGRAPHY

Akin Rabibadhana. *The Organization of Thai Society in the Early Bangkok Period, 1782–1873.* Ithaca, NY: Cornell University Southeast Asia Program Data Paper no. 74, 1969.

———. "Bangkok Slum: Aspects of Social Organization." Ph.D. diss., Cornell University, 1975.

———. *Rise and Fall of a Bangkok Slum.* Bangkok: Thai Khadi, n.d. [1978?].

———. *The Organization of Thai Society in the Early Bangkok Period, 1782–1873.* Bangkok: Bhumipanya Foundation, 1996.

Albritton, Robert, and Thawilwadee Bureekul. "Support for Democracy in Thailand." Paper delivered at the Annual Meeting of the Association of Asian Studies, Washington, DC, 4–7 April 2002.

Amara Pongsapich. *Occasional Papers on Women in Thailand.* Bangkok: Chulalongkorn University Social Research Institute, Women's Studies Program, 1988.

Anan Senakhan. *Thammai phom tong tan Banhan* [Why I must oppose banhan]. Bangkok: Sun prasanngan chaphokit ronarong nayok tong ma chak kanluaktang, 1988.

Anderson, Benedict R. O'G. "Withdrawal Symptoms: Social and Cultural Aspects of the October 6 Coup." *Bulletin of Concerned Asian Scholars* 9 (July–September, 1977): 13–30.

———. "Studies of the Thai State: The State of Thai Studies." In Eliezer Ayal, ed., *The Study of Thailand,* 193–233. Columbus: Ohio University, 1978.

———. *Language and Power.* Ithaca, NY: Cornell University, 1990.

———. "Murder and Progress in Modern Siam." *New Left Review,* May/June 1990, 33–48.

Anderson, Perry. *Arguments within English Marxism.* London: New Left Books, 1980.

Anek Laothamatas. "Business and Politics in Thailand: New Patterns of Influence." *Asian Survey* 28 (April 1988): 451–470.

———. *Business Associations and the New Political Economy of Thailand.* Boulder, CO: Westview Press, 1992.

———. *Mob Mu Thu* [The Mobile Telephone Mob]. Bangkok: Matichon, 1993.

———. "A Tale of Two Democracies: Conflicting Perceptions of Elections and Democracy in Thailand." In R. H. Taylor, ed., *The Politics of Elections in Southeast Asia,* 201–223. Washington, DC: Woodrow Wilson Center and Cambridge University, 1996.

Anonymous. *Man of Respect: The True Story of a Mafia Assassin.* Trans. Avril Bardoni. London: Pan, 1991.

(Phraya) Anuman Rajadhon. "Me Posop, The Rice Mother." *Journal of the Siam Society* 43 (August 1955): 55–61.

Anuson Limmanee. "Thailand." In Wolfgang Sachsenroder and E. Frings Ulrike, eds., *Political Party Systems and Democratic Development in East and Southeast Asia*, 403–448. Aldershot: Ashgate, 1998.

Arghiros, Daniel. *Democracy, Development and Decentralization in Provincial Thailand.* Richmond, Surrey: Curzon, 2001.

Arlacchi, Pino. *Mafia Business: The Mafia Ethic and the Spirit of Capitalism.* Trans. Martin Ryle. London: Verso, 1987.

Askew, Marc. *Bangkok: Place, Practice and Representation.* London and New York: Routledge, 2002.

Batson, Benjamin. *Siam's Political Future: Documents from the End of the Absolute Monarchy.* Ithaca, NY: Cornell University Southeast Asia Program, 1974.

Battye, Noel. "The Military, Government and Society in Siam, 1868–1910." Ph.D. diss., Cornell University, 1974.

Bidhya Bowornwathana. "Thailand: Bureaucracy under Coalition Governments." In John Burns and Bidhya Bowornwathana, eds., *Civil Service Systems in Asia,* 281–318. Cheltenham: Edward Elgar, 2001.

"Bik M (Money) haeng chumchon Bangsu" [Big M (Money) of Bangsu community] *Chan* 3 (August 1990): 59–69.

Blanchard, Wendell. *Thailand: Its People, Its Society, Its Culture.* New Haven, CT: HRAF Press, 1957.

Blumberg, Rhoda Lois. "White Mothers as Civil Rights Activists: The Interweave of Family and Movement Roles." In Guida West and Rhoda Lois Blumberg. *Women and Social Protest,* 166–179. New York: Oxford University Press, 1990.

Bunloet Suphadilok. *Sitthi kansuesan nai prathet Thai* [Freedom of communication in Thailand]. Bangkok: Thai Khadi Suksa, 1984.

Bunnag, Tej. *The Provincial Administration of Siam 1892–1915.* Singapore: Oxford University Press, 1977.

Bunruam Thiamchan. *Ruam sutyot khadi prawatsat muangthai* [A collection of the best trials in the history of Thailand]. Bangkok: Special Project Press, 1988.

Buntham Loetsukhikasem. "Khwamtaekyaek nai phakkanmuang Thai: suksa priapthiap phak Prachathipat phak Kitsangkhom lae phak Chat Thai" [Factionalism in Thai political parties: A comparative study of the Democrat, Social Action, and Chat Thai parties]. M.A. thesis, Chulalongkorn University, 1988.

Burris, V. "The Discovery of the New Middle Class." *Theory and Society* 15, no. 3 (1986): 317–349.

Cady, John. *Southeast Asia: Its Historical Development.* New York: McGraw Hill, 1964.

Callahan, William. *Imagining Democracy: Reading "The Events of May" in Thailand.* Singapore: Institute of Southeast Asian Studies, 1998.

Case, William. "Thai Democracy 2001: Out of Equilibrium." *Asian Survey* 41, no. 3 (2001): 525–547.

Chai-anan Samutawanit [Samudavanija]. *Kanluaktang, phakkanmuang, ratthasapha, lae khana thahan* [Elections, parties, the legislature, and the military]. Bangkok: Bannakit Trading, 1981.

———. *The Thai Young Turks.* Singapore: Institute of Southeast Asian Studies, 1982.

———. *Yang toek kap thahan prachathipatai* [The young Turks and the democratic soldiers]. Bangkok: Bannakit Trading, 1982.

———. *Panha kanphatana thang kanmuang Thai* [Problems of Thai political development]. Bangkok: Chulalongkorn University, 1987.

———. "State-Identity Creation, State-Building and Civil Society." In Craig J. Reynolds, *National Identity and Its Defenders*. Clayton, Vic.: Centre of Southeast Asian Studies, Monash University, 1991.

Chai-Anan Samudavanija and Suchit Bunbongkarn. "Thailand." In Zakina Haji Ahmad and Harold Crouch, eds., *Military-Civilian Relations in South-East Asia*. Singapore: Oxford University Press, 1985.

Chai-Anan Samudavanija, Kusuma Snitwongse, and Suchit Bunbongkarn. *From Armed Suppression to Political Offensive*. Bangkok: Chulalongkorn University, 1990.

Chakrit Noranitpadungkarn. *Elites, Power Structure and Politics in Thai Communities*. Bangkok: National Institute of Development Administration, 1981.

Chamlong Simuang. *Chiwit Chamlong* [The life of Chamlong]. Bangkok: Thira kanphim, 1990.

Chanwit Kasetsiri. *Kanpatiwat khong Sayam* [The revolution of Siam]. Bangkok: Praphansan, 1992.

———. *Pridi Phanomyong kap Mahawithayalai Wicha Thammasat lae Kanmuang* [Pridi Phanomyong and Thammasat University]. Bangkok: Thammasat University, 2000.

Chit Wiphatthawat. *Phao Saraphap* [Phao confesses]. Bangkok: Phrae Phitthaya, n.d. [1960?].

"Chiwit khwampenyu lae laifasatai khon chan klang nai Krungthep" [Livelihood and lifestyle of the middle class in Bangkok]. *Khukhaeng* 7 (October 1986): 119–132; (November 1986): 72–76.

Connors, Michael K. "Political Reform and the State in Thailand." *Journal of Contemporary Asia* 29, no. 2 (1999): 202–226.

Cushman, Jennifer. *Family and State: The Formation of a Sino-Thai Tin-Mining Dynasty 1797–1932*. Edited by Craig Reynolds. Singapore: Oxford University Press, 1991.

Dahl, Robert. *Polyarchy*. New Haven, CT: Yale University Press, 1971.

Darling, Frank C. *Thailand and the United States*. Washington, DC: Public Affairs Press, 1965.

———. "Political Parties in Thailand." *Pacific Affairs* 44 (Summer 1971): 228–241.

———. *The Westernization of Asia: A Comparative Political Analysis*. Boston: D. K. Hall, 1979.

Darunee Tantiwiramanond and Shashi Pandey. "The Status and Role of Thai Women in the Pre-Modern Period: A Historical and Cultural Perspective." *Sojourn* 2 (February 1987): 125–149.

———. *By Women, For Women: A Study of Women's Organizations in Thailand*. Singapore: Institute of Southeast Asian Studies, 1991.

Davis, Rebecca Howard. *Women and Power in Parliamentary Democracies*. Lincoln: University of Nebraska, 1997.

DeBary, Wm. Theodore. *Asian Values and Human Rights: A Confucian Communitarian Perspective*. Cambridge, MA: Harvard University Press, 1998.

De La Loubere, Simon. *The Kingdom of Siam*. Singapore: Oxford University Press, 1986.

Diamond, Larry. *Developing Democracy: Toward Consolidation*. Baltimore: Johns Hopkins University Press, 1999.

Doner, Richard F. *Driving a Bargain*. Berkeley: University of California Press, 1991.

Duang Prateep Foundation. "Munnithi Duang Prateep chak wan nan . . . thung wanni . . . phua kansuksa khong dek yak con lae khon yakrai . . . nai sangkhom" [Duang Prateep Foundation from that day . . . until this day . . . for the education of poor children and the poor . . . in society]. Bangkok: Nation Publishing Group, n.d.

————. "A Window on the Slums." Bangkok: Nation Publishing Group, n.d.

Editor and Publisher International Yearbook. New York: Editor and Publisher, 1989.

Ellin, Nan. "Constructing the Middle Class." *History of European Ideas* 13, no. 6 (1991): 817–824.

Fishel, Thamora. "Mothers, Teachers and *Hua Khanaen:* Gender and the Culture of Local Politics in Thailand." Proceedings of the 6th International Conference on Thai Studies, Theme V: Women, Gender and Development in Thai Society. Chiang Mai, 14–17 October 1996, 9–21.

Flood, Thadeus. "The Thai Left Wing in Historical Context." *Bulletin of Concerned Asian Scholars* 7, no. 2 (1975): 55–67.

Foreign Correspondents Club of Thailand. *The King in World Focus*. Bangkok: The Foreign Correspondents Club of Thailand, 1988.

Frykman, Jonas, and Orvar Lofgren. *Culture Builders: A Historical Anthropology of Middle-Class Life*. Trans. Alan Crozier. New Brunswick, NJ: Rutgers University Press, 1987.

Gerth, H. H., and C. Wright Mills, eds. *From Max Weber: Essays in Sociology*. New York: Oxford University Press, 1958 (o.d. 1946).

Giddens, Anthony. *The Class Structure of the Advanced Societies*. London: Hutchinson, 1980.

Girling, John L. S. *The Bureaucratic Polity in Modernizing Societies*. Singapore: Institute of Southeast Asian Studies, Occasional Paper no. 64, 1981.

————. *Thailand: Society and Politics*. Ithaca, NY: Cornell University Press, 1981.

Hanna, Willard. *Eight Nation Makers*. New York: St. Martin's Press, 1964.

Harrison, Rachel. "The 'Good' the 'Bad' and the Pregnant: Why the Thai Prostitute as Literary Heroine Can't Be Seen to Give Birth." Proceedings of the 6th International Conference on Thai Studies, Theme V: Women, Gender and Development in Thai Society, 31–48. Chiang Mai, 14–17 October 1996.

Heinze, Ruth-Inge. "Ten Days in October—Students vs. the Military." *Asian Survey* 14 (June 1974): 491–508.

Hewison, Kevin. "The Financial Bourgeoisie in Thailand." *Journal of Contemporary Asia* 11, no. 4 (1981): 395–412.

————. *Bankers and Bureaucrats: Capital and the Role of the State in Thailand*. New Haven, CT: Yale University Southeast Asia Studies Monograph no. 34, 1989.

————, ed. *Political Change in Thailand*. London: Routledge, 1997.

Hong Lysa. *Thailand in the Nineteenth Century*. Singapore: Institute of Southeast Asian Studies, 1984.

————. "Palace Women in the Reign of King Chulalongkorn." *Journal of Southeast Asian Studies* 30 (September 1999): 310–324.

Huntington, Samuel P. *Political Order in Changing Societies.* New Haven, CT: Yale University Press, 1968.

———. *The Third Wave.* Norman: Oklahoma University Press, 1991.

Igel, Barbara. "The Economy of Survival in the Slums of Bangkok." Bangkok: Division of Human Settlements Development, Asian Institute of Technology, 1992.

Ingram, James C. *Economic Change in Thailand since 1850.* Stanford, CA: Stanford University Press, 1955.

———. *Economic Change in Thailand, 1850–1970.* Stanford, CA: Stanford University Press, 1971.

International Advertising Expenditures. New York: International Advertising Association, 1963.

International Financial Statistics Yearbook, 1990. Washington, DC: International Monetary Fund, annual.

Jackson, Peter. *Buddhism, Legitimation, and Conflict.* Singapore: Institute of Southeast Asian Studies, 1989.

———. "*Krathoey*><Gay><Man: The Historical Emergence of Gay Male Identity in Thailand." In Lenore Manderson and Margaret Jolly, eds., *Sites of Desire Economies of Pleasure.* Chicago: University of Chicago Press, 1997.

Jacobs, Norman. *Modernization without Development.* New York: Praeger, 1971.

Jarvis, Darryl S. L. "Problems and Prospects in Thaksin's Thailand: An Interim Assessment." *Asian Survey* 42, no. 2 (2002): 297–319.

Ji Ungpakorn. *The Struggle for Democracy and Social Justice in Thailand.* Bangkok: Arom Pongpangan Foundation, 1997.

Jiraporn Witayasakpan. "Nationalism and the Transformation of Aesthetic Concepts: Theatre in Thailand during the Phibun Period." Ph.D. diss., Cornell University, 1992.

Johnston, David B. "Bandit, *Nakleng,* and Peasant in Rural Thai Society." *Contributions to Asian Studies* 15 (1980): 90–101.

Juree Namsirichai Vichit-Vadakan. "Not Too High and Not Too Low: A Comparative Study of Thai and Chinese Middle-Class Life in Bangkok, Thailand." Ph.D. diss., University of California at Berkeley, 1979.

Juree Vichit-Vadakan. "Women in Politics in Thailand." In *Women in Politics.* Bangkok: UNESCO, RUSHSAP Series on Monographs and Occasional Papers no. 36, 1993.

———. "Women and the Family in Thailand in the Midst of Social Change." *Law and Society Review* 28 (August 1994): 515–524.

Kamhaeng Pharitanon. *14 Tula: ratthathamanun si luad* [14 October: Blood red constitution]. Bangkok: Bangluang, 1994.

Kankheha haeng chat [National Housing Authority]. Fai prapprung chumchon ae at [Division of slum community development]. *Raignan phon samruat chumchon ae at nai Ko. Tho. Mo.* [Report of the results of a survey of congested communities in Bangkok]. Bangkok: National Housing Authority, 1997.

Kanmuang Thai kap kanluaktang [Thai politics and elections]. Bangkok: Dokya, n.d. [1983].

Kanok Wongtrangan. *Kanmuang nai sapha phuthaen ratsadon* [Politics in the House of Representatives]. Bangkok: Chulalongkorn University, 1987.

Kasian Tejaphira. *Jintanakam chat thi mai pen chumchon: khon chan klang luk jin kap chat niyom doi rat khong Thai* [Imagined uncommunity: Lookjin middle class and Thai official nationalism]. Bangkok: Phujatkan, 1994.

Kaufman, Howard K. *Bangkhuad: A Community Study in Thailand.* Locust Valley, NY: J. J. Augustin, 1960.

Kershaw, Roger. "Three Kings of Orient: The Changing Face of Monarchy in Southeast Asia (Part II)." *Contemporary Review* 234 (May 1979): 256–265.

Key Statistics of Thailand 2000 [Pramuan khomun sathiti thi samkhan khong prathet Thai pho. so. 2543]. Bangkok: National Statistical Office, Office of the Prime Minister, 2000.

Keyes, Charles F. *Isan: Regionalism in Northeastern Thailand.* Ithaca, NY: Cornell University Press, 1967.

———. "Mother or Mistress but Never a Monk: Buddhist Notions of Female Gender in Rural Thailand." *American Ethnologist* 11, no. 2 (1984): 223–241.

———. *Thailand: Buddhist Kingdom as Modern Nation-State.* Boulder, CO: Westview Press, 1989.

Khachatphai Burutphat. *Kanmuang lae phakkanmuang khong Thai* [Politics and political parties of Thailand]. Bangkok: Odeon Store, 1968.

Khin Thitsa. *Providence and Prostitution: Image and Reality in Buddhist Thailand.* London: Change International Reports, 1980.

Kim Dae Jung. "Is Culture Destiny: The Myth of Asia's Anti-Democratic Values." *Foreign Affairs* 77 (November 1994): 128–133.

King, Dan. "New Political Parties in Thailand: A Case Study of the Palang Dharma Party and the New Aspiration Party." Ph.D. diss., University of Wisconsin–Madison, 1996.

Kirsch, A. Thomas. "Economy, Polity, and Religion in Thailand." In G. William Skinner and A. Thomas Kirsch, eds., *Change and Persistence in Thai Society.* Ithaca, NY: Cornell University Press, 1975.

———. "Text and Context: Buddhist Sex Roles/Culture of Gender Revisited." *American Ethnologist* 12, no. 2 (1985): 302–320.

Kitschelt, H. "Political Opportunity Structures and Political Protest: Anti-Nuclear Movements in Four Democracies." *British Journal of Political Science* 16 (January 1986): 57–85.

Kobkua Suwannathat-pian. *Thailand's Durable Premier.* London: Oxford University Press, 1995.

Kosin Wongsurawat. *Ratthathammanun lae kanluaktang* [The constitution and elections]. Bangkok: Phrae Phithaya, 1974.

Kotfathoe muang luang. [Godfathers of the capital]. Bangkok: Matichon, 1989.

Kramol Tongdhamachart [Kramon Thongthammachat]. "The April 1979 Elections and Post-Election Politics in Thailand." *Contemporary Southeast Asia* 1 (December 1979): 211–231.

———. *Wiwatthanakan khong rabop ratthathamanun Thai* [The development of the Thai constitutional system]. Bangkok: Bannakit Trading, 1980.

———. *Toward a Political Party Theory in Thai Perspective.* Singapore: Institute of Southeast Asian Studies Occasional Paper no. 68, 1982.

Kramon Thongthammachat, Sombun Suksamran, and Pricha Hongkrailoet. *Kanluaktang phakkanmuang lae sathienphap khong ratthaban* [Elections, parties, and the stability of the government]. Bangkok: Chulalongkorn University, 1988.

Krasuang mahatthai. [Ministry of the Interior.] "Raingan khanakammakan phitjarana prayot khong thanon ruam lae krajai kanjarajon to rabob thang duan khan thisong chabap thi 2" [Report of the Scrutiny Committee on the Benefit of the Traffic Collection and Distribution Road for the Expressway System, stage 2, volume 2]. Bangkok, 1994.

Krasuang mahatthai. Krom kanpokkhrong. Kong kanluaktang. *Raingan wichai kanluaktang samachik sapha phuthaen ratsadon pho. so. 2529* [Research report on the election of members of the House of Representatives, 1986]. Bangkok: n.d. [1986].

———. *Raingan wichai kanluaktang samachik sapha phuthaen ratsadon pho. so. 2531* [Research report on the election of members of the House of Representatives, 1988]. Bangkok, n.d. [1988].

Kritaya Archavanitkul. *Migration and Urbanisation in Thailand, 1980: The Urban-Rural Continuum Analysis.* Bangkok: Mahidol Institute for Population and Social Research, 1988.

Kroekkiat Phiphatseritham. *Wikhro khrongkan phan ngoen* [An analysis of the Tambon Development Fund program]. Bangkok: Thammasat University, 1975.

Kurian, George, ed. *World Press Encyclopedia.* New York: Facts on File, 1982.

"Laifsatai" [Lifestyle], *Khlang samong* 5 (July 1987): 48–52.

Lawson, Ronald and Stephen E. Barton. "Sex Roles in Social Movements: A Case Study of the Tenant Movement in New York City." In Guida West and Rhoda Lois Blumberg, *Women and Social Protest,* 41–56. New York: Oxford University, 1990.

Likhit Dhiravegin. *Thai Politics: Selected Aspects of Development and Change.* Bangkok: Tri-Sciences, 1985.

———. "Kanchuangching amnat rawang thahan kap chon chan klang" [Contesting power between soldiers and the middle class]. *Decade* 2 (May 1992): 61–66.

Lipsky, Michael. "Protest as a Political Resource." *American Political Science Review* 62 (December 1968): 1141–1158.

Lockhart, Bruce M. "The Monarchy in Siam and Vietnam, 1925–1946." Ph.D. diss., Cornell University, 1990.

"Luk phuchai chu [C. K.]" [The man named (C. K.)]. *Khumphai* 4 (February 1989): 8–13.

Mali Bunsiriphan. *Kankhian bot bannathikan khong nangsuphim phasa Thai raiwan* [The writing of editorials of Thai language daily newspapers]. Bangkok: Thammasat University, khana warasansat lae suesanmuanchon, 1984.

Manut Watthanakomen, ed. *Khomun phunthan phakkanmuang patchuban lae phakkanmuang kap kanluaktang pi 2522–2529* [Baseline data on present political parties and political parties and the 1979–1986 elections]. Bangkok: Social Science Association of Thailand, 1986.

Marilee, Karl. *Women and Empowerment: Participation and Decision Making.* London and New Jersey: Zed, UN/NGO Group on Women and Development, Women and Development Series, 1995.

Marks, Thomas A. "The Status of the Monarchy in Thailand." *Issues and Studies* 13 (November 1977): 51–70.

———. "The Thai Monarchy under Siege." *Asia Quarterly,* no. 2 (1978): 109–141.

McCargo, Duncan. *Chamlong Srimuang and the New Thai Politics.* London: Hurst & Co. 1997a.

———. "Thailand's Political Parties: Real, Authentic and Actual." In Kevin Hewison, ed., *Political Change in Thailand,* 114–131. London: Routledge, 1997b.

———. "Alternative Meanings of Political Reform in Contemporary Thailand." *The Copenhagen Journal of Asian Studies* 13 (1999): 5–30.

———. Politics and the Press in Thailand: Media Machinations. London: Routledge, 2000.

———. "Democracy under Stress in Thaksin's Thailand." *Journal of Democracy* 13 (October 2002): 112–126.

McVey, Ruth, ed. *Southeast Asian Capitalists.* Ithaca, NY: Cornell University Southeast Asia Program, 1992.

Million Baht Business Information. Bangkok: Pan Siam Communications, annual.

Mills, C. Wright. *White Collar: The American Middle Classes.* New York: Oxford University, 1956.

Mills, Mary Beth. *Thai Women in the Global Labor Force: Consuming Desires, Contested Selves.* New Brunswick, NJ: Rutgers University Press, 1999.

Montesano, Michael. "The Commerce of Trang, 1930s–1990s: Thailand's National Integration in Social-Historical Perspective." Ph.D. diss., Cornell University, 1998.

———. "Market Society and the Origins of the New Thai Politics." In Ruth McVey, ed., *Money and Power in Provincial Thailand,* 97–122. Copenhagen and Singapore: Nordic Institute of Asian Studies/Institute of Southeast Asian Studies, 2000.

Montri Chenwithayakan [Chenvidyakan], Kunthon Thanaphongsathon, Pracha Wesarat, and Thongchai Wongchaysuwan. *Phakkanmuang Thai yuk mai* [Thai political parties in the new era]. Bangkok: Krungthai kanphim, n.d. [1968].

Montri Supaporn. "The Role Performance of Prime Ministers in the Thai Political System: Styles of Military and Civilian Rule 1932–83." Ph.D. diss., Case Western Reserve University, 1984.

Morell, David. "Power and Parliament in Thailand: The Futile Challenge, 1968–71." Ph.D. diss., Princeton University, 1974.

Morell, David, and Chai-anan Samudavanija. *Political Conflict in Thailand: Reform, Reaction, Revolution.* Cambridge, MA: Oelgeschlager, 1981.

Mulder, Niels. *Inside Southeast Asia: Thai, Javanese and Filipino Interpretations of Everyday Life.* Bangkok: Duang Kamol, 1992a.

———. *Inside Thai Society: An Interpretation of Everyday Life.* Bangkok: Duang Kamol, 1992b.

Muscat, Robert J. *Thailand and the United States: Development, Security, and Foreign Aid.* New York: Columbia University Press, 1990.

Nakharin Mektrairat. *Kanpatiwat Sayam pho. so. 2475* [The Siamese revolution of 1932]. Bangkok: Munnithi khrongkan tamra sangkhomsat lae manutsayasat, 1992.

Nantanee Jayasut et al., Survey Report. "Status of Thai Women in Two Rural Areas." Bangkok: National Council of Women of Thailand, 1997.

National Statistical Office. *Report of the Labour Force Survey 1989–2000.* Available online at http://www.nso.go.th/eng/stat/lfs/lfstab9.htm#Female. Accessed 2 November 2002.

Neher, Clark. "The Transformation of the Thai Economy." Paper presented to the Association for Asian Studies, 1991.

———, ed. *Modern Thai Politics: From Village to Nation*. Cambridge, MA: Schenkman, 1976.

Nelson, Michael H. "Thailand's House Elections of 6 Jan. 2001: Thaksin's Landslide Victory and Subsequent Narrow Escape." In Michael H. Nelson, *Thailand's New Politics: KPI Yearbook 2001*, 283–441. Nonthaburi and Bangkok: King Prajadhipok's Institute and White Lotus Press, 2002.

Neuhouser, Kevin. "Sources of Women's Power and Status among the Urban Poor in Contemporary Brazil." *Signs: Journal of Women in Culture and Society* 14 (Spring 1989): 685–702.

Nirot Khokhongprasoet. "Fakfai thang kanmuang: suksa korani kanpaengyaek fakfai phainai phak Prachathipat [Political factions: A case study of factionalism in the Democrat Party]." M.A. thesis, Chulalongkorn University, 1990.

Niti Vatiwutipong. "His Majesty the King and Thai Politics." In *The Thai Monarchy*. Bangkok: Foreign Office, Public Relations Division, Prime Minister's Office, 1999.

Nitthi Ieowsiwong. "Latthiphithi jao mae Kuan Im" [Doctrine and ceremonies of God Mother Kuan Yin]. *Sinlapawatthanatham* 15 (August 1994): 79–106.

Noranit Setthabut. *Phak Prachathipat: kwamsamret roe kwamlomlaew* [The Democrat Party: Success or failure]. Bangkok: Thammasat University, 1987.

Noranit Setthabut and Surachai Sirikrai. *Chiwaprawat nayok ratamontri Thai tangtae pho. so. 2475–2529* [Biographies of Thai prime ministers from 1932 to 1986]. Bangkok: Thammasat University, 1986.

Nuannoi Tirat and Nophanan Wanathepsakun. *Setsat kanmuang ruang thorakhomnakhom* [The political economy of telecommunications]. Bangkok: Chulalongkorn Economics Department, 2002.

Ockey, James. "Business Leaders, Gangsters and the Middle Class: Societal Groups and Civilian Rule in Thailand." Ph.D. diss., Cornell University, 1992.

———. "Thai Society and Patterns of Political Leadership." *Asian Survey* 36 (April 1996): 345–360.

———. "Thailand in 1996: The Crafting of Democracy." In Daljit Singh, ed., *Southeast Asian Affairs 1997*, 301–316. Singapore: Institute of Southeast Asian Studies, 1997.

———. "Thailand's Struggle for Democracy: The Life and Times of M. R. Seni Pramoj." *Journal of Southeast Asian Studies* 30 (March 1999): 194.

———. "On the Expressway, and Under It: Representations of the Middle Class, the Poor, and Democracy in Thailand." In Yao Souchou, ed., *Culture, Representation, and the State in Southeast Asia*, 313–337. Singapore: Institute of Southeast Asian Studies, 2001.

Parsons, Talcott, ed. *Max Weber: The Theory of Social and Economic Organization*. New York: Free Press, 1947.

Pasuk Phongpaichit and Chris Baker. *Thailand: Economy and Politics*. Kuala Lumpur: Oxford University Press, 1995.

———. *Thailand's Crisis*. Bangkok: Silkworm, 2000.

Pasuk Phongpaichit and Sungsidh Piriyarangsan. *Corruption and Democracy in Thailand.* Bangkok: The Political Economy Center, Chulalongkorn University, 1994.

———, eds. *Rat thun jaopho thongthin kapsangkhom Thai* [The state, capital, provincial godfathers and Thai society]. Bangkok: The Political Economy Center, Chulalongkorn University, 1992.

Pasuk Phongpaichit, Sungsidh Piriyarangsan, and Nualnoi Treerat, eds. *Guns Girls Gambling Ganja: Thailand's Illegal Economy and Public Policy.* Chiang Mai: Silkworm, 1998.

Phichai Kaosamran, Somchaet Naksewi, and Worawit Baru. *Kanluaktang Pattani pi 2529 suksa korani krabuankan hasiang lae rabop hua khanaen* [The 1986 Pattani election: A case study of campaign methods and the voting chief system]. Bangkok: Munithi phua kansuksa prachathipatai lae kanphatana, n.d. [1987].

Phoemphong Chawalit and Sisomphop Jitphiromsi. *Ha khanaen yangrai hai dai pen so. so.* [How to seek votes to be an M.P.]. Bangkok: Nititham, 1988.

Phonthip Usupharat and Saowapha Phonsiriphong. "Chumchon khaek jam thi yang khong longlua yu nai Krungthep" [The persistence of "Khaek Cham" community in Bangkok]. *Warasan phasa lae watthanatham* 8 (January 1989): 20–30 (abstract in English, 19).

Pisan Suriyamongkol and James F. Guyot. *The Bureaucratic Polity at Bay.* Bangkok: National Institute of Development Administration, n.d.

Plai-oh Chananon. *Phokha kap phathanakan rabop thunniyom nai phaknua pho. so. 2464–2523* [Traders and the development of the capitalist system in the North, 1921–1980]. Bangkok: Chulalongkorn University and Sang Sawan, 1987.

Prachan Rakphong. *Kansuksa kanhasiang nai kanluaktang 27 karakadakhom 2529 changwat Lampang* [A study of campaigning in the 27 July 1986 election in Lampang Province]. Bangkok: Samakhom Sangkhomsat haeng prathet Thai, 1986.

Prakan Pintomtaeng. *Kanmuang bon thong thanon: 99 wan samaccha khon jon* [Street politics: 99 days of the Assembly of the Poor]. Bangkok: Kroek University, 1998.

Prathan Suvannamongkol, ed. *Biographical Data of Thai Parliamentary Members 1986.* Bangkok: Social Science Association of Thailand, n.d. [1987].

Preliminary Report: 1990 Population and Housing Census. National Statistical Office, Office of the Prime Minister, n.d. [1990?].

Pricha Hongkrailoet. *Phakkanmuang lae panha phakkanmuang* [Political parties and problems of political parties]. Bangkok: Thai Watthana Phanit, 1981.

Prizzia, Ross. *Thailand in Transition: The Role of Oppositional Forces.* Honolulu: University of Hawai'i Press, 1985.

Pye, Lucian. *Asian Power and Politics.* Cambridge, MA: Belknap, 1985.

Race, Jeffrey. "Thailand 1973: We Certainly Have Been Ravaged by Something.'" *Asian Survey* 14 (February 1974): 192–203.

———. "The January 1975 Thai Elections: Preliminary Data and Inferences." *Asian Survey* 15 (April 1975): 375–381.

Radom Wongnam. "Opinion Leadership and the Elite in Rural Thailand: A Case Study of Two Villages." Ph.D. diss., University of California, Los Angeles, 1980.

Raikan kanprachum nitibanyat haeng chat [Record of the meetings of the National Assembly]. Session 57, 58, book 16, 1978.

Randolph, R. Sean. "Diplomacy and National Interest: Thai–American Security Cooperation in the Vietnam Era." Ph.D. diss., Fletcher School of Law and Diplomacy, Tufts University, 1978.

Rangson Prasertsri. "Women in the Parliament of Thailand: Their Characteristics and Attitudes." Ph.D. diss., University of Mississippi, 1982.

Ratchathewi District Office, Office of Community Development. "Khomun chumchon" [Community statistics]. Mimeograph, n.d.

———. "Sarup railaiat kanphattana thang kan sangkhom lae setthakit chu chumchon Kingphet (Bankhrua Nua) khet Phayathai pi ngoppraman 2521" [Detailed summary of the social and economic development of the community named Kingphet (Bankhrua Nua) Phayathai District Budget Year 1978]. Mimeograph.

Ray, Jayanta Kumar. *Portraits of Thai Politics.* New Delhi: Orient Longman, 1972.

Reid, Anthony. "Female Roles in Pre-colonial Southeast Asia." *Modern Asian Studies* 22, no. 3 (1988): 629–645.

Reinecke, Gerhard. "Social Security in Thailand: Political Decisions and Distributional Impact." *Crossroads* 8, no. 1 (1993): 78–115.

Reynolds, Andrew. "Women in Legislatures and Executives of the World." *World Politics* 51 (July 1999): 547–572.

Reynolds, Craig. "Tycoons and Warlords: Modern Thai Social Formations and Chinese Historical Romance." In Anthony Reid, ed., *Sojourners and Settlers: Histories of Southeast Asia and the Chinese.* Essays in honour of Jennifer Cushman 115–147. London: Allen & Unwin, 1996.

Reynolds, Craig, and Hong Lysa. "Marxism in Thai Historical Studies." *Journal of Asian Studies* 43 (November 1983): 77–104.

Richter, Kerry, and Bencha Yoddumnern-Attig. "Framing a Study of Thai Women's Changing Roles and Statuses." In Bencha Yoddumnern-Attig et al., eds., *Changing Roles and Statuses of Women in Thailand,* 1–7. Bangkok: Mahidol University Institute for Population and Social Research, 1992.

Richter, Linda. "Exploring Theories of Female Leadership in South and Southeast Asia." *Pacific Affairs* 63 (1990): 524–540.

Riggs, Fred W. *Thailand: The Modernization of a Bureaucratic Polity.* Honolulu: East–West Center, 1966.

Riker, William. *The Theory of Political Coalitions.* New Haven, CT: Yale University Press, 1962.

Roces, Mina. "Can Women Hold Power Outside the Symbols of Power." *Asian Studies Review* 17 (April 1994): 14–23.

———. "The Gendering of Post-war Philippine Politics." In Krishna Sen and Maila Stivens, *Gender and Power in Affluent Asia.* New York: Routledge, 1998.

100 wan wirachon prachathipatai [100 days of the heroes of democracy]. Bangkok: Thammasat University, 1992.

Roth, Guenther, and Claus Wittich, eds. *Max Weber: Economy and Society.* New York: Bedminster Press, 1968.

Rujaya Abhakorn. "Ratburi, an Inner Province: Local Government and Central Politics in Siam, 1868–1892." Ph.D. diss., Cornell University, 1984.

Saitip Sukatipan. "The Media and Politics." Ph.D. diss., University of Hawai'i, 1988.

Samak Suntharawet. *Ekkasan lakthan khamaphiprai mai waiwangchai ro mo wo. khomna-khom 21 tulakhom 2530* [Document of evidence of the no confidence debate of the minister of communications]. Bangkok: Si Phi Kanphim, 1987.

Samrit Miwongukhot. *Khumu luaktang '31* [Election Manual '88]. Bangkok: Sayamban, n.d. [1988].

Saowapha Phonsiriphong, Phonthip Usupharat, and Duangphon Khamnunwat. *Kansuksa buangton kiaokap chumchon Bankhrua Nua (Bankhaek Khrua) saphap setthakit sangkhom lae watthanatham* [A basic study of Bankhrua North (Bankhaek Khrua): State of the economy, society and culture]. Bangkok: Mahidol University, 1989.

———. "Laksana thang prachakon lae khwamsamphan phainai chumchon bankhrua nua" [Demographic characteristics and relationships within the Bankhrua North community]. In *Ekkasan prakop kansammana Thai-Farangset thang manusayawitthaya watthanatham* [Documents of the Thai-France Seminar on the Humanities and Culture]. 13–15 December 1990, Research Center for Languages and Culture, Mahidol University.

Sarakun Adunyanon. *Thaksin Chinawat: Asawin khlun luk thisam* [Thaksin Shinawatra: Knight of the third wave]. Bangkok: Matichon, 1993.

Sathit Chawanothai. "Kanluaksan phusamak rap luaktang khong phakkanmuang Thai" [Selection of candidates for elections of Thai political parties]. M.A. thesis, Chulalongkorn University, 1989.

Scott, James C. *The Moral Economy of the Peasant.* New Haven, CT: Yale University Press, 1976.

———. *Weapons of the Weak: Everyday Forms of Peasant Resistance.* New Haven, CT: Yale University Press, 1985.

———. "Everyday Forms of Peasant Resistance." In James C. Scott and Benedict J. Tria Kerkvliet, eds., *Everyday Forms of Peasant Resistance in Southeast Asia,* 5–35. London: Frank Cass, 1986.

———. "Everyday Forms of Resistance." In Forrest D. Colburn, ed., *Everyday Forms of Peasant Resistance,* 3–33. Armonk, NY: M. E. Sharpe, 1989.

Seksan Prasertkul. "The Transformation of the Thai State and Economic Change (1855–1945)." Ph.D. diss., Cornell University, 1989.

Seri Phongphit. *Buddhism, Reform and the Role of Monks in Community Development in Thailand.* Hong Kong: Arena Press, 1988.

Setphon Khusiphitak. "Ratthasapha—phumilang khong samachik saphaphuthaen ratsadon Thai run pho. so. 2476–2512" [Parliament—Background of Members of the Thai House of Representatives of the 1933–1969 Period]. In *Satkanmuang* [Political animal]. Bangkok: Suwansan, 1971.

———. *Tha yak pen phuthaen* [If you want to be a representative]. Bangkok: Social Science Association of Thailand, 1988 [original date 1976].

Sharp, Lauriston, and Lucien M. Hanks. *Bang Chan: Social History of a Rural Community in Thailand.* Ithaca, NY: Cornell University Press, 1978.

Siffin, William J. *The Thai Bureaucracy: Institutional Change and Development.* Honolulu: East–West Center Press, 1966.

Skinner, George W. *Chinese Society in Thailand: An Analytical History.* Ithaca, NY: Cornell University Press, 1957.

———. *Leadership and Power in the Chinese Community of Thailand*. Ithaca, NY: Cornell University Press, 1958.

Slum Development. Bangkok: Community Development Department, National Housing Authority, n.d. [1991?].

Sombat Chanthonwong. *Kanluaktang phuwaratchakan krungthep* [The election of the governor of Bangkok]. Bangkok: Munithi phua kansuksa prachathipatai lae kanphatana, 1987a.

———. *Kanmuang ruang kanluaktang suksa chapho korani kanluaktang thuapai pho. so. 2529* [Politics and elections: A case study of the general election of 1986]. Bangkok: Munithi phua kansuksa prachathipatai lae kanphatana, 1987b.

———. "Botbat khong jaopho thongthin nai setthakit lae kanmuang Thai: khosangket buangton" [Role of provincial godfathers in Thai economics and politics: Preliminary observations]. In Pasuk Phongpaichit and Sungsidh Piriyarangsan, eds., *Rat thun jaopho thongthin kap sangkhom Thai* [State, capital, provincial godfathers and Thai society]. Bangkok: Political Economy Center, Chulalongkorn University, 1992.

Sombat Chantornvong and Montri Chenvidyakarn. "Constitutional Rule and the Institutionalization of Leadership and Security in Thailand." In Stephen Chee, ed., *Leadership and Security in Southeast Asia*, 141–178. Singapore: Institute of Southeast Asian Studies, 1991.

Somboon Suksamran. *Political Buddhism in Southeast Asia*. London: C. Hurst and Co., 1977.

Somporn Sangchai. *Coalition Behavior in Modern Thai Politics*. Singapore: Institute of Southeast Asian Studies Occasional Paper no. 41, 1976a.

———. *Some Observations on the Elections and Coalition Formation in Thailand, 1976*. Singapore: Institute of Southeast Asian Studies Occasional Paper no. 43, 1976b.

Somrut Miwongukhot. *Sayam Olmanak 2528* [Siam Almanac 1985]. Bangkok: Sayamban, 1985.

Somsak Xuto, ed. *Government and Politics of Thailand*. Singapore: Oxford University Press, 1987.

Somsook Boonyabancha. "Causes and Effects of Slum Eviction in Bangkok." In Shlomo Angel et al., eds., *Land for Housing the Poor*. Singapore: Select Books, 1983.

Sonarong Piyakan. *52 pi khong prachathipatai* [52 years of democracy]. Bangkok: Phrae Phithaya, n.d.

Sopon Pornchokchai, *Bangkok Slums: Review and Recommendations*. Bangkok: Agency for Real Estate Affairs, 1992.

Spindler, Kanjana. "May 1992: When the Tide Finally Turned." *Bangkok Post*, 19 May 1993.

Statistical Booklet on Thai Women. Bangkok: National Statistical Office, 1995.

Statistical Handbook of Thailand. Bangkok: Office of the Prime Minister, National Statistical Office, annual.

Steinberg, David Joel, ed. *In Search of Southeast Asia*. Honolulu: University of Hawai'i Press, 1987.

Stodgill, Ralph. *Handbook of Leadership*. New York: The Free Press, 1974.

Stowe, Judith. *Siam Becomes Thailand*. Honolulu: University of Hawai'i Press, 1991.

Subramaniam, Surain. "The Asian Values Debate: Implications for the Spread of Liberal Democracy." *Asian Affairs: An American Review* 27 (Spring 2000): 19–35.

Suchit Bunbongkan. *Kanchai ngoppraman nai kanronarong hasiang lae kanluaktang* [Campaign finance and election]. Bangkok: Samakhom Sangkhomsat haeng prathet Thai, 1985.

――. *The Military in Thai Politics 1981–86.* Singapore: Institute of Southeast Asian Studies, 1987.

――. "Elections and Democratization in Thailand." In R. H. Taylor, ed., *The Politics of Elections in Southeast Asia,* 184–200. Washington, DC: Woodrow Wilson Center and Cambridge University Press, 1996.

Suchit Bunbongkan and Phonsak Phongphaeo. *Phrutikam kanlong khanaen siang luaktang khong khon Thai* [Voting behavior of the Thai people]. Bangkok: Chulalongkorn University, 1984.

Suehiro Akira. *Capital Accumulation and Industrial Development in Thailand.* Bangkok: Chulalongkorn University Social Research Institute, 1985.

――. *Capital Accumulation in Thailand, 1855–1985.* Tokyo: Centre for East Asian Cultural Studies, 1989.

Sukanya Nitungkorn. *Changing Labor Force of Thailand.* Quezon City: University of the Philippines, 1984.

Sungsidh Piriyarangsan. *Thai Bureaucratic Capitalism.* Bangkok: Chulalongkorn University, 1983.

Sungsidh Piriyarangsan and Pasuk Phongpaichit, eds. *Chon chan klang bon krasae prachathipatai Thai* [The middle class on the path of Thai democracy]. Bangkok: The Political Economy Center, Chulalongkorn University and Friedrich Ebert Stiftung, 1993.

Supannee Chalothorn. *Greater Bangkok: An Analysis in Electoral Geography 1957–76.* Bangkok: Social Science Association of Thailand, 1986.

Supatra Masdit. *Politics in Thailand with Special Reference to the Role of Women.* Singapore: Institute of Policy Studies, Regional Speakers Lecture Series, Lecture no. 4, 1991.

Suphanya Tirawanit. *Nangsuphim Thai chak patiwat 2475 su patiwat 2516* [Thai newspapers from the 1932 revolution to the 1973 revolution]. Bangkok: Thai Watthanaphanit, 1983.

Supharat Loetphanitkun. "Samakhom lap angyi nai prathet Thai pho. so. 2367–2453" [Angyi secret societies in Thailand 1824–1910]. M.A. thesis, Chulalongkorn University, 1981.

Suphawong Janthawanit. *Kanjat chuang chan thang sangkhom: Kiattiphum khong achip tang tang nai sangkhom Thai* [Organizing social structure: Status of various occupations in Thai society]. Bangkok: Chulalongkorn University, 1991.

Surachat Bamrungsuk. *United States Foreign Policy and Thai Military Rule, 1947–1977.* Bangkok: Duang Kamol, 1988.

――, ed. *Rabop thahan Thai: bot suksa kongthap nai boribot thang sangkhom-kanmuang* [The Thai military system: A study of the military role in society-politics]. Bangkok: Chulalongkorn University–ISIS, 1987.

Suraphong Sothanasathian. *Sing phim kap kanluaktang thuapai (2529)* [Printed matter and the general election (1986)]. Bangkok: Munithi phua kansuksa prachathipatai lae kanphatana, 1987.

Surin Maisrikrod. "Emerging Patterns of Political Leadership in Thailand." *Contemporary Southeast Asia* 15 (June 1993): 80–97.

Suriyan Sakthaisong. *Tamnan luat jaopho* [The bloody record of the godfathers] (part 3). Bangkok: Ngandi, n.d. [1991].

——. *Jaopho*. Bangkok: Matichon, 1993.

Suteera Thomson and Maytinee Bhongsvej. *Profile of Women in Thailand*. Bangkok: Gender and Development Research Institute, 1995a.

——. *Women Reshaping the Society*. Bangkok: Gender and Development Research Institute, 1995b.

Tambiah, S. J. *World Conqueror and World Renouncer*. Cambridge: Cambridge University Press, 1976.

Tarrow, Sidney. *Power in Movement*. Cambridge: Cambridge University Press, 1994.

Thai Government Gazette in Thai-English. Bangkok: Office of the Juridical Council's Welfare Fund.

Thailand Company Information 1990–91. Bangkok: A. R. Business Consultant, n.d. [1991].

Thailand in Figures. Bangkok: Tera International, annual.

Thailand Statistical Yearbook (Samut sathiti rai pi khong prathet Thai). Bangkok: National Statistical Office, annual.

Thailand's Budget in Brief. Bangkok: Bureau of the Budget, annual.

Thailand's Present Cabinet Ministers. Bangkok: The Public Relations Department, Foreign News Division, 1979.

Thak Chaloemtiarana. *Thailand: The Politics of Despotic Paternalism*. Bangkok: Social Science Association of Thailand, 1979.

Thawatt Mokarapong. *History of the Thai Revolution*. Bangkok: Chalermnit, 1972.

Thawisak Phansura. "Kantosu thang kanmuang khong phakkanmuang Thai: suksa korani khong phak kitsangkhom" [Political struggle of Thai political parties: A case study of the Social Action Party]. M.A. thesis, Chulalongkorn University, 1986.

Thep Prathan: Mu ban tong su [Thep Prathan: A community forced to fight]. Reprinted in Wiphak Nguanyong, "Phanthakit khong Sahakon kredit yunian chumchon phatthana Khlong Toei 79 Chamkat" [Bond business of the credit union cooperative for community development Khlong Toei 79 Limited]. M.A. thesis, National Institute of Development Administration (Bangkok), n.d.

Thim ngan Khaosot. *Rakluat Khlaeo Thanikun* [The loves of Khlaeo Thanikun]. Bangkok: Khaosot, 1991.

Thirayut Bunmi. *Suan nung khong khwamsongjam 20 pi 14 Tula* [One part of memory 20 years after 14 October]. Bangkok: Winyuchon, 1994.

Thompson, E. P. *The Making of the English Working Class*. Harmondsworth, Eng.: Penguin, 1968.

Thompson, Virginia. *Thailand: The New Siam*. New York: Macmillan, 1941.

Thompson, Virginia, and Richard Adloff. "Who's Who in Southeast Asia." Microfilm of unpublished data cards covering the period August 1945–December 1950.

Thomyanti [pseud.]. *Kham haikan khong phuying chu Oi. B. M.* [The words of a woman named Oi. B. M.]. Bangkok: Chaemaen, 1994.

Thup krusombat ratchakhru Chatchai-Praman-Kon [Breaking into the treasure room of ratchakhru Chatchai-Praman-Kon]. Bangkok: Etim, 1991.

Tilly, Charles. "Repertoires of Contention in America and Britain, 1750–1830." In Mayer

N. Zald and John D. McCarthy, eds., 126–155. *The Dynamics of Social Movements.* Cambridge, MA: Winthrop, 1979.

———. "Speaking Your Mind without Elections, Surveys, or Social Movements." *Public Opinion Quarterly* 47 (Winter 1983): 461–478.

Tilly, Charles, Louise Tilly, and Richard Tilly. *The Rebellious Century: 1830–1930.* London: Dent, 1975.

Trocki, David. "Big Men, Naklaeng and Power: The Politics of Violence in the Rural South of Thailand." Ed. Carl Trocki. Unpublished paper.

Tu Weiming. "Joining East and West: A Confucian Perspective on Human Rights." *Harvard International Review* (Summer 1998): 44–49.

Turton, Andrew. "Patrolling the Middle-Ground: Methodological Perspectives on Everyday Peasant Resistance." In James C. Scott and Benedict J. Tria Kerkvliet, eds., *Everyday Forms of Peasant Resistance in South-east Asia.* London: Frank Cass, 1986.

Ubonrat Siriyuwasak. *Rabob withayu lae thorathat Thai* [The structure of radio and television in Thailand]. Bangkok: Chulalongkorn University, 2001.

Ukrist Pathmanand. "The Thaksin Shinawatra Group: A Study of the Relationship between Money and Politics in Thailand." *The Copenhagen Journal of Asian Studies* 13 (1998): 60–81.

U. S. Congress. House Committee on International Relations. Subcommittee on International Organizations. *Human Rights in Thailand: Hearings before the Subcommittee on International Organizations.* 95th Cong., 1st sess., 23 and 30 June 1977.

Van Esterik, Penny, ed. *Women of Southeast Asia.* Rev. ed. DeKalb: Northern Illinois University Press, 1996.

van Praagh, David. *Thailand's Struggle for Democracy: The Life and Times of M. R. Seni Pramoj.* Foreword by Stephen Solarz. New York: Holmes and Meier, 1996.

Vella, Walter. *Chaiyo!* Honolulu: University of Hawai'i Press, 1978.

Vickery, Michael. "Thai Regional Elites and the Reforms of King Chulalongkorn." *Journal of Asian Studies* 29 (August 1970): 863–881.

Vilas Manivat and Steve Van Beek. *Khukrit Pramoj: His Wit and Wisdom.* Bangkok: Duang Kamol, 1983.

Vivat Prateepchaikul. "An Alternative Vision of the World." *Bangkok Post Year End Economic Review 1994,* 30 December 1994, 74–76.

Weber, Max. "Class, Status, Party." In H. H. Gerth and C. Wright Mills, eds. and trans., *From Max Weber: Essays in Sociology.* New York: Oxford University Press, 1946.

West, Guida, and Rhoda Lois Blumberg. *Women and Social Protest.* New York: Oxford University Press, 1990.

Wilson, Constance M. *Thailand: A Handbook of Historical Statistics.* Boston: D. K. Hall, 1983.

Wilson, David A. *Politics in Thailand.* Ithaca, NY: Cornell University Press, 1962.

Winzeler, Robert. "Sexual Status in Southeast Asia: Comparative Perspectives on Women, Agriculture, and Political Organization." In Penny Van Esterik, ed., *Women of Southeast Asia.* DeKalb: Center for Southeast Asian Studies, Northern Illinois University, 1982.

Wirasak Saloeyyakanon, ed. *Khumu nangsuphim thongthin* [Provincial newspaper handbook]. Bangkok: Sathaban phatthanakan nangsuphim haeng prathet Thai, 1987.

Withaya Nophasirikunkit. *Kanmuang suan thongthin nai prathet Thai* [Provincial politics in Thailand]. Bangkok: Ramkhamhaeng University, 1978.

Withayakan Chiangkun. *Khabuankan naksuksa Thai chak 2475 thung 14 Tulakhom 2516* [The Thai student movement from 1932 to 14 October 1973]. Bangkok: Grammy Publishing House, 1993 [o.d. 1974].

Withun Wiriyaphan. *108 yutthakong nai yutthachak luaktang* [108 ways to cheat in election battles]. Bangkok: Khlet Thai, 1986.

Wood, W. A. R. *History of Siam*. Bangkok: Chalermnit, 1982. o.d. 1924.

World Development Report. New York: Oxford University for the World Bank, annual.

World Media Handbook. New York: United Nations, Department of Public Information, 1990.

Wright, Joseph J., Jr. *The Balancing Act: A History of Modern Thailand*. Oakland, CA: Pacific Rim Press, 1991.

Wyatt, David K. "Family Politics in Nineteenth Century Thailand." In Clark Neher, ed., *Modern Thai Politics: From Village to Nation*. Cambridge, MA: Schenkman, 1979.

——. *Thailand: A Short History*. New Haven, CT: Yale University Press, 1982.

Yap Kioe Sheng, ed. *Low-income Housing in Bangkok: A Review of Some Housing Submarkets*. Bangkok: Asian Institute of Technology, Division of Human Settlements Development, 1992.

Yot Santasombat. "Power and Personality: An Anthropological Study of the Thai Political Elite." Ph.D. diss., University of California at Berkeley, 1986.

——. "Leadership and Security in Modern Thai Politics." In Mohammed Ayoob and Chai-anan Samudavanija, eds., *Leadership Perceptions and National Security: The Southeast Asian Experience*, 83–109. Singapore: Institute of Southeast Asian Studies, 1989).

——. *Amnat Bukkhalikkaphap lae phunam kanmuang Thai* [Power, personality and Thai political leaders]. Bangkok: Nam Thai, 1990.

Zakaria, Fareed. "Culture Is Destiny: A Conversation with Lee Kuan Yew." *Foreign Affairs* 73 (March 1994): 109–127.

Zimmerman, Robert. "Student Revolution in Thailand: The End of the Bureaucratic Polity?" *Asian Survey* 14 (June 1974): 509–529.

GLOSSARY

chumchon ae at	congested community, slum community
hua khanaen	"voting chief," a vote canvasser
hua khanaen rap jang	vote canvasser for hire
itthiphon	influence, often used for illegal forms of influence
jai nakleng	having the heart of a *nakleng* (see below)
jao mae	a female deity or spirit
jaomae	godmother, a woman with great power or influence
jao pho	a male deity or spirit
jaopho	godfather, a man with great power or influence, usually due to control over violence
je	elder sister, a term of respect
kaeng muan phuchai	"talented like a male"
kamnan	head of a *tambon*, an administrative division of about 10 villages
khakhai	small-scale trading, hawking
kharatchakan	civil servant
khunna	virtue, a form of power often associated with women
klum phuak	circle of friends, used also for a patron-client network
lukjin	of Chinese or Sino-Thai descent
mae	mother
maeban	literally mother of the house, housewife
mae kha	female market trader
nai	originally a member of the nobility, now used for mister, master, boss
nakkanmuang	politician
nakleng	a type of traditional Thai leader who is tough, charismatic, and above all, loyal to friends
phakphuak	circle of friends, members of a patron-client network
phrai	commoner
phuak	group
phudi	literally "good person," and originally associated with the nobility, now refers generally to well-mannered virtuous individuals
phunam	leader

phuyai	"big person," a person with prestige, authority, or power, a patron
phuyaiban	village leader, "headman"
rabop hua khanaen	"voting chief system," the structure of vote canvassers organized by candidates for elections
rap jang	employee, casual laborer
run	cohort, usually for a school class or age group, a generation
sae	Chinese (Teochiu) term for lineage, family in a broad sense, including relatives, ancestors, and descendants, and even those who may be unrelated yet share the same surname
sakdina	system for determining status under the absolute monarchy
samlo	a tricycle taxi, a pedicab
sangha	the Buddhist ecclesiastical organization, the monkhood
sia	Chinese (Teochiu) term for tycoon, used as a term of respect
tambon	an administrative division consisting of about ten villages
than samay	modern, modernity
thesaban	municipality
trakun	Thai term for lineage, family in a broad sense, including relatives, ancestors, and descendants who share the family name

INDEX

ABOUT THE AUTHOR

After earning his B.A. in political science and Asian studies at Brigham Young University, James Ockey completed his M.A. and Ph.D. in government and Southeast Asian studies at Cornell University. He has published numerous articles on aspects of Thai politics, including civil-military relations, parties and elections, congested communities, provincial politics, crime and politics, and "Hyde Park" style democracy. He is presently a senior lecturer in the political science department at Canterbury University in Christchurch, New Zealand.

Production Notes for *Ockey / Making Democracy*

Text design by University of Hawai'i Press production staff
using Minion and Hiroshige

Composition by Josie Herr

Printing and binding by The Maple-Vail Book Manufacturing Group

Printed on 60# Text White Opaque